In Pursuit of the Good Life.

TWO YEARS ON A BIKE

From Vancouver to Patagonia

Martijn Doolaard

gestalten

If the road is beautiful, travel the road slowly; be a turtle, be a snail and even better than this: Stop traveling; live the road fully.

—MEHMET MURAT ILDAN

ZION NATIONAL PARK, UTAH

Preface

Ten years ago, I had it all. I had moved from the south of the Netherlands to Amsterdam after securing a lucrative position at a major branding firm. It was thrilling, my new, exciting life in the big city. I bought my own apartment, lived with my gorgeous girlfriend, and commuted to a beautiful old brick building on a canal. I worked as a junior graphic designer with a team of colleagues from all over the world for big-name clients, and in my spare time, I played in a band, which I believed was my calling. And yet, I was miserable.

The job that had started so promisingly soon became constricting. The repetition of the eight-hour workday consumed me. I didn't have enough time and energy to do the things I really enjoyed, like composing for my band and making music videos. At the same time, I was coming to the realization that I lived with someone I didn't really love. But I was afraid to lose everything I'd worked for and create an imbalance in my comfortable, "perfect" life. Weeks and then months passed as I slouched at my desk, contemplating my future, not having the guts to step into the manager's office and announce my resignation. The longer I thought about leaving it all, the more impossible it seemed. I wasn't just afraid of that meeting, or that breakup: I was afraid of what would happen afterward.

Eventually the time came when I could put it off no longer. In a bout of sudden courage, I ended the job and left the relationship. Those two endings led to many new beginnings. My career developed like never before. I started freelancing at different agencies, and soon I was making more money and working fewer hours. I was excited about the greater variety of projects, which made me a better designer. I had more time for my hobbies as well. The band signed a small record deal and we toured a bit around the Netherlands. Being active across multiple disciplines kept things fresh, and I discovered new talents within myself. I became used to remote work and enjoyed switching offices all the time. I started to travel more, mostly on city trips and short outdoor adventures. Things were moving forward and it was liberating.

But before I knew it, I became a victim to this new success. Slowly, I fell back into the 40-hour workweek, doing exactly the same jobs as years ago, only as a freelancer this time. I couldn't reject jobs, because the pay was addictive, and I needed to work full-time to pay for my expensive city lifestyle. I spent money on things I didn't need; I was constantly finding reasons to buy new cameras and music production gear, convincing myself I was investing in my career, though I was actually fulfilling my hunger as a consumer. I thought I was free, but I was completely stuck in the system—and it wasn't even satisfying.

Meanwhile, our band was starting to hit the ceiling of our potential and I had to accept that I was probably not going to be a rock star. Quitting the band after years of dedication to a music career was a hard thing to do. It felt like giving up, but I knew it was inevitable. I needed to escape this routine and reimagine my life—again.

At this point, I wasn't much of a cyclist. Of course in Amsterdam, we ride bikes every day, but for me, that didn't mean more than the daily commute or riding to a bar to meet up with friends. It was during a city trip abroad that I had my first inkling that the bicycle could be more than a vehicle: it could be a home. I visited Paris with my girlfriend one New Year's Eve. We drove there in a van, but I brought my bike to explore the city. I pedaled around, and my girlfriend sat on the rear rack, legs to one side, the way Dutch couples have done for decades. As strange as it must have looked to the Parisians, who were always in a rush, it felt so familiar for me. Exploring places on my own bike gave me an incredible feeling of being at home, even in places far from home. I didn't know it at the time, but that Paris trip had planted a seed, and it was now taking root years later. What if I packed a bike to the max and rode really far? I'd always dreamed of long-term travel, but there were so many reasons to not do it. The band, the jobs, the mortgage, the income. Like most people, I was afraid that I couldn't leave it behind, let alone do without the comforts and luxuries of my life in Amsterdam. But maybe a bike was the only home I needed.

Perhaps experimenting with a short trip would give me some answers. So in 2014, I bought a proper touring bike, a Surly Long Haul Trucker, and planned a two-week trip to Switzerland. My friends laughed at me: "You won't even make it to Maastricht!" It was December when I left, but I was too excited to wait for spring. Besides, if I ever wanted to cycle the world, I needed to be able to face all types of weather. It turned out that I loved it. The sense of freedom, the exercise, the new horizons every day, and documenting the whole thing vigorously—I felt like I'd found something I could do for a long time. And so I decided to go for it. I would travel the world on my bike. I would live a simple life out of a few bags, following a routine that always delivered something new. Every day I would "work" for eight hours, but the work would be in a saddle behind handlebars, not in a chair behind a computer. I wouldn't be paid in money, but in memories.

To fund my first big trip, I took on a lot of jobs to save as much money as possible. Renting out my apartment would cover my mortgage and monthly expenses, but with my current spending habits, I still didn't know how I was going to afford, say, a yearlong journey. Certainly, my taste in restaurants and hotels needed to change. The goal of this trip was not only to see the world and indulge in all its exotic beauty, but also to take a step back from the neverending materialist lifestyle I took part in. Choosing to travel by bike was helpful in this regard because it forced me to limit what I brought with me. There was fear to overcome; there was creativity to develop. I needed to get physically stronger and mentally tougher. I needed to be able to sleep under the stars. As excited as I was, I was nervous about pulling it off. Bike touring through the Netherlands and Germany hadn't been all that challenging. The climate, infrastructure, language, and culture were familiar and safe. Crossing deserts in Iran and getting over the Himalayas on a loaded bicycle would be a different game.

Once I set off, life was very clear to me.

On April 16, 2015, I handed over the keys to my apartment and pedaled out of Amsterdam. I had vaguely informed family and friends that I was cycling to China, only to give an idea of the direction and magnitude of my travel intentions. Travel visas, political unrest, and troublesome areas would be addressed on the way. There were no routes, no plans, and no destinations. In the coming weeks and months I would play it by ear and figure out if this was something for me. It made sense to approach it that way. It felt liberating to not have a plan; it was the only way to really live in the moment.

Once I set off, life was very clear to me. The simplicity of traveling the world by bike gave me focus. Everything had a purpose. All the things loaded onto my bike had been carefully thought through. I knew exactly what was in each bag and where everything was packed. I was fueled by a desire to produce stunning photos and writing. I camped in beautiful places, crossed Europe's green fields and forests, and moved toward the Far East. I lost weight, got a tan, looked better, and felt great.

Of course, not everything was easy. There were days of saddle pain, aches in my right knee during the first long climbs in the Carpathian Mountains, and occasional stomach bugs. I stayed in many ugly hotels, and I longed for communication in places where no one spoke English or where internet connection was not prioritized. I had to

give in to many moments of hardship, and give up the level of comfort and luxury I was used to. Yet overcoming these obstacles only made me stronger, and all of the difficult moments grew into powerful memories. I gained mental resilience and discovered a new, expansive version of myself.

After a thrilling journey from Amsterdam to Singapore through 18 countries and over 17,000 kilometers, I arrived home, rich in memories and quite broke. Frankly, I'd started missing my job after one year. The design agencies booked me again, and normal life slowly took over, as if nothing had changed. The big difference, however, was that *I* had changed. I was better able to appreciate the little things and the larger comforts of life in the Netherlands, with its healthcare system, good infrastructure, my nice apartment, and everything I used to take for granted. I started to work on a book and film about my journey. Six months after my return home, *One Year on a Bike: From Amsterdam to Singapore* came out, and it is now being sold all over the world.

After about a year in Amsterdam, the inevitable itch to travel again returned. This time, I wanted to see if I could combine my working life with cycling. Since most of my work was done behind my laptop, I just needed a chair, a table, and Wi-Fi, and I knew I could find those things anywhere in the world. Convincing my clients was not easy, since most of the agencies I worked for were used to having me in their offices. They were afraid that the time difference and my physical absence wouldn't work for them. But I strongly believed that it would be possible and that the traveling would open even more doors down the road.

Since I had already cycled the farthest I could overland from Europe, the choice for this new route was obvious: North and South America. I needed an extreme distance, with a destination that would always seem out of reach. It would be even better if it crossed continents. The simplicity of a single line from north to south, from one side of the globe to the other, sparked my imagination in the same way that biking to Singapore had. I had always wanted to explore the Western United States—the most geologically interesting part of the country. And I had never been to Latin America. I chose Vancouver, British Columbia as my starting point. It was a bit late in the season to start from Alaska, and Vancouver would be a better place to get all the parts for my new bike setup. Besides, I had friends there and some freelance work to finish up. This time, my design work would dictate my planning, so I could keep my income while on the road. If there was work for me, I would settle in a town. If there was no work, I would cycle, take photos, and write my way from one end of the world to the other.

DEAD HORSE POINT, UTAH

Endurance setup — an ultralightweight setup with minimal luggage to race long distances unsupported. This setup prioritizes speed and performance over comfort and leisure.

Cycle touring setup — The classic bike touring setup with panniers and racks that can haul plenty of luggage. This is widely considered the ideal setup for long journeys around the world, where comfort and versatility are more important than speed.

Bikepacking setup — For bikers who continue when the road runs out. The big tires have maximum control on rough terrain, and light luggage is directly strapped to the frame instead of with racks and panniers, allowing for clearance in narrow gullies and bushy trails.

Preparation
—*Choosing a bike*

It goes without saying that the bike itself deserves thorough contemplation before setting off on such a big journey. I've met dozens of bike travelers from all corners of the world, and each one does it differently. It's best not to get bogged down in fretting over the "right" setup. When I remember meeting local bicycle travelers in India or Bolivia, navigating long distances on cheap Chinese racing bikes with their belongings stuffed in cardboard boxes and strapped onto self-fabricated racks, I see that it ultimately doesn't matter much. If there's a will, there's a way.

At the same time, there are more options than ever, and as a cyclist with access to them, settling on the optimal setup is a fun puzzle. Decades ago, it was simpler. You had city bikes for commuting, mountain bikes for dirt, and race bikes for speed. In today's world, there's a plethora of newborn subcategories that mix and match tire sizes, geometry, handlebar shapes, and packing opportunities—the choices are dazzling. You may have found your perfect bike to spend your Sundays in the local backcountry, but as it turns out, the forest department has just repaved the trails with a slightly finer type of gravel, and it just so happens that your favorite bike brand has released a new gravel bike which would just be perfect for it... and before you know it, you have 10 bikes in your shed. The upside of the wide variety of choices is that you can personalize your setup in detail. The first thing, then, is to learn what you like and need.

Obviously, there are a few bikes to rule out for the journey described here. That ultralightweight racing bike of yours would most likely snap under the weight of heavily loaded panniers. Your favorite fixie that gets you around town and looks so good with your coat and scarf won't get you up steep climbs. Consider your riding posture, too: a sportive position might break your back in the long run and have you seeing fifty shades of tarmac instead of the wonders of the world. On the other hand, an upright position will be unbearable in a relentless headwind. You will probably end up somewhere in the middle. With good bike geometry, you can spend a long day in the saddle without too many aches. A handlebar that offers multiple riding positions prevents strain in wrists and shoulders, and a strong frame will easily carry you and your belongings. Mounting options for screwing on luggage racks or cages are also helpful. And you will want gears: the more the better. You will use "granny-gear" more often than you think, climbing those endless cordilleras.

Many long distance riders opt for steel frames, which are the strongest and easiest to work with. If a steel frame breaks on a back road in Iran, someone will be able to weld it together again in the next town. Steel is also flexible and absorbs some of the shocks and shakes, which makes

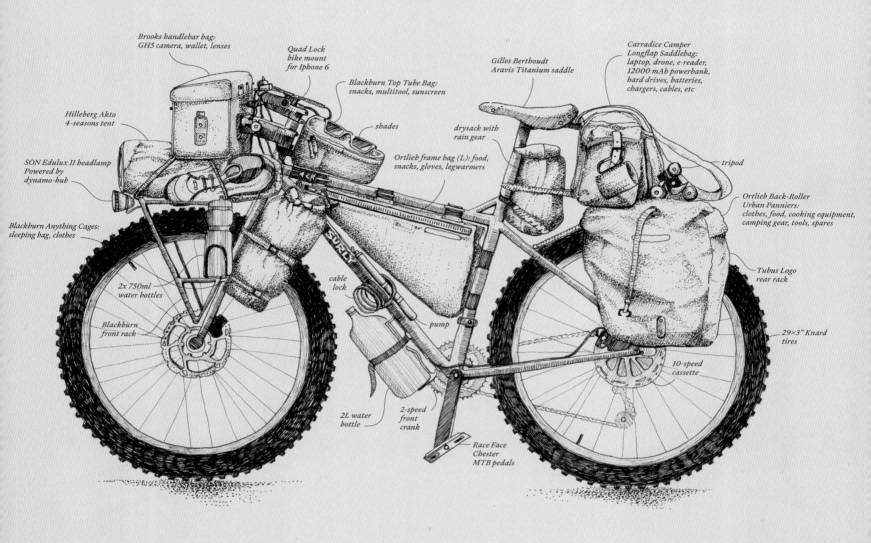

Brooks handlebar bag:
GH5 camera, wallet, lenses

Quad Lock
bike mount
for Iphone 6

Blackburn Top Tube Bag:
snacks, multitool, sunscreen

Gilles Berthoudt
Aravis Titanium saddle

Carradice Camper
Longflap Saddlebag:
laptop, drone, e-reader,
12000 mAh powerbank,
hard drives, batteries,
chargers, cables, etc

Hilleberg Akto
4-seasons tent

shades

drysack with
rain gear

tripod

SON Edulux II headlamp
Powered by
dynamo-hub

Ortlieb frame bag (L): food,
snacks, gloves, legwarmers

Ortlieb Back-Roller
Urban Panniers:
clothes, food, cooking equipment,
camping gear, tools, spares

Blackburn Anything Cages:
sleeping bag, clothes

2x 750ml
water bottles

cable
lock

Tubus Logo
rear rack

Blackburn
front rack

pump

29×3" Knard
tires

2L water
bottle

2-speed
front
crank

10-speed
cassette

Race Face
Chester
MTB pedals

the ride more comfortable compared to stiffer materials like aluminium or carbon. The downside? Steel is by far the heaviest material. More and more, bikes are being made from aluminium or carbon, which are much lighter than steel. Aluminium frames are affordable, lightweight, and strong enough so that they rarely break. Ultralightweight carbon, previously only used for racing bikes, is getting stronger too, and is now also used for touring bikes. But you have to be more careful with a carbon frame when doing something like throwing your bike on top of a Landcruiser in Africa to escape a pride of lions. While carbon is very strong, it's difficult to repair when damaged. Finally, many brands are moving toward premium titanium frames. The material is lightweight, ultrastrong, and sleek, but you'll need a deep wallet.

I have toured extensively on my Surly Long Haul Trucker (LHT), a sturdy, classic touring bike. Standard 28-inch wheels, 35-millimeter tires, no-nonsense V-brakes, steel frame. Many extras that could break on a bike are not present on this one—it's the bare minimum, but all I've needed. I considered taking it on this trip as well, but on rocky or sandy roads, the thin tires have made the riding hard or even impossible, and I've often ended up pushing it on the roughest roads. So I looked into mountain bikes and fat bikes, both of which are capable of rougher terrain. The Surly ECR, a so-called "camp-bike," caught my attention.

Its tires, at 29 by 3 inches, had a lot more rubber than the LHT's, which would make dirt roads more butt-friendly and potentially keep me pedaling through sand. People advised against it, saying it would slow me down on pavement. After some test rides, I saw they had a point, but I felt a connection to the bike. It was so comfortable on dirt, I felt like it was inviting me to adventure. Besides, it wasn't my intention to be the fastest. I wanted to be comfortable and feel confident. Despite all the rational advice, at the end of the day, I just needed to feel good in the saddle. More than my bike, it was my mindset that would take me around the world.

Bike:	Surly ECR, Large
Saddle:	Gilles Berthoud Aravis, Titanium, Cork
Tires:	Surly Knard 29x3.0"
Rims:	Rabbit Hole 50 mm
Brakes:	Avid BB7, 180/160mm front & rear
Brake Levers:	Avid FR-5
Shifters:	SRAM NX Eagle
Handlebar:	17º aluminium bar
Pedals:	Race Face Chester, Red

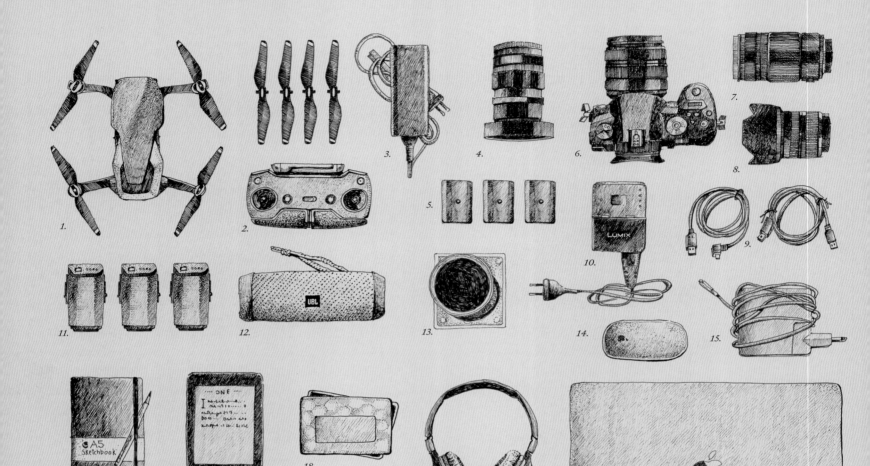

Gear
—What to pack and how

Climbing the first hills with the sheer weight of a fully loaded bike always makes me reconsider everything I am carrying. "Do I really need this bluetooth speaker? Should I lose the Bialetti and settle for instant coffee? Is a drone worth the extra kilos? Maybe I could ditch the heavy tripod and forget about time-lapse photography?" I thought long and hard on what to bring with me. A few nonnegotiables emerged. First and foremost, I wanted to be 100 percent independent, having a shelter and the means to cook my own food at any moment. Second, because documenting my journey in film and photography was going to be a key part of traveling, I needed the tools to process and store content on the road. Finally, I needed to be able to do common repairs on the bike, like patching tubes and replacing gear cables.

As far as how to pack a bike, there are two main setups worth considering, ruling out the endurance setup. The best-known is the classic touring setup, with most belongings carried in panniers attached to racks. Panniers fit a lot of luggage and you can quickly remove them for convenience when you check into a hotel or visit a restaurant and don't want to leave all of your belongings on the street. But the system is slightly heavier and not ideal on rough terrain because of clearance issues and potential rattling and shaking. The other option, which has gained popularity, is the bikepacking setup, which employs smaller, lighter bags smartly strapped onto various parts of the frame and handlebar. This setup reduces weight and maintains better clearance for narrow trails in the woods and river crossings. Nowadays, these setups are often com-

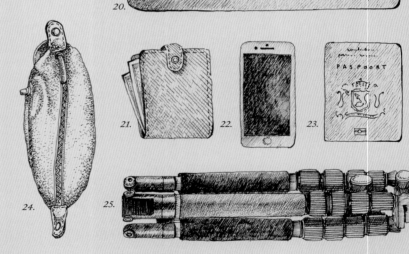

1. DJI Mavic Air	16. notebook	30. bike tool
2. DJI remote control	17. Kindle e-reader	31. Leatherman multitool
3. drone charger	18. hard drives	32. adjustable wrench
4. Voigtländer 25mm f/0.95	19. JBL headphones	33. allen keys
5. camera batteries	20. Macbook Pro 15" Retina	34. tube repair kit
6. Panasonic Lumix GH5	(2012)	35. spare nuts and bolts
7. Lumix 35-100mm f/2.8	21. wallet	36. disc pads
8. Lumix 7-14mm f/4.0	22. Iphone 6	37. 2 drybags
9. various cables	23. passport	38. tubeless sealant
10. camera charger	24. pouch with bike parts/tools	39. bungee corts
11. drone batteries	25. Sirui tripod	40. pump
12. JBL Flip 4 speaker	26. gear and brake cables	41. chain oil
13. lens filters	27. spare chain	42. bike lights
14. Apple mouse	28. pliers	43. Carradice saddle bag
15. Macbook charger	29. spare inner tube	44. seat post drybag

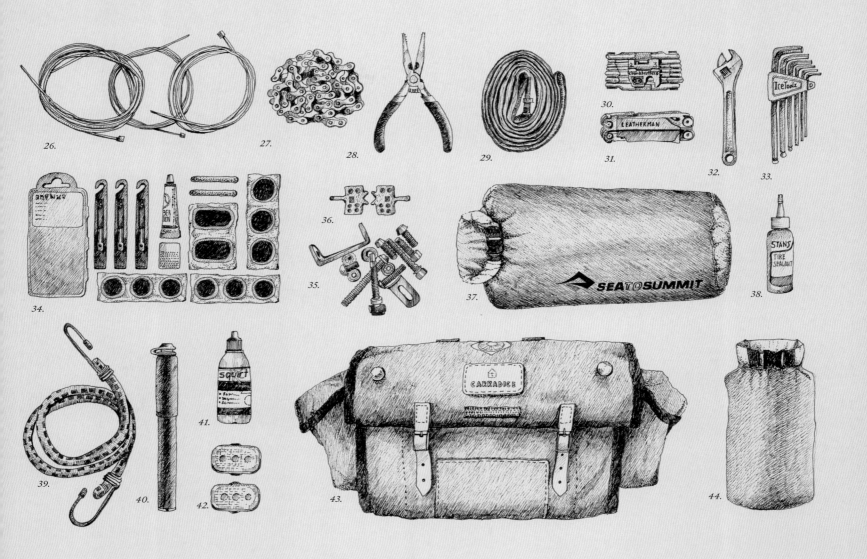

26.   27.   28.   29.   30.   31.   32.   33.

34.   35.   36.   37.   38.

39.   40.   41.   42.   43.   44.

bined, so I went for a bikepacking setup with racks and panniers on the back for more space. The handlebar bag on the front held my camera, so it would be easily accessible. I learned this from my previous trip: the more effort it takes to get the camera, the more valuable moments you miss capturing. The bag was attached to a second stem, so it rested on the tent and was positioned at an ideal height. The Carradice saddlebag held all of my other electronic equipment. Both bags had quick releases and were easy to take off when I stopped and left the bike unattended. This way, I kept my most valuable belongings at my side.

Photography — I started off with a full frame mirrorless camera, the Sony A7r, with one 24–70 mm f/2.8 zoom lens (Sony G-Master). A flexible setup suited both for landscapes and portraits. I thought I could do with that one lens, because it's fairly wide, and the 42 megapixels that are captured by the Sony would give me some room to crop the image, if I wanted a longer shot. However, eventually I missed an ultra wide lens and better video- and timelapse capabilities, that I had with the Panasonic Lumix cameras I used previously. So in Mexico City I ended up switching to the Panasonic GH5. The compromise was losing some megapixels and quality in low light situations, and carrying three small lenses instead of one big one, but I knew this setup worked on my previous journey.

Additionally, I carried a GoPro and a drone. First a Mavic Pro, and after it broke a Mavic Air. The drone especially seemed like a no-brainer considering the quality of today's landscape photography. With smartphone cameras and drone technology evolving so fast, it is getting much easier to carry high quality, lightweight equipment on a bike. You can fly a drone up without even dismounting and instruct it via your smartphone to fly around you while you cycle. Despite the incredible potential of drones and smartphones, they still don't beat a larger sensor photo camera, especially when it comes to depth of field and low light capabilities. For editing and backing up files, I used a 15-inch Macbook Pro. I backed up most of my content on Dropbox and external hard drives. Sometimes I shipped the latter home to save weight and keep the content safe.

Bike parts — The great thing about traveling by bike is that if something breaks down, you can most likely fix it yourself. I carried a patch kit, brake cables, brake pads, gear cables, lube, allen and torque keyset, pliers, chain breaker, tubeless sealant, a spare tube, and a Swiss army knife. The tires were not tubeless ready, but I could still put tubeless sealant into them to prevent many punctures. (I discovered this after I found about 30 punctures at once after cycling through some goatheads in California.) Later in the journey, I used tubeless ready tires, which for me was the way to go. Generally, wide tires are more prone to punctures, and in thorny landscapes, tubeless is a blessing from above.

Clothes — I try not to overpack on clothing and carry only what the season demands. Cycling across two hemispheres means going through varied climates, and it doesn't make sense to carry down jackets, sweaters and gaiters across the jungles of Central America. Outdoor goods stores can be found everywhere, and because my trip started in the summer in the US, I packed lightly. I prefer to cycle in casual outdoor clothing that dries fast but doesn't look too sporty. I want to go out in the city without looking like I just got off my bike.

Camping
—Do I need an axe..?

One of my favorite aspects of bike travel is being able to wild camp at any given moment. I can count on two hands the number of times I camped on official campgrounds on this trip. I preferred to scroll the maps, searching for a secluded spot in the forest, on the beach, or along a steep cliff. There, I pitched the tent, watched the sunset, and felt the freedom of sleeping outside. I camped roughly two-thirds of this journey. The rest of the time, I stayed in hotels, hostels, Airbnbs, or on people's couches. But nothing beats starting the day by brewing a cup of coffee in the morning dew with the smell of pine needles wafting about, or stirring hot porridge on a snowy mountain pass, or toasting potatoes in the embers of a crackling campfire, dreaming about the road ahead.

My tent is a four-season Hilleberg Akto. It's meant for one person, but fits a friend if you leave the inner tent out. I've used it for years and it has served me well. It's strongly built and its double layers and compact design make it one of the warmer tents. That does make it a little too hot in the tropics. With most tents, you can remove the rain fly to gaze at the stars and catch a cool breeze. This is more difficult with the Akto, because you'll need to reattach the lines, and the inner tent fabric is not mesh. It also needs to be staked to the ground, which is a problem if you camp on a concrete floor.

For cooking I use a multi-fuel stove that burns white gas, normal gas, diesel, and kerosene. It's reliable, even at freezing temperatures and high altitudes, where propane canisters might fail. You can keep it at a soft simmer or a rolling boil, and you can buy fuel anywhere. I've used several brands, but my favorite is the MSR Whisperlite International, which is the quietest. Most of the other ones sound a

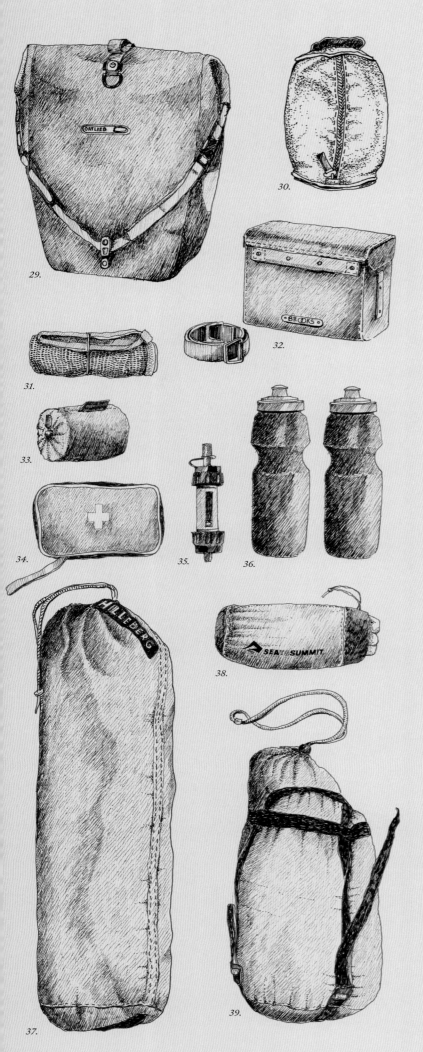

1. Bialetti 2-cup coffee maker
2. MSR Whisperlite Int.
3. Buck cocobolo hunting knife
4. coffee pouch
5. dish scraper
6. Primus cooking pot
7. olive oil
8. various spices
9. Petzl Tikka headlamp
10. lighters
11. cup
12. titanium spork
13. toothbrush for dishes
14. Greenland wax
15. cream
16. toiletries
17. Fjällräven jacket
18. Ziploc bags
19. sunscreen/deodorant
20. Palladium boots
21. Trousers and bib shorts
22. down jacket
23. beanie
24. sunglasses
25. GORE-TEX rain jacket
26. Rapha gloves
27. socks
29. Ortlieb Urban Panniers
30. toiletry bag
31. camping towel
32. Brooks Handlebar Bag
33. Cocoon travel pillow
34. first aid kit
35. water filter
36. water bottles
37. Hilleberg Akto tent
38. Sea to Summit ultralight pad
39. Sea to Summit sleeping bag

bit like a rocket launcher. To save weight and space, alcohol stoves are a good solution, as are good old propane canisters, but the latter are not available in all countries.

Camping in winter — For most, camping is a summer activity. Winter is often considered too cold, too dark, or too wet to sleep outside. It's true that it comes with challenges, but with the right preparation and mindset, winter camping can be an enjoyable and beautiful experience. As a start, it's important to dress well with the right technical garments, maintaining a three-layer principle: a quick-drying base layer, an insulation layer, and a wind and rain stopper. For sleeping, a thick down bag is just the start. Most of the cold will come from direct contact with the ground. A reflective foam pad with an aluminium layer will help a lot, which you can combine with an insulated air mattress to help trap warm air between your body and the ground. To preheat your sleeping bag, add a bottle of hot water or some stones from the campfire. Do a workout just before you go inside the tent. The blood flow makes sure all of your body parts are warm and instantly heats up the sleeping bag. Finally, don't forget to pee before you go to sleep: otherwise your body will use extra energy to keep all that liquid warm.

Finding a camping spot — If I have cell service, my favorite way to find a camping spot is to scroll Google Earth for some space in nature. In rural areas, there's always a place not too far from the road, but even in urban areas, the map tells me a lot. With a bicycle it's easy to disappear and set up camp somewhere unnoticed. I usually arrive late in the day and leave early in the morning. If I have the chance, I ask the owners for permission. On some occasions I've been caught by a farmer, but it has always ended with a laugh and a handshake. I admit that not all places I've slept have been 100 percent legal, but not all illegal things are wrong. If you respect nature and leave no trace, I see no harm in camping on private property. If you want to play it safe, there are helpful apps with extensive libraries of places to spend the night, including wild camping spots. Two I frequently use are iOverlander and park4night, which are supported by reviews from travelers.

It's impossible to give a full list of what you really need for camping. It also depends on how comfortable you want to be. If you like spending time in the saddle most of the day and are going for the maximum distance, you might want to stick to the bare necessities, to keep the bike light. I enjoy spending quiet time at camp, preparing food, going for a walk, reading, and hanging out. If you want a chair to sit in, why not bring it? You can always ship things home or donate them. On my first trip, I cycled all the way to Kyrgyzstan with an axe before I got rid of it. I had used it only twice, and though it made me feel safer when I heard strange sounds in the dark forest, I ended up being fine without it.

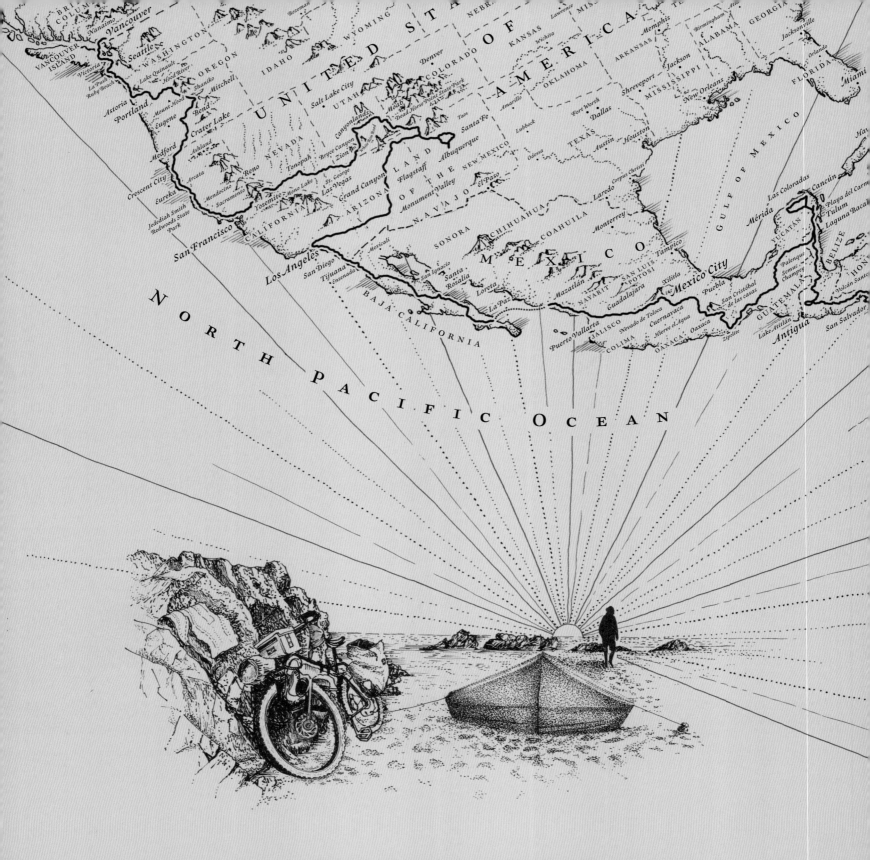

THE ROUTE

*It was simple to draw a straight line from the North to the South
following the Pacific coast. But inevitably, the route grew more
complex, including many detours and excursions, resulting in
a total travel log of 19,778 kilometers.*

CORDILLERA BLANCA, PERU

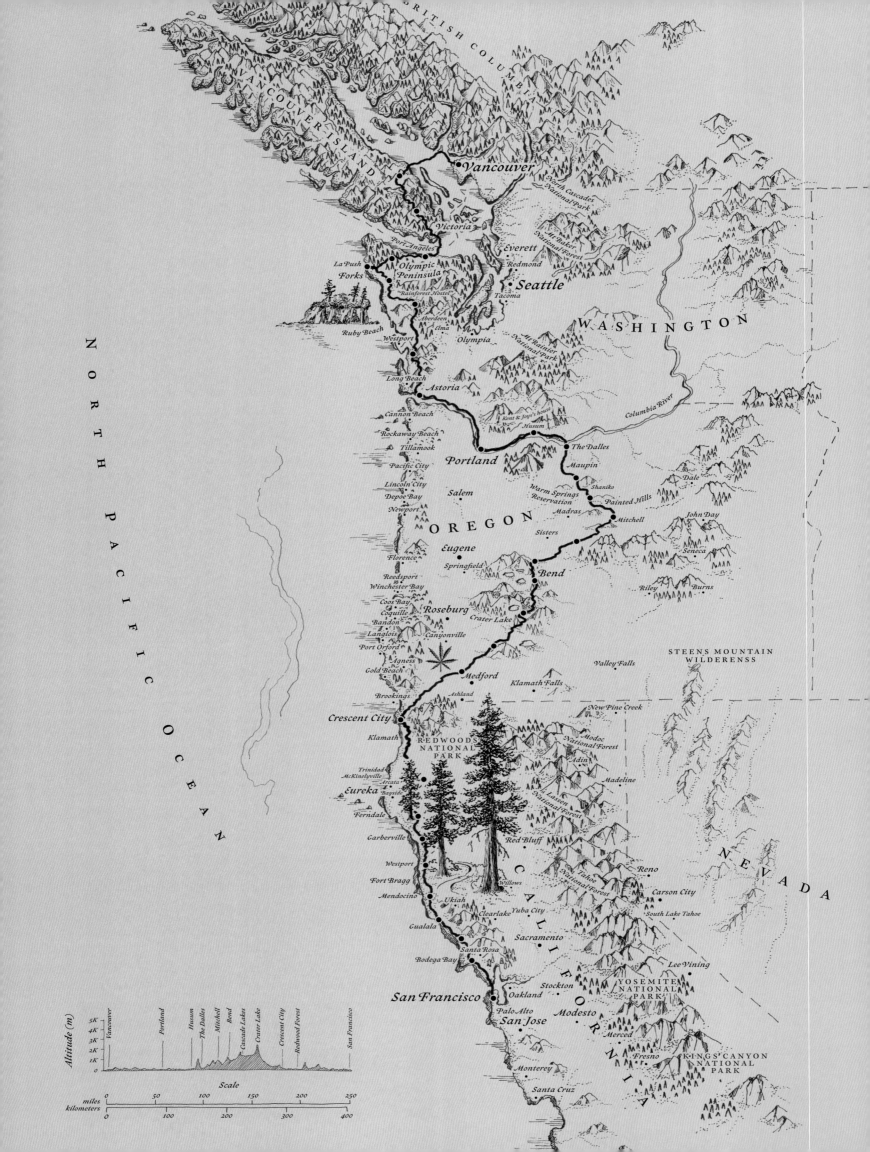

BRITISH COLUMBIA

VANCOUVER ISLAND

Vancouver

North Cascades
National Park

Victoria

Mt Baker
National Forest

Everett

Port Angeles

La Push
Olympic
Forks *Peninsula*

Redmond

• **Seattle**

"Rainforest Hostel"

Tacoma

Ruby Beach

Aberdeen
Elma

Westport

Olympia

WASHINGTON

Mt Rainier
National Park

Long Beach

Astoria

Kent & Joy's house

Columbia River

Cannon Beach

Husum

Rockaway Beach

The Dalles

Tillamook

Portland

Maupin

Pacific City

Dale

Lincoln City

Salem

Warm Springs
Reservation

Shaniko

Painted Hills

Depoe Bay

Newport

O R E G O N

Madras

Mitchell

John Day

Florence

Eugene

Sisters

Seneca

Springfield

Bend

Reedsport
Winchester Bay

Riley

Burns

Coos Bay

Coquille

Roseburg

Crater Lake

Bandon

Langlois

Canyonville

STEENS MOUNTAIN
WILDERENSS

Port Orford

Agness

Valley Falls

Gold Beach

Medford

Klamath Falls

Brookings

Ashland

New Pine Creek

Crescent City

Klamath

REDWOODS
NATIONAL
PARK

Modoc
National Forest

Adin

Madeline

Trinidad
McKinelyville

Arcata
Bayside

Eureka

Lassen
National Forest

Ferndale

Garberville

Red Bluff

Westport

C A L I F O R N I A

Fort Bragg

Willows

Tahoe
National Forest

Reno

Mendocino

Ukiah

Carson City

Gualala

Clearlake

Yuba City

South Lake Tahoe

Santa Rosa

Sacramento

Bodega Bay

Lee Vining

San Francisco

Oakland

Stockton

YOSEMITE
NATIONAL
PARK

Palo Alto

San Jose

Modesto

Merced

Monterey

Fresno

KINGS' CANYON
NATIONAL
PARK

Santa Cruz

N O R T H   P A C I F I C   O C E A N

N E V A D A

Altitude (m)

5K
4K
3K
2K
1K

Vancouver
Portland
Husum
The Dalles
Mitchell
Bend
Cascade Lakes
Crater Lake
Crescent City
Redwood Forest
San Francisco

Scale

miles   0   50   100   150   200   250
kilometers   0   100   200   300   400

PACIFIC NORTHWEST

DAY 1 - VANCOUVER, CANADA - 0 KM

The plan is to follow the coast, possibly venturing inland at some point. On my way are the rainforests of the Olympic Peninsula, the city of Portland, the high deserts of Central Oregon, the Cascade Lakes, and the famous redwood forests. San Francisco is my first goal.

The view from Lions Gate Bridge, with views over Stanley Park and downtown Vancouver.

*On the way out of Vancouver,
ready to go with zero mileage.*

—Taking off

Gasping for air, I take one last look from the Lions Gate Bridge over Vancouver. My friend Paul has been waiting for me in the middle of the bridge for a few minutes already. He's clearly in better shape, despite being two decades older than me. He and his wife have been hosting me for the last few weeks in the city, and now he joins me on his bike for two days on Vancouver Island. I'm struggling as I work myself up the bridge in first gear. The bike feels heavy. The leather saddle—fresh out of the box—is rock hard. It's going to take a week or two to become comfortable. The rubber handlebar grips are sticky, and the zipper on the frame bag is stiff. My body is stiff too: I haven't trained at all. I feel saggy, with a bit too much body fat. But I know it's only a matter of time until I feel comfortable. These first days, I will fine-tune the position of everything: the height and angle of the saddle, the position of the handlebars, the placement of my luggage. It's like moving into a new house.

I'm starting the journey with a detour. Paul knows some good trails on Vancouver Island, so we take the ferry north to Nanaimo instead of the much faster overland route to Seattle via Interstate 5. The border crossing into the US at Port Angeles will be quieter, and the route will be much more scenic. My aim is to choose interesting routes over economic routes. I'd rather see the bike as a way to *be* somewhere, rather than a way to *go* somewhere. Time is no factor; destinations are vague. San Francisco is my first goal, but the more I think about that, the more it takes me out of the moment. I remind myself to enjoy where I am and to embrace and accept each challenge as it comes. I will have to actively surrender to each long climb, unexpected traffic jam, boring hour, and hot day. If my mind can find its way through, my body will follow. All those things are part of everyday life, and I have to try to understand their purpose. Of course, I will revel in the beautiful moments too: the views, the freedom, the wind in my face, the endorphins spiking in my brain. Every day will be full of new scenery, new prospects, and a new horizon.

In the evening we find a camp spot on a hill, deep in the forest on Vancouver Island at a small lake. It's easy to find a wild camping spot here, because there are many logging roads with no residences. We go for a swim, make a fire, and cook our dinner. It's a beautiful early summer night. A perfect, easy start to the journey.

↗ *Filling up water bottles in Olympic National Park in Washington.*
→ *A map showing the trails on Vancouver Island.*
↘ *First camp on Vancouver Island with Paul. In the middle of the photo you can see the fire.*

I'm more nervous to wild camp here than in any other country.

It's evening when I enter the US by ferry at Port Angeles. It's a small crossing and I'm given a friendly welcome. After buying some groceries, I camp in a fenced-off field along the road. As in Europe, or perhaps even more so, it's hard to find a patch of land that isn't fenced off. Night has fallen by the time I make camp and I feel uncomfortable. This is the United States, where normal people own guns. It's a part of the culture I will never really understand since I'm not from here. Traffic signs are pockmarked with bullets. Maybe for practice, but more likely out of boredom. I'm more nervous to wild camp here than in any other country, from Iran to India to anywhere in Central Asia. Having recently read Bill Bryson's *The Lost Continent* where he describes his journey through small-town America doesn't help either. I tell myself it's probably not as bad as I think it is, and my tired body falls asleep quickly.

In the morning, I wake up and pack the tent undisturbed. I haven't seen a soul. Highway 101 is the main coastal road through Washington, Oregon, and California, and I now follow it toward the Pacific Ocean. It is a beautiful ride through temperate rainforest with the biggest conifers I've ever seen looming overhead: western red cedar, Douglas fir, and Sitka spruce. The road meanders through valleys with moderate climbs and descents. Where I can, I take a trail off the highway, although there is not much traffic to avoid here in this isolated corner of the US.

A few days later I reach the Pacific coast at La Push, a sleepy town on the Hoh Indian Reservation. It's a quiet place with mostly indigenous inhabitants, cut off from the busy urban sprawl of Seattle by the Olympic Mountains. The sea is rough and too uninviting for a swim. The water of the Pacific is cold this far north. Big logs wash up on the shores and get bashed against the sharp rocks. The smaller driftwood is sanded smooth by the water. In a convenience store, I buy a Budweiser to celebrate the minor achievement of reaching the ocean. They only have 700 ml size "tallboy" cans—this must be America.

Jimmy in his self-fabricated greenhouse.

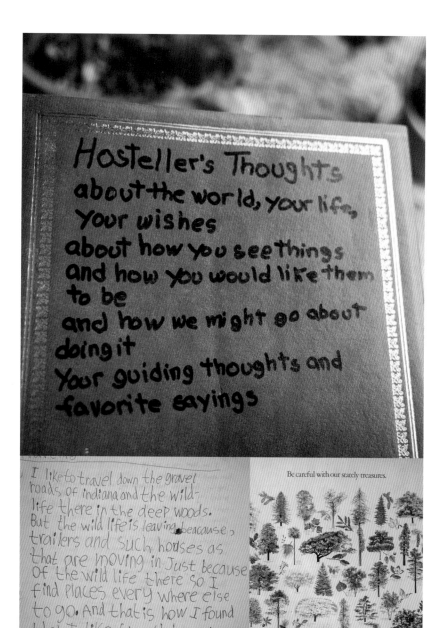

—Jimmy's hostel

The last few days have been rainy, and because most of my camping equipment is wet, I decide to look for a hotel. I end up in the Rain Forest Hostel, situated on Highway 101 but far from any town.

I knock at the door and step inside. An older man—Jimmy—and three girls, who appear to be travelers too, are sitting on a couch in a cozily lit living room. It's intensely warm inside. Everywhere are books, photographs, drawings, notes, letters, pots, pans, tools, toys, firewood, maps, fishing rods. Everything is old, well-used, and cared for. It's debatable whether this is really a hostel, or just a home with some spare bedrooms. Jimmy greets me with a friendly "Welcome!" Without getting out of his chair, he gestures for me to join on the couch.

As I take my place on the sofa, he delivers an introductory speech about the hostel, which he does to all new guests. It consists of three points: the first is about the payment, which is based on donations. The base rate is 10 dollars per night, and guests may decide for themselves if they want to pay less or more. The idea is that the ones who pay more cover for those who pay less. (Jimmy is a Bernie Sanders supporter, and this payment policy is based on his political leanings.) The second point is about judging people—I'm not sure if I completely understand it, but he tells me that he catches himself judging new guests when they come to his house. He wants to be more open, less judgmental, and less afraid of people. He says there is a lot of fear in the US of strangers, particularly of foreigners, because the US has a lot of enemies. I've noticed this fear myself on the countless signs declaring, "NO TRESPASSING," "VIOLATORS WILL BE SHOT," or even stronger, "THERE IS NOTHING HERE WORTH DYING FOR," alongside a picture of a gun barrel aimed at the reader. Jimmy has seen his fair share of violence. He says he served in Vietnam, but he won't talk about it, even when I ask him about it later. He ends his monologue with the third point: guests should do a 15-minute chore before leaving each morning. This could be doing the dishes, sweeping the floor, getting firewood, or helping in the garden. If we don't want to do the chore, we have to pay five extra dollars. I share my thoughts with the other guests, and we all agree to pay 20 dollars for the night and do a chore in the morning.

I end up staying for two nights so I can explore the forest around the house and all the objects inside. There is a guestbook in which people have written their stories since 1992, a time when people still knew how to write with a pen. I write a little story too, and thank Jimmy for the hospitality.

IT'S THE FIRST TIME I RIDE ON THE BEACH COVERING SOME DISTANCE — A BLISSFUL FEW HOURS BEING AWAY FROM THE TRAFFIC OF THE HIGHWAY.

A wild camping spot along Highway 197 in Oregon. Mount Adams is in the distance.

This trip is about simplifying life and minimizing luxury.

After cycling for a while on the Washington side, I cross the Columbia River to the south back into Oregon and ask about a room at one of the motels in The Dalles. It's a charmless place with a view of the parking lot, and it costs 135 dollars. Still, I'm tempted by the promise of a soft bed and a shower after a long day of cycling, especially since it's getting dark. But I deny myself the room. It's not that I can't afford the motel; it's just not worth it. It's too easy, giving in to luxury. It's the same way I feel while shopping in a supermarket. Honestly, I could eat whatever I want, given that I burn about 4000 calories a day. But I want to limit my cravings. This trip is about simplifying life and minimizing luxury. By reducing choices, my life can be easier and more straightforward. I do my Wi-Fi things at a McDonald's and set out in the night, climbing up into Oregon's high desert. After 15 kilometers, I set up camp just behind a hill. I'm probably trespassing, but so be it. I feel like a little boy, doing something excitingly illegal but ultimately harmless. The previous nights were all at hosts' homes or designated campsites. I've missed this sense of adventure.

COLUMBIA RIVER GORGE, WASHINGTON / OREGON

↑ Shaniko is a ghost town—most of it, at least. Only a few call it home and run the general store for people who take Highway 97. At Goldie's, you can get a plate of food and an ice cream. People there say, "Shaniko is a great place to do nothing."
← Bakeoven Road, likely the most appropriately named road in Oregon's high desert. Temperatures during the day are much higher inland than near the Pacific coast.

↑ The Painted Hills, Oregon. Not the work of some modern artist but the result of erosion and climate changes over a long period of time.
→ High walls of snow next to the road at Crater Lake (2316 m). A stark contrast to the hot desert roads from the past days.

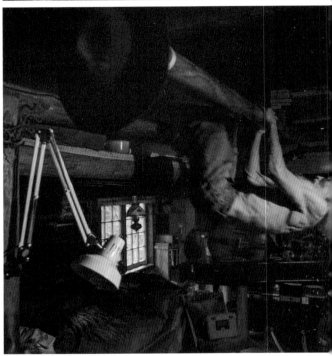

There's no sense in building a big home when you are surrounded by such lush nature. When you live small, you tend to spend more time outside.

← *Joy's outdoor kitchen.*
→ *The Norwegian style cabin Kent built himself.*

Kent & Joy
A home off the grid

Back in Portland, I was welcomed for a few days by Tanja and her husband. They told me about her parents, who have lived independently in the forest for 42 years. I was intrigued and asked if I could visit them once I was in their area, since it would be more or less on my route. Tanja helped me pinpoint the house on Google Maps, and now, I find myself struggling through the thick forests and rough roads to get there—my legs aren't ready for rugged terrain yet. I'm pushing my bike up the hill when I arrive and see Kent, a small, bearded man with giant hands that make him look like he's straight from the Shire. I see Joy inside the little house preparing dinner. "I've got an ice-cold pond here you might wanna jump into," Kent calls to me by way of greeting.

Kent and Joy hardly ever welcome people on their property, and they hardly ever leave it. It's quite a journey to reach the nearest town, and here in the forest, they have everything they need. Kent sits down on a tiny bench underneath a wall of instruments. The wood of the bench is bowed by many hours of the same person sitting there for decades. The small Norwegian-style cabin is detailed with carvings he made himself. It's not bigger than 20 square meters, with a ladder to a small nook underneath the roof where they sleep. He takes away the ladder and shows me that he's still able to climb in the bed without it. From his perch, he says, "You see, the cabin is kinda tiny, but we actually live big. Let's go outside!"

Trails sprawl across the forest as we take a walk around the property. A manmade pond stores their water that comes from the stream, which also generates their electricity. There's a little treehouse they built for their daughter Tanja, some decades ago. Kent keeps rambling on as we follow the trails, his giant hands hanging still alongside his body as he walks. "There's no sense in building a big home when you are surrounded by such lush nature. When you live small, you tend to spend more time outside."

In the evening we sit inside. Joy is chopping veggies and tells me about her study of herbs. She makes her own herbal creams and salves from what she finds in the forest. While Joy cooks, Kent writes down the outside temperatures in his book. He has done this every day since 1970. On some pages, there are blank lines. These are from when they were away, which rarely happens. If they leave the property for too long, nature will take over. Once, they returned from a three-week family holiday in the winter. It took Kent weeks to fix all the problems created by the heavy snowfall and freezing temperatures. The water pump froze and a few structures collapsed. As they and their home grow older, the problems build up. One of the cabins is slowly sinking away and they are trying hard to save it. As youthful as their spirits are, it's a lot of work to fight against the elements and maintain a life in the wilderness.

THE REDWOODS

It hasn't been boring. In a relatively short period I've been through rainforests, pine forests, high deserts, and snowy alpine roads, and now, I'm back on the Pacific coast in California.

My first encounter with the redwoods is an otherworldly experience. I have heard of the mythic trees, but I haven't known exactly where to find them. It's late in the afternoon when the main road I'm cycling goes through the forest. As the forest deepens and evening falls, the trees grow larger and larger. Mighty giants rise straight up right next to the road, with trunks as wide as a single lane. Some are nearly 2000 years old. Like little toys, the cars disappear in between the trees as the road winds down to the sea. Once, these trees grew across the entire Northern Hemisphere, but now they only remain in California where they are protected. It's incredible how much history those trees carry, how much they've seen. Many of them were here long before Europeans arrived on the continent.

Although I'm tired after the long ride, I'm giddy like a child, going off on trails through the woods while the sun sets. The fresh smell of the trees and the fog of the Pacific does me good. I reach Crescent City late in the evening having cycled 132 kilometers—my longest day on the road so far. I couldn't wish for a better welcome into California.

The collision of the cold air from the Pacific and the warm winds from the land often results in beautiful mornings with fog among the tall redwoods.

The wilderness makes me more alert. My senses sharpen and I feel alive.

I'm sitting against a tree trunk in the middle of a wide, dry riverbed. It's almost dark and there's a strong sidewind dancing over the plain and whipping the drawstrings of my hoodie against my face. In front of me are the redwoods, tall and dark, their silhouettes grim against the fading sky. Somewhere in those tall trees is my tent, which I have just set up. It's a bit of a haunted place, but in a beautiful way. It's not a place I would normally wish to be at first—in the dark, alone, exposed in the wind and the cold—but I've missed it. Lately, I have been staying on campsites, often with other cyclists. Being in a group is comfortable and safe, and comes with its own routines. I have a chat, cook some food with people, take a hot shower. Here on my own, it's much different. Things have the potential to be more unnerving—and more exciting. The wilderness makes me more alert. My senses sharpen and I feel alive. I'm able to turn deeper into myself, discover new things, overcome obstacles, confront fears. It all makes my heart beat faster. I think the fact that I never get used to this makes it so exciting. Later, I will go for a walk, and then I will crawl into my tent and tuck myself in. When the silence returns, I will worry for a while if the panniers, storing my food are closed properly against animals. Bears, elk, raccoons, skunks—there is so much wildlife here that I'm not familiar with in Europe. I will tell myself not to worry about them, and then, I will fall asleep.

Warmshowers
—A *worldwide bicycle community*

What do you do if you love traveling and meeting new people, but you have a job, a family, or other things that keep you in one place? Well, you could sign up as a host on warmshowers.org and let bicycle travelers visit *you*. On my trips around the world, this community has been invaluable. From Germany to Iran to Malaysia, people on this platform have welcomed me in their homes and helped me with route information. A few days ago, when I entered California on the coast, I was welcomed by Katie, the senior secretary of a small church. Over the years, she has welcomed hundreds of bicycle tourists who want to rest for a few days and use the church facilities for free.

Today, I'm staying on a farm in Arkata, California. Albert (in the red shirt) has cycled a fair bit through the US and Mexico, but he currently owns and runs an organic farm which leaves him with little time to travel. To fill the void, he has opened up his place for cyclists, who can camp on his property or stay in one of the cabins at no cost. This is a busy time of year for him, and today is no exception. I meet José from Brazil and Eve from California, who are cycling north together. While we have a chat in the garden among the flowers and fresh strawberries, being gazed at by the chickens and cows, Rafael, also Brazilian, comes pedaling down the driveway—I met him a few days ago along the coast. In the evening, Josh and Katie from Massachusetts also surprise me with their arrival. We have all met on the road or at a campsite before. Cycling the coastal Highway 101 is a popular route in the summer. Almost every day I meet

cyclists packed for the long haul. Most of them are traveling from north to south, following the direction of the wind. Everyone except José—he's coming from the south, complaining about the wind.

Cass, one of the workers on the farm, shows me around on the property. At the foot of the hill is a yurt where guests can stay. A walking trail goes up under the trees to an outdoor shower. Next to it is a composting toilet, which strangely smells of chocolate. Cass tells me that after doing my business, I'm to pour a scoop of cacao shells through the hole, which masks the smell. Farther up on the hill is where I will sleep. It's no more than a wooden awning over a platform to put an air mattress on. The hot outdoor shower is a gift from heaven. It's been a few days since I had a chance to bathe, and the hot water on my back and the cold sea breeze in my face is priceless. Next to the garden are the barn and kitchen, as well as a little shop where local customers can buy fresh milk, eggs, and

organic vegetables from the garden. The shop is unattended. You come in, stock up, write your purchases in the book, and leave your payment in a safe. The level of trust within this community is worlds away from the aggressive "NO-TRESPASSING!" language in the rural north of the country.

We don't see Albert very often, as he is busy tending the farm. But he comes by now and then for a chat and to make sure there is fresh milk in the morning for his guests. I'm always amazed by the hospitality of Warmshowers hosts. All around the world, I've been blindly trusted by strangers on their property. Everyone is in it for their own reasons. Sometimes it's to meet people, to bring some life to their home. Many elderly people sign up as hosts once their children leave the house. Others are interested to learn more about bike traveling. Sometimes, it's simply to give or share something.

—California summers

I've been avoiding Highway 101 as much as possible,
and trying to take smaller roads if they aren't too out
of the way. During the first days in Washington, this
same road was fairly quiet. Now, as I approach the Bay
Area, there's a lot more traffic. In the summer, the coast
is a popular destination, because the ocean brings
cooler temperatures.

Right now I'm on the historic Highway 1. It's a slow
ride, cycling up and down along the steep coastline.
A glance at my statistics tells me I've already climbed
30,000 meters in 2700 kilometers. The hills are short,
so on the downhills I try to get as much momentum as
possible before reverting to "granny gear" just before
the next hilltop. But there's nothing to complain about.
The farther south I get, the brighter the colors and the
warmer the temperatures. I'm starting to understand
what they mean about those California summers.

Staying healthy
—Cooking on the road

Often, I wonder if I am eating enough, because cycling seven hours each day burns a lot of calories. I don't think of myself as an athlete, so I don't keep close track of my diet. My goal is simply to feel good, to stay healthy, and to keep it simple.

Bike travel limits what food I can carry. I have no fridge, little space in my bags, and one small cooking pot. I'm very much dependent on what's available in grocery stores I pass on the road. During the day, I eat a lot of tortillas. They are a compact form of carbs and they stay fresh for a long time. In my panniers I always have a jar of peanut butter, which is high in fat and protein. I also try to eat a lot of fruit, whatever is available. Olive oil, fresh garlic, salt, and pepper stay good in hot weather for a number of days. I'm also a big fan of dried fruits mixed with nuts and cereals. These are all high in nutrition, are compact, and don't melt or perish. In the

morning, I have yogurt with cereal and dried fruit—so far, the nights are still cool enough to keep the yogurt from spoiling. I also cook six eggs, three for breakfast and three to bring on the road. Carrying uncooked eggs on a bike is asking for trouble. Sometimes I crack them into a small bottle if I want to make an omelet later. In the evening, I often cook a big plate of spaghetti, sometimes adding a can of tuna. This is the simple setup for if I don't pass any well-stocked supermarkets or restaurants and have to rely on what's in my panniers. It's tempting to stock up when I'm in a supermarket, but I must ask myself how much weight I'm willing to add. My diet will probably change once I'm out of the US and eating in roadside restaurants becomes more affordable.

One day, I stay at a hike and bike site, where I share the camp with other cyclists. It's always nice to have some inspiration and see how others eat on the road. Mariam, who is cycling the coast from Canada, loves to cook and proves that meals on a bike tour can be elaborate affairs. At the upscale organic supermarket in Point Reyes, we stock up, and along Highway 1, we find plenty of wild blackberries. Another cyclist, Tom, has bought some big sausages, so we fire up the barbecue too. This time, the peanut butter and tortillas stay in my panniers.

↑ Potatoes in aluminium foil on the campfire, with olive oil, garlic, salt and pepper.
↗ Wild berries grow plenty along Highway 1 in California.
↓ Sharing a meal with other bikers at a hike and bike campsite.

Your dreams are bigger when you look at the stars before falling asleep.

DAY 52 - OCEAN COVE, CALIFORNIA - 2497 KM

I'm almost in San Francisco, my first destination, but not after one last night at the seaside. I can spend endless hours on beaches without getting bored. Alone, I listen to the waves and the crackle of the fire. I cook food, go for a walk, set up camp, take pictures. I do everything slowly, aware of the process of simple chores. The noise of the sea purifies me and brings me to rest by absorbing every other sound, including that of my thoughts. In front of me is nothing but half a globe of water. Behind me are the cliffs, and behind them, half a globe of roads going south. Above me is a dome of darkness. I'm already looking forward to go to bed, because your dreams are bigger when you look at the stars before falling asleep. The best sleeps have been on soft sand, hushed by the soothing swell of the ocean.

In the morning, I pack up for the ride to San Francisco. Before entering the city I cycle up to Hawk Hill, a viewpoint overlooking the bay and the Golden Gate Bridge. But what I see from there could hardly be called a view. The fog has blown over the hills and through the bay. Hot, inland summer air mingles with the cold breeze from the Pacific, creating San Francisco's cool, notoriously foggy microclimate. 30 meters below me in a parking lot, tourists take selfies with the unrecognizable gray backdrop. The two pillars of the iconic bridge are never in view for more than a few seconds at a time in the shifting clouds. I change from my cycling clothes into dry ones to avoid catching a cold after the steep climb. The wind rushes over the hills and the temperature drops as the sun sets. I was planning on camping here, but now it doesn't appeal to me at all. Besides, my camera has just died and I forgot to charge my

battery. I'm sitting here with the wind at my back, looking at a colorless void which could have been an incredible view. There is no epic picture coming out of this. I'm unlucky.

Still, I enjoy the view. Because I can *hear* it. The noise of the city, the dense traffic moving over the bridge, through the hills, and all the way to the Victorian houses far in the distance. Sometimes the mist gets a little thinner, and I see a white sailboat on the dark blue water, just for a few seconds. Then it closes in again. After a half hour, I start pedaling downhill into the city. I have some design work to do, so San Francisco will be my home for the coming weeks.

Time to stay put for a while.

SAN FRANCISCO

DAY 81 - SAN FRANCISCO, CALIFORNIA - 2794 KM

The marvelous city of fog has disrupted my plans and taken the wind out of my sails—in a good way. It's the first time that I'm reconsidering my journey's goals. I am left in a state of internal debate, contemplating whether to stay or to move on.

The marvelous city of fog has disrupted my plans and taken the wind out of my sails—in a good way. It's the first time that I'm reconsidering my journey's goals. I am left in a state of internal debate, contemplating whether to stay or to move on.

"Meet me in Club Deluxe on Haight Street when you're done," Rachel texts. It's the end of the day and I am wrapping up some things on my laptop at WeWork, a coworking space where I'm renting a desk for the month. "Okay. I'm hungry, you want to eat something together?" I reply. "I already have; come when you've eaten." I put my laptop in a locker and walk out to get some falafel around the corner. As I make my way down Market Street, I sidestep the breathing bodies lying on the ground. It always surprises me to see how many people in America live disconnected from the system. People everywhere camp on the streets, their belongings in a shopping cart. Some yell at each other, some at themselves. There's no city in Europe where I've seen this many homeless people. I thought Brussels would compare, but it's got nothing on downtown San Francisco, Portland, and Vancouver.

After a quick dinner, I pedal up to Haight Street via Market and Golden Gate Avenue, climbing gradually up the hill. I've heard people talk about The Wiggle, an unofficial bicycle route through the city that avoids the steepest hills, but I'm not bothered by going up and down, so I don't stick closely to it. I became used to hills following Highway 1 along the coast.

Haight Street's colorful sixties vibe becomes more visible once I'm out of downtown. I'm in a neighborhood full of blasts from the past. Club Deluxe is located on the famous corner of Haight and Ashbury. Coming closer, I reduce my speed, catch my breath, and hope I don't look sweaty. I want to be relaxed when I meet Rachel for the first time. From the street, I look through the windows of the club. It's crowded at the bar, and I can hear live music. I lock my bike to a tall street lantern, text her, and enter the club. It's an intimate, European-style bar setting: seating is free, and there are no waiters. In front of the stage, people sit at small bistro tables. Behind that, it's standing room only—the place is packed. But I see Rachel right away. She is the only girl sitting alone, on

Bernal Heights Park

a table right in front of the stage. I immediately recognize her jet black hair and defined jawline. Squeezing through the crowd, I touch her shoulder and quietly greet her. Rachel stands up to hug me and flashes a bold, beautiful smile. I smile back, and then slip away to the bar to order an IPA for me and another glass of wine for her.

The band is undoubtedly American. They are all older men from the neighborhood who have been playing this stage for decades, and their passion and technical skill are unmatched. I have never experienced jazz and blues like this. It feels like I'm in the Deep South. Rachel and I listen, applaud, chat, and sit close to each other like magnets. It gets late, but the night isn't close to ending. It's hard for the audience to sit still when the band cranks it up a notch. A nearby couple gets up to dance. There's hardly any room, which makes it even more intimate. Rachel and I dance too, carefully shuffling in between the tables that are full of glasses. As most of the audience is older and more elegant than us, we don't want to be the young drunks knocking things off their tables. I think I'm fitting in here just fine. I'm glad I was able to score a nice blue striped shirt and brown leather loafers at the secondhand shop, and that I don't have to dance center stage in my hiking boots and bleached-out shirt with sweat stains. From the neck down, I look like a decent young man from the nineties.

"This is amazing, but I really should get going," Rachel says a few songs later, when the musicians finish their set. She is a nurse in the hospital, and has an early shift in the morning. "One more song!" I insist. She flashes that smile again: "Okay. I'm going to get another drink. You want a beer?" I nod, and watch her saunter to the bar. She doesn't seem in a hurry at all. Soon, there is a new jazz band up, and they outplay even the previous one. They have a contrabass, two guitars, a mandolin, two singers, and a dancer. No drums, but the group somehow transmits enough rhythm and groove without them. Having been in bands for years, I have never witnessed this raw power and energy in Dutch musicians. Their third song is a fierce cover of "Viva Las Vegas," the first song I actually know. I love it, but Rachel doesn't—perhaps it's too gratuitously American for her taste. I admit that it's a bit of a frantic song. "Come," she says. "Let's go now!" She stands up, leaving our full glasses on the table. "You can tuck me in..."

The next morning, I briefly wake up when Rachel gets ready for her seven o'clock shift, and then I sleep in. Later, after taking a shower, I walk downstairs to my bike. The neighborhood looks gray and foggy as I roll down States Street from her house, passing the Castro Theatre and taking Market downtown to WeWork. When I arrive, I open my laptop and pour a coffee. I am hungover, but San Francisco's cool morning air has invigorated me, and I am euphoric about Rachel. She is an absolute treasure. It has been a while since I felt this excited about meeting a girl. She is different. My plans are off the table. As of last night, cycling to Patagonia is on hold.

I can't focus on work this morning, but there is a lot to do. Just before starting this trip, I accepted a big project redesigning a Caribbean beer brand. I started the first phase during my month in Vancouver, and on the road I have grown accustomed to staying in motels for a few days at a time to work on it. I've also grown partial to greasy spoon diners.

I drape my tent over my bike to dry from the morning dew, and log on while I enjoy an omelet, hash browns, and drip coffee. I do the requested design tweaks, send out the PDF, answer all the other emails, and get back in the saddle. Luckily, this client is in Santa Lucia, so our time difference is only two hours. I have other clients in Amsterdam, and the nine-hour time difference sometimes gets complicated. I end up having conference calls during breakfast when they are already signing off for the day.

To be honest, most of my clients don't even know I'm on a bicycle trip. I thought people wouldn't understand that I could combine the work and the travel. But it works out fine, and this break in the city is really welcome. The WeWork provides a comfortable, well-designed coworking space. It has nice furniture and materials, fast Wi-Fi, reasonable coffee. They even have free IPA on draft. There is nothing wrong with working at an office, as long as it's not 40 hours per week, all year round. For the moment, I feel I've struck the perfect balance.

Two days later, a text from Rachel pops up. "Lets go to Yosemite! We could hike Half Dome." I have talked to her about going to some hot springs in Point Reyes, and also visiting the iconic park, so of course, I say yes. The following day, she picks me up at WeWork. Before leaving the city, we stop at REI to buy extra supplies. All her camping gear is still in Portland, where she's from originally. She has only lived in the city for a month after landing a full-time job as a nurse in the USCF hospital. Before that, she held part-time jobs waiting tables and picking weed during the summer in Northern California. She has traveled the world as well, mostly solo as a girl in her early twenties. She backpacked on her own in South America when she was 19, and took trains all around India after that. I can't imagine how much stamina and resilience one would need to travel alone in those countries as a young white girl. "I have a big mouth, which helps a lot," she says with a laugh. "You just need a thick skin, and you will get it after a while." I admire her for it, as I only started taking road trips on my own after I was 26. She makes me think I didn't live enough when I was young, that I should have put myself out there more.

We leave the city via the Oakland Bay Bridge and drive through the endless urban sprawl of the Bay Area, into the Central Valley with its prominent wineries. The landscape becomes drier and more yellow as the sun sinks in the sky. We arrive at Yosemite Valley early in the evening, after five hours of driving. Majestic granite peaks rise up from the forested slopes on our left and right. This is one of the most popular national parks in the US, and being just a few hours from the densely populated Bay Area, the camping rules are strictly enforced: we are only allowed on established campsites, which are expensive and fully booked in the summer. So instead, Rachel and I backtrack to look for a spot just outside the park. Near the Merced River, we stop for the night. It's a warm, bright evening, and there's no need for a tent, so we zip our sleeping bags together and lie down under the stars. But I can't sleep. The full moon is bright on my face and makes me restless. It feels like there is a car shining its headlights from the top of a cliff. I'm thinking about the black widow spider we found a few meters away when we arrived— Rachel recognized it. She's much better educated about the plants and wildlife here than I am. I look at her face. She is sleeping peacefully, her black eyebrows gently curved. She has done this more often than I have. Having grown up near the Cascade Lakes in Oregon, she is a nature girl, and has explored many of the wild places in this part of the US. We have our beautiful historic cities in Europe, and some forests, and the Alps, but we're always in close proximity to towns and infrastructure. It's nothing like the wide wilderness of the West.

We plan to wake up early to hike, but instead we sleep in and enjoy a beautiful morning at camp. We want to hike to Yosemite Falls, but we aren't alone: there's a whole crowd at the trailhead when we finally arrive. Our initial plan to hike Half Dome we've abandoned, because we would need to register and buy an extra permit, which have all sold out. Rachel leads the way; she is clearly faster. Despite all the hikers, it's a really beautiful walk. At one point, she hands me some tree bark. "Smell it. Ponderosa pine—it smells like vanilla." Admiring her knowledge, I take the bark—it does smell incredibly sweet. The whole time, I am taking pictures of the scenery. I take some of her as well, but she doesn't like it at all. I don't understand why, because she doesn't strike me as insecure. She is feisty and confident. She says she hates the self exploitation of social media, but in my experience, not wanting to be photographed is more about being afraid to be seen. When it comes down to it, most people are insecure. It usually hasn't much to do with beauty: the most stunning models I have photographed have been self-conscious about their looks. But maybe that's not what this is. There is a mystery about Rachel that I just can't grasp, though I will find out more sooner than later.

Reaching the top of the waterfall, we can finally indulge in the full view over Yosemite Valley. The white granite rock, the tall pine trees, the iconic cliffs. As John Muir, who was responsible for turning Yosemite into a protected park in 1890, lovingly said,

> Climb the mountains and get their good tidings. Nature's peace will flow into you as sunshine flows into trees. The winds will blow their own freshness into you, and the storms their energy, while cares will drop away from you like the leaves of autumn.

We hike a little farther to Yosemite Point, which provides more breathtaking views over the valley. North Dome, our initial goal, looks tempting from here, but we are both tired and it will be a long walk back. Back at the waterfall, I take another rest and we sit on the flat rocks near the stream. She asks me why some guys can't get erections. We talk about that for a while. She always asks these kinds of questions out of nowhere.

Exhausted, we return to the trailhead. We have brought food and wine, so we linger in the valley for a bit to enjoy a snack. When we drive out of the park, we dip raw broccoli in hummus, which is delicious after the long hike. Too tired to find a new spot to camp, we go back to our previous place along the Merced River just outside of the park. It is late afternoon and still light and warm, so I suggest we bathe in the river before cooking. We take off our clothes and naked, we climb over the round boulders to the river. Everything looks golden in the late afternoon light. The water is refreshing. I chant the song "Down in the River to Pray" from *Oh Brother, Where Art Thou?* as I walk over the stones in the stream. Rachel laughs at my silliness. I watch her from the middle of the river while she washes her hair, her white skin turned gold in the sun glinting through the trees. Everything looks magical. For a brief moment my heart aches, because I feel that life cannot get better than this. In the infinite beauty of this moment, I feel the vulnerability of attachment. I am afraid of the future, afraid of losing this, which will inevitably happen at some point. I will look back at this moment of euphoria, where everything has come together—the beauty of nature, of friendship, of love, and of adventure, all together at once. I wish I could photograph it, but maybe sometimes, an image is stronger if it just exists in the memory.

In the following days, I'm back at my rented WeWork desk, still excited about the adventure with Rachel. I am still not thinking about traveling or cycling. I am now staying in Bernal Heights, being hosted by one of my Instagram followers for a few days. Josh is a bike enthusiast who has an extra room in his colorful, richly ornamented 1870s Victorian house, where he lives with his Japanese wife and four-year-old son.

One evening, Rachel and I have a dinner date in the neighborhood. I meet her on Cortland Avenue in the Lucky Horseshoe, an old café with a round bar in the middle, where she is sipping a glass of whiskey. I am hungry so we make our plans quickly and call for a table at Red Hill Station, a seafood restaurant. It's crowded, so while we wait for a table, I join her for a whiskey. We talk about social media again. She describes her aversion to it. "It's so fake, how people pose for pictures at Yosemite for the perfect Instagram post, and how actually enjoying the view seems secondary!" She has a point, but as I always do when someone is outspoken on a topic, I play the devil's advocate. I don't find it so harmful and defend my own point of view by explaining how well it works for me. It's a massively useful tool, and a way to express myself. I even have a nice room with a view over the city thanks to social media!

When we get to Red Hill Station, we order a lot of seafood. The white wine makes us lightheaded, and we fool around with the crab and mussel shells. We are getting quite buzzed. At some point, she throws her legs on mine under the table and gets a little too loud. It doesn't seem to bother anyone around us—the small restaurant is packed and everyone's in a Friday-afternoon kind of mood. I find it entertaining but at the same time, I think we might be drawing too much attention. When the bill comes I offer to pay, which Rachel aggressively refuses. We split it instead and leave too big of a tip.

When we walk out, we are pretty sloshed. I have a bad feeling about how this evening is developing. We wobble down the hill to Mission Street and check out the Royal Cuckoo, an old jazz bar. Inside, it's incredibly dark. A big deer head is mounted on the wall above the bar. There is no stage, but two old guys are playing jazz in some kind of nook next to the bar. I order a whiskey and a beer for us to share. We sit down on a bench in the back, watching the musicians and chatting about all sorts of things. Rachel seems full of fire. I don't know how it starts, but soon we are talking about governments and wars and the problems of the world—as drunk people do—and she concludes that men are responsible for most of the evils in the world. I can't disagree with that. She states that women should rule everything instead. Maybe I should have just nodded, but instead I challenge her to explain how that should manifest. That sends our discussion through the roof. I can't get a word

With Rachel in Yosemite National Park.

Lee the "Truthsayer" in his house on Haight Street.

in or change the topic. With everything I say, I throw fuel on the fire. I don't even fully know what we are fighting about. We are both furious, agitated, and drunk. At some point it gets so tense I walk out of the bar to cool off and think about what to do. I want to go home, but I don't want to give up. After a few minutes I go back inside. She is sitting next to the door, her face still angry but less tense. She asks me to come with her. Instead, I leave her and walk home.

I am in bed, alone and awake. A part of me wants to pack my bags immediately and leave San Francisco. Deep down I know I have to cut this little adventure off and leave at some point. Rachel is trouble; I can't make any sense of her. But she is also exhilarating. She challenges and inspires me and forces me out of my comfort zone. How can I let that go? This journey has no deadline: I'll give it another chance.

This weekend, Josh and his family are off to Colorado, so I have the house to myself. In the morning, Rachel texts and apologizes. I let her wait for an hour, then send a reply saying I am alone. "Sweet!" she texts. "Can I come over?" I am expecting to have a conversation, but as soon as she arrives, she takes her clothes off and we have sex. No more words are needed. It seems like we are good—for now. We go for a walk up to Bernal Heights Park, along the wooden staircases and private gardens of the small Victorian houses. Californian flowers drape over the pastel-colored pergolas. On top of the hill is another little park, where liberals with jobs at tech companies walk their designer dogs. We sit and enjoy the view from a tree stump. On the left is the neighborhood of Twin Peaks, barely visible in the fog. Ahead of us is the Mission, and farther away downtown is the Fisherman's Wharf. Folsom, the street I take to get to WeWork, is buried in trees.

Rachel breaks the silence: "I'm probably not going to see you anymore." My heart sinks. "I have to accompany John on his trip to Idaho for the eclipse." She has told me about this extra little freelance job of hers. She is responsible for taking medical care of John Perry Barlow, the 70-year-old retired lyricist for the Grateful Dead. He is going on a road trip to Idaho with a few friends and muses to watch the 2017 solar eclipse, probably while tripping on acid. Rachel's job as a nurse is to make sure the old rock star doesn't die of high blood pressure and drug abuse— while doing this, she will probably take a hit or two as well.

I feel the moment to say goodbye has arrived, and it makes me melancholic and quiet. Back in the house, we hang out on the sofa and watch the sunlight cast shadows of the trees on the high ceilings. It looks like a typical Sunday morning after a night out. A moment between moments. Flashes from the past days go through my head: dancing to live jazz in Club Deluxe, sleeping under the stars in Yosemite, swimming in the Merced River at sunset after our hike. I remember her golden skin while she was sitting on a rock wringing the water out of her hair—the sun now streaming in through the windows lights her up in the same way. All those memories that made me feel euphoric and sad at the same time. Some say not to get attached to people you meet on your travels, that it is best to simply attract, embrace, and let go. It makes sense, but I can't do it. Having feelings for someone is valuable. I don't want to stay on the surface of my relationships; I want to immerse myself.

Rachel leaves the next day. I think I will never see her again. To finish work I need to stay a bit longer in the city, so I book a room in the Red Victorian, just a few blocks from Club Deluxe, where a commune of young artists and creatives live. They have a room or two on Airbnb. The main floor behind the high storefront windows is a vintage clothing and antique store, and behind that is a living room and communal kitchen combined in a large, shared open space. One night, I am invited to a small party at Lee's house. I don't know who Lee is, but a party would be good for me. So I join two girls who live in the hotel and walk through Haight Street with its colorful flickering lights and extravagant storefronts, where everyone buys their outfits for Burning Man. All of the tenants in the Red Victorian are talking about preparations of the extravagant art festival in the desert, which is coming up soon. We arrive at Lee's house and hit the buzzer. All front doors in San Francisco have iron gates to protect the homes from crime and from people wandering in off the street. An extra level of security I'm unfamiliar with in Europe. The girls tell me that we are waiting for Jim to open the door. I don't know who Jim is, either. Once inside the house, everything is bathed in a crimson glow. It's like the red light district in Amsterdam, but without the smell of lubricant. The party is not really a party, but more a small get-together. Lee, a self-appointed "Truthsayer," is a musician, art collector, and creative polymath. He has a dressing room full of Victorian robes, and everyone wants to try them on. San Francisco is full of these peculiar people, these relics of the Summer of Love. After drinks and weed from a dab pen—there are more smoking toys here than in Amsterdam—I go back to the Red Victorian. I've forgotten to write down the code of the front door, and there is no buzzer. I climb over a homeless man and work myself over the iron gate. Luckily the front door is unlocked. I look back at the man sleeping against the gate but he doesn't open his eyes. The night is full of weird dreams.

When I make plans to continue with my journey, to my surprise, Rachel returns earlier than planned. We spend more days together, going out of the city for some small trips. I seriously consider staying longer. I want to invest more time with her. Something valuable is growing. On the other hand, I have been here for five weeks, my work is finished, and staying in the city is taking a toll on my credit card. I don't have much to do while Rachel is at work. It's time to move on. And so we agree to take a little road trip in Utah once I arrive there by bike. With mixed feelings, I finally say goodbye and set out to the east.

Sometimes, I'm afraid that I'm leaving something behind which I will regret in the future. I don't want to lose Rachel. Now and then I fantasize about staying and building my own place in the forest, having a family and the space to create things. On this bicycle trip, I'm constantly inspired by people who have created a beautiful life together, like Kent and Joy. There are so many great ways to establish an alternative way of living without being constantly on the move. I wonder if I could do it. But this is not the time. Maybe I am addicted to the freedom, to being bound to nothing beyond myself and whatever is ahead of me, to always being in charge of my course and doing what I feel is best with my time. There will be long moments to mull it over as I head to Nevada and Utah. The next weeks will be full of solitude and isolation on the empty roads of the Great Basin. I'm preparing for one of the longest desert rides I've ever done. It will be harsh, but I believe it will do me good.

DEAR SAN FRANCISCO,

YOU MADE ME THINK ABOUT LIFE, ABOUT FUTURES, ABOUT GOALS, ABOUT LOVE. YOU'VE CONFUSED ME, SEDUCED ME, SURPRISED ME. YOU'VE PLAYED WITH ME, PROVOKED ME, ARGUED WITH ME. YOU WOUNDED ME AND YOU HEALED ME.

I DON'T WANT TO, BUT I HAVE TO LEAVE NOW. YOU'VE LET ME IN, AND I'VE LET MYSELF OUT. INEVITABLY, UNWILLINGLY. THANK YOU FOR LETTING ME NEAR YOU, SMELL YOU, FEEL YOU.

THANK YOU FOR YOUR FRIENDSHIP, YOUR EMBRACE, YOUR FLATTERING. I'LL LEAVE A PIECE OF ME HERE AND TAKE SOME OF YOURS WITH ME. ONE FOR THE ROAD, ONE FOR THE SOUL.

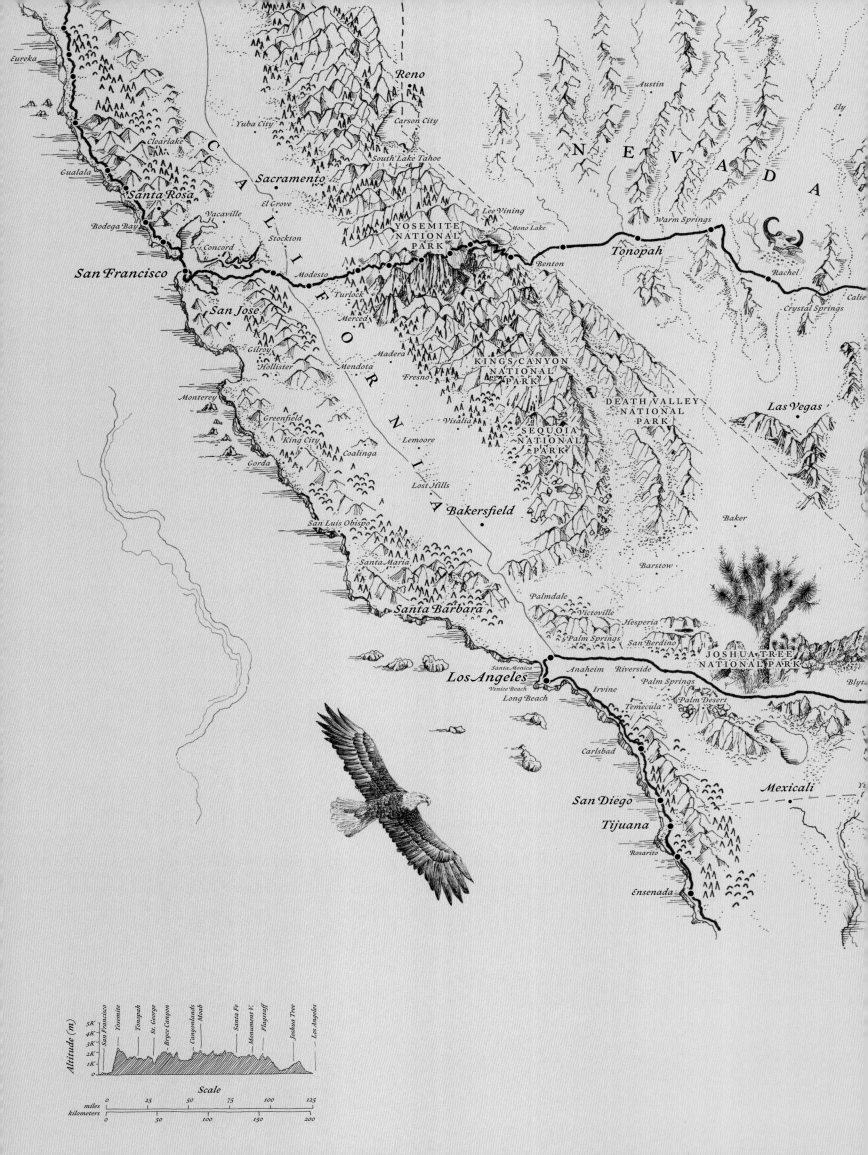

Eureka

Reno

Yuba City

Carson City

Clearlake

South Lake Tahoe

CALIFORNIA

Gualala

Vacaville

El Grove

Santa Rosa

Lee Vining

Bodega Bay

Concord

Stockton

Modesto

Mono Lake

Benton

Warm Springs

Sacramento

YOSEMITE
NATIONAL
PARK

NEVADA

Austin

Ely

Tonopah

Area 51

San Francisco

Rachel

Turlock

San Jose

Merced

Crystal Springs

Calie

Gilroy

Madera

KINGS CANYON
NATIONAL
PARK

Hollister

Mendota

Fresno

DEATH VALLEY
NATIONAL
PARK

Las Vegas

Monterey

Greenfield

Visalia

SEQUOIA
NATIONAL
PARK

King City

Lemoore

Gorda

Coalinga

Lost Hills

Baker

San Luis Obispo

Bakersfield

Santa Maria

Barstow

Palmdale

Santa Barbara

Victorville

Hesperia

Palm Springs

San Berdino

JOSHUA TREE
NATIONAL PARK

Santa Monica

Anaheim

Riverside

Los Angeles

Venice Beach

Irvine

Palm Springs

Blyt

Long Beach

Palm Desert

Temecula

Carlsbad

Mexicali

San Diego

Tijuana

Rosarito

Ensenada

Altitude (m)

5K
4K
3K
2K
1K
0

San Francisco
Yosemite
Tonopah
St. George
Bryce Canyon
Canyonlands
Moab
Santa Fe
Monument V.
Flagstaff
Joshua Tree
Los Angeles

Scale

miles   0   25   50   75   100   125
kilometers 0   50   100   150   200

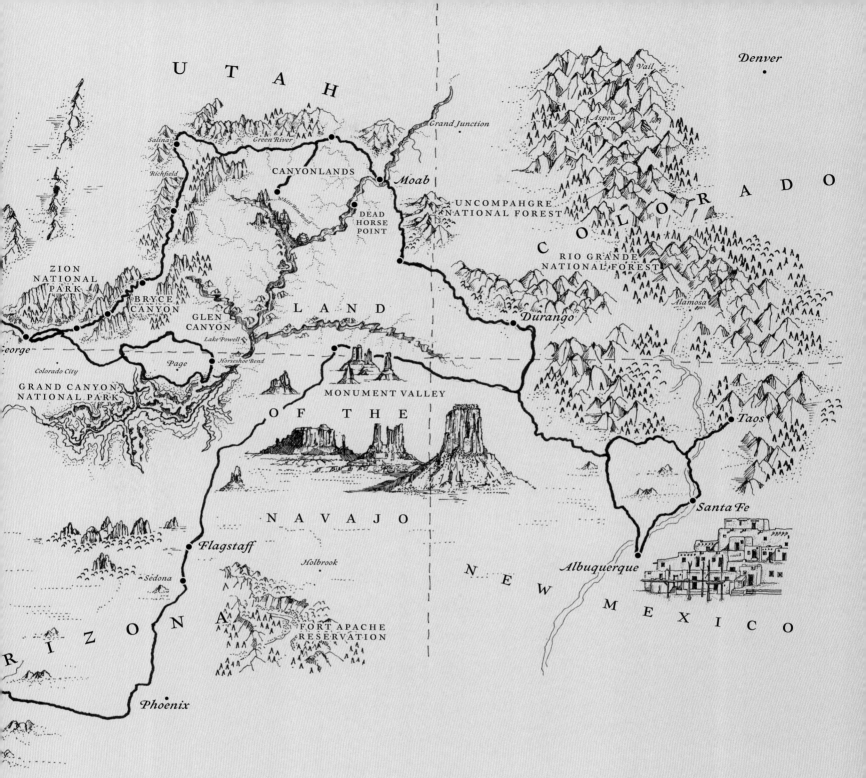

THE WILD WEST

DAY 94 · MODESTO, CALIFORNIA · 3088 KM

I've always dreamed about the far-stretched plains of Nevada and the red rocks of Utah and Arizona. Summer is at its end and the scorching-hot deserts are about to cool down. It's the perfect time to stray from the coast and head due east from San Francisco over the Sierra Nevadas, on toward the Great Basin.

"*The mountains are calling
and I must go.*"

—JOHN MUIR

YOSEMITE NATIONAL PARK, CALIFORNIA

A beautiful morning in Yosemite, preparing a nutritious breakfast while the sun rises in between the pine trees. Cereal with nuts and apple, bread with peanut butter, and freshly made coffee. You're not allowed to wild camp inside national parks in the US, but sometimes you need an extra day of cycling to cross the park and can't help spending a night. In such cases, it goes without saying to respect the rules as much as possible and leave no trace.

—*Coyote encounters*

I'm zipped in my tent in the middle of Yosemite National Park, and I'm having trouble falling asleep. This is bear country, and I'm worried I didn't take the right precautions. My food is in my panniers, which should be airtight. To be safe, I've stashed them far from camp. I'm camping farther from the road than usual. The faint noise of cars passing by is normally reassuring, but because I can't hear any cars now, I feel anxious. Now, if a bear attacks, no passerby will be able to hear or notice me. Earlier in the evening, I prepared dinner about 60 meters from my camp, but I'm storing my cooking equipment in my tent. Maybe I should have packed it with the food. The little pan is rinsed, but there might be a little leftover Kathmandu Curry, a strong smell I'm sure bears would notice. There are also some apples still in my frame bag.

I remember my last "run-in" with wildlife a few days ago in the Central Valley, where I camped in the middle of a field. It was warm enough to sleep in the open without setting up my tent, which allowed me to avoid being seen by farmers in the flat landscape. As I lay in my sleeping bag, exposed under the stars, convinced I was safe, I heard the howl of a wolf not far from me. My heart leapt; blood rushed through my veins. Just as the howl stopped, there were even more, all around me. I recorded a voice message to share with Paul from Vancouver. He replied, "Hah, those are coyotes! You shouldn't worry about them. They don't attack people." It calmed me down a bit, but just to be sure, I opened Google on my phone and read everything I found under "coyote encounters."

It is the same here in Yosemite. My inexperience worries me. I wouldn't know what to do if a bear came near. Should I keep quiet, pretending to sleep? Should I get out of the tent and start making noise? What if a bear is nearby right now, sniffing around my tent pegs? I'm focused on every little noise in the forest around me. Once the night fell and the steady traffic died down, a new world of sound opened up. Now, I hear the tiny crackles of wood, a branch falling from the canopy, a critter under the tent fabric, a bird rustling through the leaves. Every unexpected noise makes my heart beat faster. I'm cold because of the higher altitude. Or maybe I'm cold because I'm scared. Every few minutes, I clap my hands to keep the bears at a distance. Make some noise now and then, that is what I've read on all the plaques in the park. Then suddenly, I hear something rustling—it sounds like it's in my tent! But it's my own beard scratching my sleeping bag—I'm a joke.

↗ *Mono Lake. The unique formations called tufa formed after the water levels receded in the past century.*
↘ *These desert flowers are found all over this part of California and Nevada and have a fresh, basil-like smell.*

NEVADA DESERT

DAY 101 - GREAT BASIN DESERT, NEVADA - 3112 KM

Nevada welcomes me with grand gestures that bring new levels of excitement and fear. I am prepared for the long, straight roads under the sun, but the desert surprises me with a new challenge: thunderstorms.

The horizon lit by thunderstorms. Lightning strokes are not visible because of the long exposure capture. The red light is light pollution from my head torch.

—Two perfect storms

Descending from the high altitudes in Yosemite, I plunge into the desert after a brief break in Lee Vining. It's all sunny and friendly when I arrive the next day in Benton, on the border of California, where I take a break for lunch. Benton is a sleepy junction town along the highway with a gas station, diner, and grocery store, all located in one corner building. A stream runs through town, which is why a few people still live here even after the silver and gold mines were exhausted around 1900. This is the only access to water for miles around. I leave with six liters of water in PET bottles on my bike, enough for two days. With altitude increasing, temperatures become slightly milder, otherwise I would need more. Tonopah, the next town, is 130 kilometers ahead, and in between the two towns there will be no trace of human presence other than pavement, traffic signs with bullet holes, and a small sign saying "Welcome to Nevada." The open space is daunting, but I swallow my fears and pedal out of town. Now and then, I glance back over my shoulder, feeling the safety of human civilization drawing me back. After a bend in the road, I'm all on my own.

Nevada is the driest state in the US, but that's not the case today. A few hours after I've left Benton, the skies behind me morph into a threatening vortex of clouds. The views reach so far across the valley that I'm able to analyze the direction the storm is heading. The skies demand all my attention; there's simply nothing else to look at. Behind me in the distance, a thick blanket of rain washes over the land. A strong tailwind kicks up and thrusts me forward faster than I can pedal. Eventually I'm in the middle of it and the rain pours down. All the dust accumulated over the months gets washed off my bike—I haven't ridden in the rain since I was in Washington. The storm doesn't take long. As fast as it has come, it blows over, and the sun returns. At a deserted gas station, I change into dry clothes.

The Great Basin is a vast desert ribbed by north-south mountain ranges. Between the ranges are false flat arid plains with little to no vegetation. The iconic desert highways of Nevada cut straight through them, vanishing at the horizon, without a bend in sight. Because I'm crossing from west to east, I'm always on a mild incline or decline.

I set up camp about 200 meters from the road, almost exactly in the middle of the valley, which is reminiscent of a very shallow bathtub. I haven't had to search for the perfect spot; anywhere is good. Occasionally a car passes, but no one notices me. I see the cars first as they come over the hill about ten kilometers away. Then a few quiet minutes pass as I watch the headlights slowly approaching, until the car passes by and the red taillights fade toward the other hill. It takes about 15 minutes for a car to cross the entire valley at 100 kilometers per hour, and I can see its entire path. It's a sobering realization of how outstretched and remote this valley is—and I'm in it all alone.

As I prepare some food, the roar of my gas stove is the only sound there is. Far away, ominous clouds rise up again. Lightning jabs at several places across the horizon. Another storm? It looks like it will blow over far from here, so I poke around in my pot and finish my Shepherd's Potato Stew with Beef, enjoying the show. I've never seen so much continuous lightning: it's an astonishing spectacle. There's no thunder, just beams of light shattering across the entire horizon. But as time passes, I start to feel less comfortable. The lightning hasn't stopped, the storm is slowly drawing in, and I am the highest point in the area. Only my tent and low shrubs surround me; there's not even a traffic sign in the near distance. As a precaution, I tie some extra ropes to the tent to withstand the coming storm. Dark clouds drift over like a large spaceship, covering the stars and the light of the Milky Way. I hide in my tent when the wind starts to blow up sand. It pounds against the tent fabric, trying to cut through. There's neither thunder nor rain, just a howling wind and the lightning. I've never experienced anything like this. I calm myself by emptying a flask of Jack Daniels, and I fall asleep holding onto the tent pole while the storm tries to sweep me away.

In the morning, I wake up and stick my head out of the tent. Apart from the thin layer of sand covering everything, it looks like nothing happened.

I'm surrendered to the vastness,
and being in the middle of it,
I'm bound to it.

—Unbearable Silence

The views are unchanging for the majority of my time cycling through the stretched-out, lifeless valleys of Nevada. Often, there is more to see in the sky than on land. Clouds fly over. Storms evolve in the distance and disappear again. Tonopah is still 25 kilometers ahead on the other end of the straight line, behind the mirage glittering. I'm losing myself in the rhythm of pedaling, unaware of making any progress at all.

I feel small and vulnerable, but I also feel raw and pure. I am not part of the "real" world as I traverse this moonscape surrounded by space and dust, far from humanity. I'm surrendered to the vastness, and being in the middle of it, I'm bound to it. The way back to the beginning of the Great Basin is now as far as the way forward. It's both liberating and suffocating. I have to stay sane and keep pushing, enjoying the silence, the void, the beauty of it.

Aliens
—legends from Area 51

The desert makes the mind wander. Its secrecy feeds conspiracy theories in the small mining towns across this part of Nevada. Area 51 is a highly classified and guarded US Air Force base where weapons and aircraft are tested. It dates from the Cold War, but was only officially acknowledged by the CIA in 2013. No wonder myths are born here as strange lights appear on the horizon at night. I've been seeing the lights from my bike, but never know what to make of them. At least, not until I experience one of the strangest nights on the entire journey.

Before entering Nevada, I marked all the places on the map where I could potentially find water. Warm Springs is one of them. I assumed it was a small town, but a miner in Tonopah told me I would find nothing more than an abandoned bar with a hot spring and the remains of a settlement. Still, a hot spring sounds like an attractive place to spend the night, because I haven't showered for days.

When I arrive in Warm Springs at the end of the afternoon, I see that I am not alone. Rich and Felicia, a young couple from Ohio, have brought their car to camp here. The property is fenced off, but the gate is unlocked. Amidst the shrubs and junk of leftover building materials is an old pool fed by the hot spring, which itself is up a hill. Next to the pool is a small changing room, with big letters on the door saying "KEEP OUT." I touch the translucent mineral water and guess it's around 40 degrees Celsius, just a little too hot to jump straight into. Despite the state of the buildings, the water looks surprisingly clean.

An old truck arrives a few hours later. Rich, Felicia, and I can see the driver talking to himself as he parks and gets out. He's a man in his forties with a black beanie, a long thin beard, and a thick German accent, and he approaches us, still muttering. We aren't sure at first if he is speaking to us, but it appears that he is. He introduces himself as Tom, and tells us he is on a road trip from Calgary, Canada, where he currently lives, visiting hot springs on his way. He is recovering from a car accident, and he can't sleep well because of muscle pain. The hot springs offer him some relief. The dashboard of his truck is loaded with bananas, and we ask him why. It is the only thing he eats, he tells us. I quickly tire of listening to him, but it's hard to walk away since he won't stop rambling. I'm not sure when I stop believing his stories. Probably when he tells us about a wolf climbing into his tent.

I prepare dinner over the fire, and to our relief, Tom disappears to the pool. Rich and Felicia explain that they are on their honeymoon. I wonder how they came to select such a dilapidated "resort" in the middle of the desert, which officially is off-limits, as a honeymoon destination. We laugh about it. As we enjoy dinner on a trashed sofa, the skies darken again: another storm is about to drift in. We can feel the electric-ity in the air. When it comes, we take shelter in the shed. Tom doesn't bother. He just keeps standing in the middle of the pool with his arms crossed while the storm rages. He is still talking. We can't understand a word.

Down the property toward the road is an abandoned bar, and I go for a look. The back door is open and I use my headlamp to light the way. It's a mess inside. Broken glass, a pool table, a fridge, and some old kitchen stoves are strewn about. In small stacks on the bar are some magazines from 1980, the colors all bleached out. I pick my way over toward a side room and hear something rustling. I hold my breath to hear better and not make any noise. The room is pitch black inside. When my headlamp illuminates the floor, I see that it's covered with what seem at first to be chocolate sprinkles. I slowly lift my head, and see that the entire ceiling is covered with bats, staring at me as they hang upside down. I'm out of the building again in seconds.

The storm goes on but it has stopped raining. I sit down watching the fire. The strong wind blows the sparks far away and I worry about it setting the dry grass on fire. Rich offers me something to smoke. I exchange it for some bourbon. Tom is *still* in the pool, though he has stopped talking. Felicia softly sings in her tent. I can barely hear it through the noise of the storm that rattles the buildings, but it comforts me. Once everyone else goes to bed, I decide to take a dip in the pool myself. The winds are still going at full speed and give me the chills, but the pool is now a perfect temperature. It's surreal to hide in the hot spring while the storm blows over. Lightheaded from the hot water, the bourbon, and the weed, I set up my tent. When I'm almost asleep, I hear Tom shouting that there is a police car coming. I stick my head out of the tent and look over the plains. In the far distance, we see red and blue flashing lights. We watch them for a while, but we can't decide if they are really moving. It's probably something else. Something we aren't supposed to see, from a place we aren't supposed to be.

The morning starts slowly. Tom points to something in the field far away, something that wasn't there the day before. We walk toward it to check it out. It's a dead bull. It's still bloated, so it must have died very recently. I've seen traffic signs about cattle roaming freely, but this one is the first I've seen. I start to get a weird taste in my mouth. I've had enough of this place. I need to move on as soon as possible.

Tom, the peculiar German traveler, with his endless conspiracy theories.

Area 51 is a highly classified US Air force base. Nobody really knows what's going on here, but it seems to be a test area for experimental aircraft and weapons. As I cycle through this part of the desert, I hear the sounds of jet fighters, and even explosions. The people in the little towns nearby are obsessed with aliens, having witnessed all kinds of strange lights in the skies at night. Recently, motorcyclists have been stopped at gunpoint when they were trying to get close to the area via a dirt road—it's truly a place rife with conspiracy.

—The Grand Canyon

For millions of years, the Colorado River has carved over 1800 meters deep into the Colorado Plateau, revealing a plethora of sediments and colors, layer upon layer. It's not on my route—in fact, it's 500 kilometers out of the way—but I simply have to see it. I rent a car for a one-day detour, but it turns out to be an unsatisfying visit.

When I arrive at the parking lot at the North Rim, I see that everything caters to large groups of visitors—the opposite of what I'm looking for in nature. I don't like it. I feel like I'm just ticking boxes on a to-do list. I have been so spoiled by natural beauty in the last months. Simply driving here, stepping out of the car, and taking a few pictures doesn't do it for me anymore. The most memorable places are those I've worked hard to find, or places that show up as a surprise. A view is more rewarding after hiking or biking there, with one's legs burning from the effort. Just sitting here on the edge of the cliff, being chilly because I just stepped out of a heated car, confirms to me that the bicycle is the perfect vehicle for travel. Another lesson learned.

Zion
—Sharing the road

"You're going the wrong way!" is often the response I get when I tell fellow cyclists I'm going to Patagonia. They are right: Patagonia is in the opposite direction. But now that I have finally arrived in Zion, I don't regret this detour at all.

Utah is different. I've never seen so many deep reds and browns. I noticed it by zooming in on Google Earth and turning off all the labels. (It's a great way of exploring landscapes and planning a journey, because one can discover little-known mountains, canyons, and scenic roads.) In St. George, I am hosted by Chris and his girlfriend for a few days. On

my way forward, he joins me for a day en route to Zion National Park. Chris is a "hard case-only guy," and has been creative in rigging out his bike with repurposed plastic containers, like cat litter buckets. They serve as panniers, chairs, and a kitchen table when camping. A chair is a big luxury after cycling all day. Usually, cyclists sit on the ground to take breaks or when they stop for the night. Personally, a foam pad and my saddle—to serve as back support—work well enough.

On our way we meet Robert, a Dutch cyclist doing a recreational version of the Trans Am Bike Race, a popular cycling route crossing the US from east to west. Funnily enough, he lives in the village where I grew up in the Netherlands, though I've never heard of him. On the road into the park, we realize that we will have to hitch a ride, because cyclists are not allowed through the dark, narrow tunnels. It doesn't take long before a truck stops to take us all through. As we zip along, I notice—not for the first time—that the US is a car country, even with respect to its national parks. They are designed to be easily accessible to drivers, but not cyclists or walkers. I would love to see more of an

impetus to get people on bikes or out for a walk. That would be the best way to explore the stunning rock formations of Zion.

In the evening we camp in a field just over a hill at the end of the park, still in the gorgeous landscapes, and swap camping tricks we've learned on our travels. Robert teaches us to make a fire by putting wood on his gas stove for a few minutes, without bothering to start with kindling. Chris is able to get my greasy pot, which I just cooked an Indian dish in, totally clean by rubbing it with soft sand. It takes a while, but what else do we have to do besides sit around a campfire all evening sharing stories? Robert has been on the road alone for a long time like me, so meeting other cyclists means instant family bonds. Whenever I share camp with other cyclists, great friendships are born, and I deeply appreciate the company.

Chris with his cat litter buckets-turned panniers.
Camping tip: if limited water is available, clean your pots and cutlery by rubbing them with fine sand. The sand will scratch off any grease or dirt without the use of soap.

BRYCE CANYON, UTAH

Canyonlands
—A road trip with Rachel

From the edge of the cliff, I watch the clouds cast their shadows over the plains in the lower canyons. I'm overlooking what was once a sea, millions of years ago. These canyons were carved out over time by wind and water. It's midnight, and it's chilly. Rachel has just crawled into the sleeping bag. I'm staying up because I love the nights at viewpoints like these. The quietness grants me perspective and clarity, and I can let my thoughts wander. I recall the events of the day: hiking the arches in Moab, smoking weed through an apple, walking through the strange sandstone formations in Goblin State Park, and driving deep into Canyonlands.

Rachel has taken a flight to join me for this small road trip. To be honest, I've been looking forward to this every day since I left San Francisco two months ago. It's great to have a friend who shares the same adventurous spirit. She challenges and inspires me to approach things differently, and as a local, she knows much more about the landscape and geology. In the months we've known each other, we've been on dates in the city and microadventures out in nature, and it is during those times outside, being spoiled by the beauty, that I feel our strongest connection. The nights under the stars, the long walks into canyons, sharing sunsets together at the Pacific... knowing we love those things allows us to create a bond and share memories whose power will only grow with time. The intense fights we had in San Francisco are still in the back of my mind, but the last two weeks together in the city we were growing together, and any bad memory simply melts away sharing moments together in these awe-inspiring landscapes.

We're sleeping in my tent, which is way too small for two people, so we keep the inner tent in the bag to have a bit more space. The alarm is set before sunrise because as usual, we're not actually allowed to camp here in the park. We want to have the tent packed before any park ranger might appear. I'm sitting outside to edit some photos on my laptop and finish our bottle of wine. All the clouds are gone now, and the moon creates sharp blue shadows in the ravine. The mountains in the distance are hazy. There's a crack in the earth with a white rim around it. Tomorrow we are planning to hike down, descending 400 meters into the steep canyon and hiking to the next one. I've never seen a landscape like this; it's eerie and sublime. No birds, no insects, no signs of life at all, just the wind sweeping

View on the lower canyons that look like the footprints of a giant monster, flanked by the White Rim Road.

between the walls. I lie down on the edge of the cliff and let my head hang off, feeling the wind cradling my neck. Finally, I crawl in our warm sleeping bags, which we have once again zipped together. Rachel mumbles something and turns toward me. I indulge in her warmth. Usually my sleeping bag is cold when I enter it. All I feel is simple happiness. Her scent is planted in my brain, and hasn't left me since I left San Francisco. I have missed it every night since I left. I fall into a deep sleep.

When the alarm goes off, Rachel is up instantly. I need a few minutes. The air is crisp and cold. At the edge of the cliff, we prepare breakfast with dusty views of the Wild West. A spectrum of unusual colors ranges between chocolate brown, burgundy, and teal, contrasting with the soft greens of sage and rabbitbrush. The sun peeks over the horizon and warms us up. Mango, sweet cereal, and Greek yogurt are for breakfast. Coffee percolates cheerfully in the Bialetti. Another day of blissful adventure is ahead.

Arches National Park, Utah.

—Back on my own

After four days together, Rachel returns to her job in San Francisco. I reach Dead Horse Point alone, where I set up camp on the edge of the table rock. It's still warm from absorbing the sun all day. I stare into the waning light for an hour, trying to get my mind straight. I am not sure which direction to go from here. I feel lost.

Since I left San Francisco, I have been living on a cloud. Everything has been going so well. I feel like I've reached a high point in my life. I've been traveling through the most amazing landscapes, I've had lucrative freelance work, and I'm in love with the most gorgeous girl. And yet, even though I recognize that I have everything I've ever wished for, I feel alone and unhappy. I think it is the same internal conflict I felt in San Francisco: stay with Rachel, or pursue my dream of the road? I cannot have both. Usually I'm in my element when I'm out camping alone. I feel neither fear nor loneliness. But tonight, I only long to be with her. My plans about the journey are again unsure. My compass is jammed.

The next day, I try to distract myself by listening to podcasts, but there is just too much time to kill on the lonely roads of Utah. The desert offers few distractions; often, the only sign of life is my own beating heart. The slow progress of my bike is frustrating, because I've been in a car the last several days. It's incredibly demotivating to cycle in days what a car could do in hours. With, I might add, comfortable chairs, air conditioning, music, and refrigerated snacks. I know this is a temporary funk, that it will all get better later. Like a flesh wound, it takes pain and time to heal. I try to relish the moments with Rachel and simply enjoy the memories, rather than stew in the loss, and I look to the south to contemplate my next move. Rachel recommended a trip to Taos, a native enclave in New Mexico. But it's far off my route to the east, and at some point I need to head back to the coast. Perhaps if I had a faster way to get there... I write "South" on a piece of cardboard and wait by the road. Dozens of cars pass; nobody stops. After only 10 minutes of flaunting the sign, I give up and hop back on the bike. I don't want to be dependent on other people.

DEAD HORSE POINT STATE PARK, UTAH

Enjoying lunch with Sarkis and some of his friends at the Hanuman Ashram in Taos.

New Mexico
—A home among natives

As it turns out, I end up hitching a ride after all, by a Trump support-er, no less. Almost all the people I have interacted with in the US have been Democrats. In a roadside bar at the border of Utah, he and I start chatting. Not about Trump so much, but about fishing, which he just returned from in Lake Powell. Minutes later, my bike is in the back of his boat, on a trailer behind his double-axle Ford pickup. We sip Coors Lights and discuss the American dream as we cross into Colorado, and then New Mexico.

Once in Santa Fe, I continue cycling toward Taos, following Rachel's advice. Early in the day, I cycle through a reservation where the police stop me and escort me out. Apparently I'm not welcome as a white tour-ist—fair enough. Later, I reach a small, dusty town called Kewa Pueblo on a dirt road, and it feels like I've left modern America. I'm not rushed out of here; in fact, I have a chat with the locals and enjoy some Navajo tacos, which are made from thick frybread. The native population here still speaks their own language, Keres, and everyone has two names: an official registered name, often in Spanish, and a Keres name which cannot be written with the Latin alphabet. I try to connect with the older locals to take their portraits, but most are hesitant. It's not in their tradition to be photographed, as it's considered a sort of capturing of the soul. I can respect that. Eventually, I make it to Taos, known for its native Pueblo community. They still live in a historical mud clay village, a style of building seen all across New Mexico.

If it weren't for Sarkis Gorial, I probably wouldn't have come here. But he has graciously invited me to stay in his home. Sarkis, 56, is a Persian artist and traveler. He has resided in Taos for the past 14 years. We have never met in person before, but we share acquaintances in Iran and he has been following my travels since I cycled through his country of birth two years ago. I couldn't ask for a better host. He introduces me to the intriguing community of Taos, and tells me stories as we wander the historic village.

Later at his apartment, a large open space full of paintings, Sarkis tells me his life story. He grew up in Iran as an orphan. His father passed away when he was four, and his mother wasn't financially capable enough to take care of him, so he moved between families. At age 17, he started to travel the world. This was, of course, before the existence of social media and mobile phones, in a time when one had to talk to

people on the streets and in bars instead of googling everything or connecting on Instagram. When the revolution started in Iran in 1979, Sarkis knew he couldn't return because his Assyrian name betrayed a Christian lineage. His home country became off-limits for him, and so his traveling became a search for a new home, focused on spending more time with people and establishing deeper friendships. He lived for periods of more than a year in countries like Greece, Italy, the Netherlands, India, Guatemala, and, for the past 32 years, the United States. He maintains an especially strong connection with the Netherlands. In his twenties he lived there for two years and met a family in Arnhem, who unofficially adopted him as a son. It's the closest thing he has to a family, and he tries to visit them every year.

Sarkis has been painting for most of his life, and has mastered several styles. Some of his works are Rembrandt-like in their detail and soft yet

> "As a painter, I think of myself as an imitator of the Creator, who has created all and everything we are surrounded by. It gives me joy and a purpose to live."

dramatic light. Others are rougher and more expressive. In the corner of the room is a beautiful black and white painting of his mother, perhaps his most personal work. I ask if I may photograph him while he works on a painting. He takes an older piece from the wall and continues on it. To him, a painting is never finished. As I point my camera, he tells me, "Painting is a spiritual journey for me. I think of myself as an imitator of the Creator, who has created all and everything we are surrounded by. It gives me joy and a purpose to live."

I consider how fortunate I am to have a family in my home country, the Netherlands, who will be there for me if or when I go back. That makes my way of traveling different from Sarkis's. The connections I make are more like gathered experiences, which may or may not extend to the future. I keep things open. Since I met Rachel two months ago in San Francisco, I've felt myself slowly disconnecting from Amsterdam. It might not be permanent, but more than ever, I feel open to new adventures and possibly to establishing a home somewhere for a while, wherever that might be. I feel inspired being in another culture. Creating a new home elsewhere for years at a time is a form of travel, too. When I live and work somewhere for a longer period, I discover the subtler differences of my new, chosen culture. It can be a risky thing to settle down in an unfamiliar atmosphere, because it leads one to reexamine his own origins, or, like Sarkis, to conclude that one's old home needed to be abandoned. But for me, living elsewhere usually just makes me appreciate where I came from.

TAOS PUEBLO, NEW MEXICO

The path to longevity is in a youthful countenance.

"You hippies are always late," John grumps when I finally arrive on his property. He is Sarkis's friend, and I met him in a bar in Taos a week ago. I am indeed late, but it wasn't easy to find his place amidst all the trashy settlements in this part of the desert. John's place is a junkyard of scruffy self-made buildings, car parts, chairs, an old washing machine, desks, tires, mattresses, and all other kinds of detritus laid out in the dry scrubland. I'm curious to learn how he has lived here for 20 years, so isolated and exposed to the elements.

John takes me into a dilapidated house. It's barely standing, and the ceiling sags in the middle, forcing me to bow my head. On the walls are colorful, psychedelic works of art. He makes sure all of them hang perfectly straight before granting me permission to photograph them. He still seems grumpy. I want to win his respect, so I ask about his painting. Willingly but haltingly he answers; his mind seems to work slowly. His voice is raspy and there are long pauses between every sentence. Proudly, he introduces me to all his paintings then shows me his own small temple, which is dressed up with carpets, handmade jewelry, and figures of Hindu gods.

I try to imagine how it must be to live here, out in the open, in the stillness of the desert. I often cycle through these landscapes, but it's different to be moving, heading forward. John's mind must be resilient to withstand living in this void. He shrugs it off and tells me that people get used to it, learn to slow down. I ask to take his photo in his handmade native robe he showed me earlier, and eagerly he walks to his trailer to put it on. I buy a necklace from him, too. When I leave, he is full of joy, compared to when I arrived. He has a daughter who's 53, but he jokes that he's younger than her. "The path to longevity is in a youthful countenance." I give him a hug and we take a selfie. As I pedal away, he stands in the middle of the road, disappearing into the dust.

MONUMENT VALLEY, ARIZONA

Navajo man, Oljato-Monument Valley, Arizona.

—Exiting the United States

If you wanted to cycle from Vancouver via the coast directly to San Diego, a navigation app would calculate a 2714 kilometer trip with 16,492 meters of elevation gain. I reached San Diego by cycling 5109 kilometers and climbing 57,582 meters. It's fair to say I took the scenic route—and I even didn't cycle everything. Most of the way from New Mexico to Los Angeles, I took a car. If you factor the driving in, I've traveled about 7000 kilometers, but I only have registered cycled distances. I don't keep a strict rule that I have to cycle every little bit, otherwise this journey would take a year or two longer. My primary goal is to cycle a wide variety of landscapes. From highways to cattle tracks, capitals to hamlets, jungles to deserts, canyons to mountaintops, I want to see it all. I still am not adhering to a schedule. Sometimes work has slowed me down, and of course, Rachel ruined my travel plans—but I've loved all of it.

I'm writing this up now as I sit on a beach in San Diego. I've just returned from a short trip to San Francisco to see Rachel before I leave the country. Since we met, we've been in touch on a daily basis. Our relationship never fully established itself; we have been in the early stage of drunken excitement, constantly wanting to see and talk to each other. It has made the ride difficult. Cycling through these unforgettable landscapes has been bitter-sweet because I haven't shared all of it with her. When we texted or called, it lifted me up. When she didn't answer for a few hours, it killed me.

My mind has constantly been somewhere else. Cycling long distances requires determination, which has been in short supply. In between the highlights—which are what this book mainly consists of—have been many dull moments, dozens of days where the landscape hasn't changed and my camera has stayed in the bag. Days with overcast skies, busy roads, and ugly towns. The neverending time in the desert in Nevada, Utah, and New Mexico, while initially a welcome change of scenery, soon became boring and challenging, and then, I was left only with the rumbling of my mind.

This last visit to San Francisco turned out to be the final chapter for Rachel and me. At first, we couldn't wait to see each other. When I landed in the city, I felt like I was home. The cold gray weather and the old neighborhoods reminded me of Amsterdam. She and I went to museums in the day and jazz bars in the evening. We found ourselves closer than ever, and we lived together in the city for a bit, imagining what it would like to have a future. But at the same time, things became difficult as we had a taste of everyday life, with its busy schedules and humdrum obligations. Our differences, while at first exciting, turned against each other. We found out we were much less compatible than we thought we were. The dreams of living and traveling together soon faded. One night, I couldn't sleep, so I took a long walk over the hills of the Castro, sitting on top of Corona Heights park in the November drizzle, trying to find a way to make things work. No answer satisfied me. The magnificent views of San Francisco from the hilltop were melancholic. Ironically, it resolved something inside me and made me smile. What a life! I deeply valued our time together.

Two days later I left, earlier than planned. All our future plans were canceled. Somehow, I felt relieved. I could focus on the trip again. I love Rachel, and I'm grateful we got to know each other. But here on this California beach, the bright warm sun on my face makes me forget the fog of San Francisco. It's time to move on. Mexico is smiling at me.

C A L I F O R N I A

Long Beach

Carlsbad

San Diego
Chula Vista
Tijuana

Tecate

Mexicali

Ensenada

BAJA
CALIFORNIA

Puerto Peñasco

SONORA

Punta Colonet

Vicente
Guerrero

San Quintín

Puertecitos

El Rosario

Bufeo

Punta Final

Isla Ángel de la Guarda

Bahía de
los Ángeles

Hermosillo

El Marrón

Santa Rosaliíta

El Rosarito

Guerrero
Negro

Bahía Tortugas

SEA OF CORTEZ

Guaymas

Ciudad
Obregón

Del Vizcaíno

BAJA
CALIFORNIA
SUR

Santa Rosalía

Navojoa

M E X I C O

Bahía
Asunción

Mulegé

N O R T H   P A C I F I C   O C E A N

La Bocana

Loreto

Los Mochis

Parque Nacional
Bahía de Loreto

MEXICO 1

San José
de la Noria

Ciudad Insurgentes

San Carlos

Puerto Cortés

Ferry to Mazatlán

La Paz

Los Barriles

Todos Santos
El Pescadero

Cabo San
Lucas

Altitude (m)

5K
4K
3K
2K
1K
0

San Diego
Ensenada
Punta Colonet
Cataviña
Guerrero Negro
Santa Rosalía
Loreto
La Paz

Scale

miles   0   25   50   75   100   125
kilometers   0   50   100   150   200

THE BAJA DIVIDE

Baja California is a peninsula in the far west of Mexico, a rich palette of cactus-covered wilderness and dizzying colors, weathered under the burning sun. Banda music plays loudly from the car radios. Everywhere there are freshly prepared fish tacos: cheap, spicy, and delicious.

Entering Mexico
— *"People will be a lot nicer here."*

Coming from the "safe" West, the border town Tijuana is usually avoided by travelers, who associate it with drug dealing, dangerous traffic, and general criminality. A lot of Americans seem to have some sort of Mexico-phobia. "Be careful out there!" I have been warned many times. I heard similar remarks from Western Europeans when I told them I was going to cycle the Middle East: "Are you sure you're going to cycle through Iran..?" Many people experience trepidation about other cultures and religions, but on my travels, it's always the "scariest" places where I receive the warmest hospitality, being treated as family by complete strangers. Not that I'm ignorant and unaware of danger, but I try to balance common sense with an open mind. The fear is often unfounded. When I spoke to Latino people in California about heading

south, I always heard the same thing: "Oh, people will be a lot nicer there!" So I am not too nervous to enter Mexico.

The border crossing is smooth, and I receive a stamp in my passport allowing me 90 days. To leave the crowds as soon as possible, I follow the main road south on the peninsula, out of Tijuana. It's dusty and narrow, and it reminds me of the chaotic traffic in Iran and Kyrgyzstan, where the cars rattle with age and emit black exhaust. Sometimes I have to hold my breath in the dense traffic. But I'm excited. Mexico is vibrant. Advertising is painted on the buildings, weathered away by the sun. Banda music, with its typical, ear-shredding Mexican brass and percussion, plays loudly from car radios and roadside stores. As I slowly grind up the hills, I look over my shoulder to keep an eye on the larger trucks that pass so closely. It's hot, and the veins on my forehead swell and dust cakes onto my skin. Once most of the chaos is behind me, I stop at an Oxxo. I buy an ice-cold Pacifico and sit next to my bike on the pavement. Traffic rushes by. There are even horses on the road.

This roughness makes me feel alive and away from it all. It recalibrates my mind. Once I'm out of the urban region of Tijuana, I will join the Baja Divide, a newly mapped mountain bike route crossing the entire peninsula from north to south. It's time to start riding on dirt.

—Low pressure

It's my first time spending multiple days on trails and dirt roads. The surface is rough, and I need to let quite a bit of air out of the tires to make the ride somewhat comfortable. With three-inch tires that's easy, as they have a lot of clearance with the rims. On a hillside, I meet a couple of cyclists from Hong Kong on classic touring bikes with thin tires and full loads. They are struggling with the inclines. I pinch their tires, as one does during casual roadside conversations. They're as hard as carrots, and I make the suggestion to let some air out. It will help, even if it's just a little bit. High pressure makes a cyclist fast on pavement, but on this rocky surface, every little pebble makes the bike bounce, and there are a lot of pebbles ahead of us. It's hard to say precisely what pressure is ideal in general. Lower pressure is more comfortable because it absorbs the shocks and keeps the bike rolling through sand, but it's also a lot slower and heavier to pedal because of the higher rolling resistance. On downhills, however, soft tires are exponentially better—I fly over the rocks as if I'm on a paved road.

—Perks of the secondary roads

The best thing about these dirt roads is the silence. No noise, no exhaust fumes, no loud horns. Many sections go straight along the beach. Now and then, I throw the bike in the sand and take a dip in the ocean. I don't have to bother digging out my swimwear from the bottom of my panniers: there's no one around. I swim, read a few chapters on my Kindle until I'm dry, and move on. Today, I've only seen three cars. There are no worries about passing traffic, staying on the right side of the road, or looking over my shoulder.

The progress is slow, but I'm okay with that. It's a more active style of cycling, constantly scanning for the smoothest bit of surface, avoiding potholes and rocks, keeping the bike in balance. At some points, I slide away into soft sand. If I do 40 kilometers in a day, I can be proud of myself.

I often pass time by making these nightly pictures at my campsites. The camera shoots continuously from a tripod. The exposure could be half a minute or longer, which you can tell by the motion of the stars. The red color is the light from my headlamp. In this scene, I'm moving around camp and inside my tent to light subjects, and eventually I walk out of the frame, which explains the light ray.

Killing time collecting sand dollars.

MULEGÉ, BAJA CALIFORNIA, MEXICO

MEXICO CITY

*The Mexican spirit is seductive, lively, and contagious,
and it all comes together in the capital city. The fiery
flavors of the street food, the sun-kissed colors of its painted
advertising, and the stately aristocratic neighborhoods
keep me entranced for four months—and once I decide to
leave, my bike is stolen.*

I'm in Plaza La Romita, a quaint little pocket of the bigger neighborhood Colonia Roma. The Airbnb I'm in belongs to a young artist. I haven't met the host; the doorman handed me the keys. The apartment has a sixties vibe with antique furniture, iron windows, and green tiles in the kitchen, reflecting the charm of the historic area. Together with neighboring La Condesa and Juárez, Roma is one of the more Europeanized, gentrified areas of Mexico City. With plenty of bars, boutique stores, and informal taquerías lining the green streets and pocket parks, there is something for all who can pay for it.

I have just sent off some design work, so I walk downstairs and out onto the plaza. As always, the sun is shining brightly. I'm seeing Martha, whom I met a few weeks ago in the queue for the *tortillería*. She's

coming out for brunch and a walk around town. I see her right away: she's waiting with her little dog El Barto, named after the *Simpsons* character. I've been trying my best to get along with El Barto, but he always stays away from me. I think he doesn't like me much, although Martha reassures me that he's just shy. El Barto's suspicions aside, I think Martha and I fit together quite well; we look like a hippie couple. I'm wearing baggy, shredded denim jeans, and my hair is so long, it's starting to look ridiculous. I need to find a barber soon. Martha's a tall Mexican woman, fiercely dressed in all black, wearing a turtleneck, tight, high-waisted jeans, and white Adidas sneakers. The ethnic variety in Mexico City seems greater than what I've seen in the rest of the country. Martha, for instance, doesn't look like what I'd have thought of as typically Mexican. I'd have guessed she was Greek or Israeli. She has a

"Luxury under a thin layer of dust, and Latin radio from the taquería downstairs"

friendly face with soft curves, high cheekbones, wide brown eyes, and long, thick, black hair with blunt bangs.

We take our place at a picnic table in a small pop-up restaurant. Or maybe that sounds too fancy, it's more like a street food joint, with basic local food. Everybody can eat here for two dollars a meal. That's why I like these neighborhoods so much: there's a healthy mix between the working class and the rich and famous. Food carts and *fondas* are democratized spaces where people from every stratum of society eat together. In these neighborhoods one can sit down on plush, high-end designer furniture and order a flawless latte for a European price. Or, for a few pesos, one can buy a quick snack from the *camotero*, the camote man, whose deafening whistle you can hear from several blocks away. His rolling cart is basically an oven on wheels with a chimney and a steam whistle where the camotero cooks *camotes* (sweet potatoes) and *plátanos machos* (baked plantains), slides it onto a polystyrene tray, and covers them in sweetened condensed milk before jamming a plastic fork into it—probably one of the most iconic sights of Mexico's street food scene.

The little square in La Romita reminds me of a Spanish colonial village. Everything is built around a small stone church surrounded by pine trees and a little fountain. The houses are colorful and charmingly dilapidated. It's Sunday morning and fairly quiet, at least as quiet as it can get in a city of 21 million people. The doors of the chapel are open and churchgoers are filing in to attend mass. Martha and I order the staple of the day, quesadillas with black beans and rice, and talk about work. She is a ceramic artist. She designs, makes, and sells pottery for individuals and local businesses under her own brand name. It's hard to make a full living from it, so she also works as a barista. She talks about growing up in her country, and about how lucky she is to come from a family that is well-to-do. She lives in a bubble in this megacity, in a nice apartment in Roma Norte, close to Parque España, where she walks her dog every day. That's another thing that makes this part of the city different: domesticated, well-cared-for dogs accompany every other person here and signify affluence. Everywhere else I've been, dogs are just part of the street, like pigeons.

Life in Roma is incredibly well portrayed in the black and white movie *Roma* (2018) by Alfonso Cuarón. It portrays the life of Cleo, a domestic worker for a rich family in Roma Norte in the early seventies. The avenues, the fences, the tiles, the marble floor inside the house, the concrete rooftops with the laundry, the greenery in the streets, even the tap in the kitchen: it showcases luxury under a thin layer of dust, and Latin radio from the taquerías downstairs. All these small details situate the viewer in this unique enclave.

I scoop extra chili sauce on my quesadilla. Cilantro, diced onions, chili, and fresh lime juice are always unlimited condiments, giving Mexican food its intensely rich flavor. That flavor is one of the reasons this city has grown on me so much. Suddenly, a sinister sounding alarm snaps me out of my reverie. I see people rushing out of buildings onto the streets. I have no idea what's happening. All sorts of alarms go off every day

in Mexico City, usually cheap car alarms that can be ignored. "Earthquake!" shouts Martha as she grabs El Barto's leash. I follow her out into the growing crowd. All around us people are emerging from buildings. There's nothing to feel yet, but the distinctive alarm keeps echoing eerily. Then, slowly, the earth starts to move. It's something I've never experienced. The ground softly sways left and right. It's not the shaking I'd expect from an earthquake, but a gentle undulation, like standing on spent chewing gum. I can hear small bangs and pops in the distance. The potted plants and chandeliers hanging in the restaurant on the opposite side of the street swing dangerously. The people continue pouring out, stopping all traffic. The telephone poles squeak and crack as they move around, yet nothing major seems to break down. Then, small explosions happen above us as electrical wires snap off the poles. I can read the fear in people's eyes as they make phone calls. It's strangely exciting, standing next to Martha in the crowd as she squeezes my hand. Slowly, the swaying fades out again. The pots hanging from the ceilings are still swaying, but the worst is over.

I check the time: it must have taken only around 10 minutes. I wait with Martha as she makes a few calls to family members, and then she goes home to check on things. I take my bike and cycle around the city to see the situation. The streets remain filled with people, like there's a parade or national holiday. Apparently, it's not safe enough to go back inside. People drink tea and have meals on their porches. Some have brought their TVs outside to follow the news. It's actually quite a festive atmosphere in the warm light of the setting sun, an afternoon I won't soon forget.

Mexico is one of the most seismically active regions in the world and earthquakes happen often. It has only been six months since Mexico City was hit hard by the Puebla earthquake where 370 people lost their lives, thousands were injured, and many more lost their homes. One of the hosts I stayed with told me he returned back home after work to find his apartment in ruins. Some neighborhoods were out of water and electricity for more than a week. Luckily, this time it was only a small earthquake. I can't imagine what it feels like for the people who live here to hear the sound of that alarm again and again, anticipating how bad it could be.

Weeks go by as I establish my place in the city, eventually moving nearby to La Condesa. I work from my Airbnb, go out for lunch and dinner, and hang out in the park with Martha. Even El Barto grows fond of me. I've been in the city long enough that I've started running again to stay in shape. It's enjoyable because the city is much greener than I expected, and nowhere more so than in La Condesa, with its oval Avenida Amsterdam lined with Art Deco buildings from the 1920s. It's my favorite running path because it has a bike lane in the middle canopied with tall trees and bordered by exotic plants.

Mexico City has served as the perfect place for me to cultivate the dream I felt so taken by in the US, the dream of establishing a short-term home somewhere else. A bicycle trip of this magnitude entails endless hours on the road and near-constant physical movement. It

Roma Norte, Mexico City.

sometimes makes me restless. After these many months, new friends, and thousands of kilometers, the experiences and impressions have stacked up and created an overload of memories in my head. On my first bike journey, I discovered that the slower I traveled, the more I experienced and remembered. Soaking up all of the details and witnessing the gradual change in landscape, architecture, infrastructure, and people—that was where I found the true beauty of bike touring, rather than in maintaining an efficient, destination-driven travel style. The road itself became my destination. This time, I'm taking it a step further. Not only am I traveling slowly, I am choosing to stop and settle in places along the way. I want to give myself time to breathe, process, remember. Being here in Mexico City lets me take part in the same pattern of life that everybody else follows. I keep up with the local news, discover local gems, read books in the park, go to birthday parties, meet for drinks after work, and so on. I am connected to the city and its people, and I am connected to myself.

Thanks to services like Airbnb, it's easier to establish a home in between trips. A local apartment adds something to the experience that an anonymous hotel chain can't. Family photos on the walls, curated art, and personal touches make a place much more personal and welcoming. Booking a place has become so easy that I often do it the same day, while stopping at a traffic light with the bike between my legs. The first things I look for are a good table and chair to work on, Wi-Fi, windows that let natural daylight in, a nearby bakery, and a good supermarket.

The first few days in Mexico City, I slept on someone's couch in the historic center whom I found through warmshowers.org. The center is a traditional Mexican neighborhood in the oldest part of the city, where the lifestyle is quite a bit rougher. The streets are clogged with traffic, vendors, and garbage. The atmosphere of chaos and noise is unbearable. Stores often have large speakers in front of their doors and salesmen prattling on into microphones, trying to persuade customers to come in and buy whatever they're flogging. When the microphone isn't in use, the speakers blast commercials or music. In Mexico, that music is usually reggaeton, played at an obnoxiously loud volume. Reggaeton is not just for the younger generation—everyone loves it, or at least tolerates it. I don't love it. After four days it drove me completely nuts, which is why I'm now in La Condesa.

Another day, I get a text from Toño, a local cycling enthusiast who wrote to me on Instagram. He has toured in Turkey and Iran like I have, but now he is in between trips and living with his parents in Juárez, a neighborhood north of La Condesa. He's also a freelance designer, so I look forward to meeting him and sharing experiences. I'm waiting in La Botica, a hole-in-the-wall mezcal bar in Roma Norte. The music is loud, but at least it's not reggaeton. Mezcal is the specialty here; they even have a separate menu for it. Tequila is known as the worldwide exported Mexican drink, but mezcal is the more popular regional favorite. It used to be known as the poor man's tequila, but has gone through a marketing renaissance in recent years. Like tequila, it's a smoky spirit made from the agave plant, but it is a specialty of Oaxaca, not Jalisco. It's served at room temperature alongside a saucer of orange slices, salt, and chili pepper. Whenever I have a meal, I love to order a mezcal along with a cold Pacifico beer.

Toño is impossible to miss: he arrives on a ridiculously tall bike. He has a mustache like Mexican men from previous generations, but with his large glasses, he'd look more at home in Berlin. I have to try out his bike. It's basically two frames welded on top of each other so he can sit twice as high. At first, it seems impossible to get on or off, but once I get some momentum, it's not too hard. As soon as I get on it I notice that all eyes are on me and that the cars keep a safe distance. After a few spins we sit down at La Botica and he throws a book on the table: *Home Is Elsewhere: 50 Years Around the World by Bicycle*. It is about the bike touring record holder Heinz Stucke, who cycled 650,000 kilometers around the world across 196 countries. Aside from the compelling story, it's the historical aspect of the photography that draws me in. There are pictures from the eighties of rural India and Istanbul, from a time when people hardly carried cameras and the world population was half the size it is now. Traveling abroad has become much more accessible since then, and everyone owns a smartphone to document their experiences in vivid detail. Even people in the poorest regions of Mexico walk around with them. But it makes me wonder if we've lost something along the way. Anyone can share anything online whenever they want to. People make a living as "influencers," a job title that until recently did not exist. Does producing so much content—most of which is bound to be forgotten in 24 hours—somehow cheapen the art of photography and the experience of encountering the unknown?

—Xilitla & Las Pozas

Winter has fallen in the city. When I walk through the streets of La Condesa, I notice people in stores and offices wearing their jackets and scarves inside. Because temperatures only drop for a few weeks in the winter, indoor spaces are never equipped with heating. At 2300 meters above sea level, Mexico City's weather is always pleasant and mild, with temperatures staying between 20 and 25 degrees, during the day. The only difference between seasons is that the summer is rainier and slightly warmer than the winter. It's one of my favorite climates, which is another reason I'm still here. One day, it is 13 degrees, one the coldest days of the year. I light the kitchen stove to warm up the house and return to my laptop, where I see a text from Alejandra. She is inviting me to join her in Puerto Vallarta, on the Pacific coast. Her father owns an apartment at a beach resort and it's free for a few days. I text her that I have work to do, but before it's sent I erase it. Why not? I could bring my work with me. To be honest, I've been wanting to get out of town and continue cycling anyway. And this sounds like a better alternative. Before we buy tickets to Puerto Vallarta, I ask if she's up to first visiting Xilitla, a place I have heard a lot about. It is located in the green hills north of Mexico City and contains a famous garden called Las Pozas, a tropical paradise filled with surrealistic architecture and waterfalls. She's never been there either, so we switch up our plans and book bus tickets, planning to meet the next day.

I met Alejandra a couple months ago in Guadalajara, Mexico's second largest city. It is rumored that the most beautiful women in Mexico are from Guadalajara, and Alejandra proves it. She's nearly as tall as me and her eyes are brighter than the Caribbean Sea. She's a Mexican model, but her ancestors are Europeans who moved to Mexico during the Spanish Civil War. With a French mother, Spanish father, and grandparents from former Yugoslavia, she speaks six languages, three times as many as me. Not that I'm good with languages at all—anything beyond English and Dutch and I'm in trouble. In Spanish, I can barely get a hotel room and a quesadilla.

After storing the bike in my apartment building's garage, I take an Uber to Terminal del Norte for the midnight bus. I see nothing from the windows the entire journey, but the endless swinging of the bus on narrow, winding roads tells me the hills must be steep. After five hours and countless switchbacks, I'm in Xilitla. It's 4:00 in the morning when I arrive at the hotel, which leans into a verdant hillside. Despite the impossible hour, the host greets me cheerfully and shows me to my room. I want to sleep a bit before Alejandra arrives in the afternoon on her bus from Guadalajara. Because of the lower altitude it's hot and humid, and I'm glad I didn't come here by bike.

After a rest, I pick up Alejandra from the bus stop and we walk into the old town of Xilitla, inadvertently taking it by storm. She is talkative and charismatic, and effortlessly connects with everyone. The hotel owners, people at the fonda around the corner, taxi drivers, shop owners... with everyone, she shares a smile and a chat. The local village people are two heads shorter than her and her magical blue eyes make all the old men melt. It doesn't take long before the whole town knows there is a model from Guadalajara and a foreign photographer in town. We get even more attention when I realize I've forgotten my camera charger and Alejandra launches a campaign to find one. She tells the hotel host,

who generously calls around asking to borrow a Panasonic charger. Nobody in town seems to own this camera—most local photographers use the outdated but more affordable Canon models. Nevertheless, the people in Xilitla prove to be extremely kind and helpful. I just have to be cautious with the little battery power I have.

The next day, we visit Las Pozas. The gardens are only a 15-minute taxi drive out of town but feel like they're in another world. The whimsical structures rise from the thick jungle. There are numerous natural pools and waterfalls that are interlaced with concrete bridges and towers in a Gaudí-like fantasy. It's all the work of Edward James, a wealthy British poet who designed and commissioned the creation of the gardens and its buildings half a century ago. A mystical gem to wander and explore the rich plant and bird life. Alejandra has connected with a jewelry brand on Instagram, so we take some photos for them. We draw too much attention from the guards for "public indecency" because she takes off too many pieces of clothing, and we're almost sent away. But I apologize and they let us stay.

Back in Xilitla, we have lunch on the central plaza. While I take off for a moment to work in a café, Alejandra visits the old church and gets acquainted with the priest, who offers to take us to Sótano de las Golondrinas (Cave of the Swallows). Later in the afternoon, he picks us up from the apartment. Padre, as we call him, looks far from a typical priest, but his kind voice and heartwarming generosity make him credible enough. He wears flip flops and an oversized yellow football jersey over his large beer belly, which hangs out over his sweatpants. While he drives, he drinks. He reaches out under his seat and pops two Coronas with a Hello Kitty beer key for us as well. The windows are open and the radio is at maximum volume, playing the heartrending Mexican ballads of Los Bukis. Padre tells me I look like their lead singer when he was young, which makes Alejandra laugh out loud. On our way, we stop at someone's house in a little village to join for a birthday toast in the garden. We sit around the table with the men, who are being served pork and tequila with lime and salt. Alejandra is the center of attention. She regales them with tales of my journey, though I don't follow most of it. The vibe is cheerful and I enjoy sitting back, sipping tequila, and laughing with the men. But it takes much longer than we expected, and Padre has to step on the gas to arrive at the caves before dark.

At sunset we are there. Alejandra and I rush down the short trail. There are local villagers that let tourists look over the edge while they lie on the ground with a rope around their waists. From a distance, it looks like a small round canyon, tucked in the green jungle, but once I stretch my head over the edge, I'm looking straight into a gaping pit 370 meters deep. The cave opening is about 50 meters wide, and opens up even wider underground. It's impossible to see the bottom because the light doesn't reach that far, but a cold fog rises up from the depth and I feel the darkness pulling me into the abyss. As Alejandra and I lean over the edge, tightly roped up, we wait for the swallows to enter the cave for the night, the daily phenomenon that tourists come to witness. Soon, we hear someone shouting. A moment later, like a storm, the bright green birds appear from all directions out of nowhere, and torpedo down into the cave with dazzling speed. We hold our breaths until the overwhelming sound, like whips right next to our heads, fades out. The sun has set and the brief spectacle is over. We catch our breaths and are pulled back to safety, then start the hike back up to the car. Padre is waiting for us with some peanuts and a bottle of tequila.

145

→ Alejandra leaning over the edge of the Cave of the Swallows. ↘ The whimsical reality of Las Pozas. It's a subtropical garden area with surrealistic structures created a few decades ago by the British poet Edward James. A mystic gem, perfect for wandering down numerous trails and exploring the rich plant life.

—*Puerto Vallarta*

After three days in Xilitla, Alejandra and I travel
to Puerto Vallarta. Winter hailstorms are ravaging
Mexico City, but it's warm and tranquil on the
coast. Our beachfront condominium is a small
paradise. The building dates from the sixties and
seems to have not been updated, which lends it
an air of old world luxury. It's furnished with taste
and quality from a time before the plastic era, with
chipped brown tiles, iron fences, arched windows,
and stained glass. Just outside, an abundance of
palm trees and flowers frame a magnificent view of
the blue Pacific. We're the youngest people in the building. Most of the
tenants are retired American snowbirds enjoying the tropical climate.

It's midnight. A mighty palm tree in front of the balcony is lit from the
apartment windows below. Even at night, it's hot in the room, and I
walk outside to catch the salty breeze. The waves slam on the short,
steep beach in front of the condominium. Alejandra stirs and climbs
out from under the blanket, still with her jewelry on. Outside on the
balcony, the air is fresh. I lean against the cold iron fence. She joins me,
wearing only a short fur coat and panties. I light a cigarette and listen
to the sea's lulling, omnipresent swells. The noise absorbs everything
else and keeps me in the moment. The bike journey is a distant dream.
She leans against me. An interesting relationship, or whatever you may
call it. We are by no means made for each other, and we both know it.
It's a temporary thrill. She's a model; I'm a photographer. "Every artist
needs a beloved, a lover, and a muse," she says into the night. Her accent
sounds Eastern European, perhaps because of the many languages she
has mastered. She sounds like Sabina from the film *The Unbearable
Lightness of Being*. There's something cinematic about her, and I can't
put a finger on why. Maybe because she always says my name when she
talks to me. I steal a glance at her crystal-blue eyes that twinkle by the
light of the swimming pool below us. I think about what she just said
and which one of the three she is to me. I think about other lovers I've
met on the road—what they have meant to me, and what I've meant for
them. Travel relationships evolve fast and are filled with excitement;
there is wonder in dating someone who grew up in a different culture.
At the same time, they disappear like the wind. I indulge in the memories as they form and try to keep them close, even as I struggle to withstand the dreadful longing for a person when I am on my own again. I'm
slowly learning to control those feelings. Or maybe I'm simply getting

used to the rhythm of meeting and parting. I've long since disowned the
idea most of us are raised with, that each person is meant to have one
partner their whole life. It's a fragile, impossible concept that doesn't
fit in our time, a time characterized by self-discovery and individual-
ism. Accepting this is the only way to deal with the suffering, which is
the suffering of not finding the perfect connection, because it doesn't
exist. Once we think we've found it, we always strive for more. We are all
alone, and at the same time, all together. It's nothing sad.

After Alejandra returns to bed, I light up another cigarette. I'm not
living a very healthy lifestyle at the moment. I eat badly, drink too
much, and occasionally smoke. During this bike journey my metabolism
is so fast that I always recover well, but since I've been off the bike for
a few months, I feel more sluggish. Perhaps it will be time to continue
soon, perhaps not. At the moment I have no idea where this little adventure is going to lead. A few weeks ago, or even a few days ago, I'd never
have expected to be here, in this retro resort, far off my route with a girl
I've only known for a few weeks. Not knowing is part of the thrill.

During our stay on the coast, Alejandra wants to shoot some photos
for a swimwear brand. I leap at the chance to capture something other
than my bike or tent in a landscape, which comprises the majority of
my social media content. I don't have to explain why a woman is more
fun to photograph than a bicycle. After sharing some of my favorites, I
browse through my Instagram inbox and read messages from disturbed
followers who don't appreciate the half-nudes I posted. Sometimes I
forget I have the reputation of a bicycle traveler and that people don't
follow *me*, but a selection of expected content, like they'd follow a mag-
azine. I ignore the messages. They're going to have to wait for bike pics.

PUERTO VALLARTA, MEXICO

—Understanding climates

It is common knowledge that it's warmer in countries closer to the equator, but it's not always that simple.

There are many factors that influence climate. Elevation is a key player. Quito, the capital of Ecuador, is very close to the equator, but it has a much colder climate than Los Angeles. This is because Quito is situated at 2850 meters above sea level and Los Angeles is at sea level. Temperature drops roughly one degree Celsius per 150 meters of elevation gain.

The seas are another factor. Why is it that summers are hotter in Bend, Oregon, at 1104 meters than in the coastal town of Coos Bay, which is at the same latitude? This has to do with the cold, wet air coming inland from the Pacific Ocean. And not every sea has the same effect. Going for a swim in the refreshing waves of the Pacific in Puerto Vallarta is a completely different experience from swimming on the opposite coast in the Gulf of Mexico, which is soothingly warm.

In the same way, humidity influences temperature differences. The more moisture is in the air, the less extreme the temperatures will be between day and night, or sun and shade. Nights are much cooler in the desert than in the rainforest, where the humidity keeps the temperatures more equal.

The seasons and their severity vary greatly by latitude. In the north, there's a clear distinction between summer, fall, winter, and spring. The same goes for the far south, where the seasons are reversed. When it's high summer in Vancouver, it's winter in Patagonia. Countries near the equator are not familiar with these seasonal changes. The amount of rainfall signals the changing of the seasons, but the temperatures remain more or less the same all year.

Mural by Jorge Tellaeche, on Orizaba and Tabasco in Roma Norte

—Bike stolen!

I have cycled 25,000 kilometers around the world, and nothing has ever been stolen except for a bike tail light in India. I have parked the bike outside in Prague, Istanbul, Tehran, New Delhi, Bangkok, Singapore, Paris, Berlin, Vancouver, San Francisco... and there has never been a problem. People have tried to steal things, but not thoroughly. Over the years, the cable lock has gained lots of little scars in its plastic from people attempting to cut it, probably with small, dull knives, but it has remained my property. Until now. Something I have been afraid of many times has finally become reality: my bike, my home, is gone.

Back in Mexico City, some weeks after Puerto Vallarta, I'm having dinner with Toño at a restaurant in Roma Norte one Friday night. We have both parked our bikes in sight, locked against a pole. I do it all the time. Roma is one of the safer neighborhoods in Mexico City and there are plenty of cyclists. After dinner, I meet Martha at her house, and we decide to go to the movies. We ought to leave the bike there and take an Uber, but we don't. I think it would be fun to ride together, so we hop on the bike. She sits on a towel on the rear rack, legs to one side, like we are a Dutch couple cycling through Amsterdam. At the cinema, I ask if I can park the bike inside, but the guard doesn't allow it. We walk to the parking garage next door, but bikes aren't allowed there either. We eventually park it in front of Café La Lombarda, a bustling restaurant with large, open windows and a terrace, where people and staff can see the bike. I lock the frame with a cable lock to a streetlight. The movie is a little longer than expected, and we leave the cinema just after midnight. In contrast to a few hours ago, the street is now deserted, and I suddenly have a bad feeling. We walk to the corner of Chiapas and Manzanillo where it was parked. I crane my neck, trying to see it. "Don't worry, your bike will be there," Martha soothes. We take 10 more steps, and we both see: it is missing. My heart sinks. For a second I wonder if we parked it elsewhere, but I know it is gone. I feel stupid and careless. I loved this bike. So many memories, so many challenges we've been through together...

The lock is still there, tossed into the middle of the street. I pick it up: it's been cut clean through. It requires a big cable cutter, but if you have that, it's only two seconds and the bike is yours. There are some taco stands around, which are still cleaning up. I've eaten there a couple of times, and I know the guys from my time living in this neighborhood. Martha talks to them, but they haven't seen anything. I feel guilty for leaving the bike outside. I should have been more careful. But then again, there have been so many unguarded moments—this could have happened at any time. Every day when I'm cycling, I leave it outside when I go to a supermarket or store. Most of the time, I just take the front and rear bag with me, which contain the most valuable belongings, but at small stops like at convenience stores in villages, I don't even bother with those.

I walk home on my own and try to recall what exactly has been stolen. Luckily, most of my luggage is in my room, but some camping equipment was still in the frame bag on the bike. Not to mention all the extras attached to the frame, which more than double its value. All of these are top-quality products and probably impossible to get here in Mexico.

The next day, I visit the police office to report the theft, though Martha insists that they will be of little help. Toño posts photos of it in bike-related Facebook groups. The post is widely shared through Mexico, but I have little hope. I gather the material to open a claim with my travel insurance. In the meantime, my plans to continue the journey are now on hold—and this time it's not by choice.

Then, on the third day, a glorious turn. Pipe Llanos, a member of the Facebook group MTB Friends, offers me his almost new mountain bike for free to continue my travels. This isn't a brand that wants to sponsor me, just a guy with a heart of gold. We meet the next day at La Bici Urbana, a bike shop in the city center. Pipe says he bought the bike recently, but he doesn't use it very often. It's a good mountain bike—aluminium, a lot lighter and less robust than the Surly ECR. I take it for a lap around the block. It's a size smaller than mine, but it doesn't feel too bad. The biggest challenge will be fitting all the luggage on this bike, because it's a regular mountain bike, without any braze-ons or attachment points for racks and cages. But at this point I can only be grateful. Pipe allows me to try the bike for a few days to see if it's a realistic solution for the long journey to Patagonia.

The generosity doesn't stop there. La Bici Urbana donates a heavy u-lock to prevent a second robbery, and plenty of offers come in on social media from people who want to help out. Joe from Take A Hike Shop in St. Louis, Missouri offers to send me a load of items from his store, from racks and cages to pedals, straps, and lights. A follower from Australia ships a quick-release for my phone. Gear comes from everywhere. In the meantime, there is still no sign of the stolen bike. I'm getting around on Pipe's donation, but it isn't ideal. The frame is too short and it feels too light to pack heavily. I would feel less confident to go to remote places on this bike. There are already enough things that can go wrong out there on the road. If there's one thing that needs to be perfect, it's the bike.

Weeks pass as I wait for more gear to be shipped in. Some packages are stuck at customs; some are God knows where. I keep visiting various post offices to ask for news. Tax fees are sometimes outrageously high. I have no control over it—I just have to pay up. I can only be grateful to all the people who have helped me get a new kit together. Eventually, there's great news from Surly. They're willing to sponsor me and ship a new Surly ECR to Mexico City. This is an incredible relief; I was having more and more doubts about the donated bike. The guys at La Bici Urbana offer to assemble everything for me. I return Pipe's bike and thank him for his kindness.

More days go by as the last parts make their way to Mexico City. The bike theft has kept me in the city an extra 9 weeks. In the meantime, the rainy season has made its introduction. Almost every afternoon, it pours from 4:00 to 6:00; you can set your clock to it. This further disrupts my plans: I will no longer be traveling in ideal weather. The Central American summer ahead of me promises to be hot and wet. I tell myself that it doesn't matter, that the rainy season has its own perks. I hope I'm right.

The new bike on the way out of Mexico City. It's pretty much the same bike as the first one. The framebag was sponsored by Nature Bird Designs, and the leather saddle by Selle Anatomica.

Leaving Mexico City
—*Disturbing headlines...*

On my last day in Mexico City, I am confronted with disturbing news. In the hills of the southern state Chiapas, two cyclists have been found in a ravine, brutally murdered. A German and a Polish man, both experienced bike travelers in their forties, were cycling together and went missing some weeks ago. I follow one of them on Instagram—lately, he's been mute. And now, their bodies have turned up. The strange thing is that the authorities have tried to sweep the incident under the rug by stating that it was an accident, that they fell off the cliff. However, all of their cameras and electronic equipment were gone and they were found far away from each other, their bikes accidentally swapped. All signs indicate that this was set up and that they had been deliberately robbed and murdered.

Shaken by this horrifying story and the theft of my own bike, I at last continue my journey to Patagonia. I feel paranoid. The darker side of the country has come to the surface, confirming Martha's chronic suspicion of the police. Everyone is always warning me on social media: "Be careful! Be safe!" Questions run through my head. *How* can I be careful? Were those cyclists *not* being careful? Could they have known? More than ever, I'm aware of the dangers of the road. I don't let my bike out of my sight anymore. During hotel stays, I don't even leave it in the garage; I bring everything to my room. I'm suspicious of everyone, and I don't like it. Hopefully I relax as I move on and the flashy new bike gets some dust and scratches.

CENTRAL AMERICA

DAY 336 - MEXICO CITY, MEXICO - 5835 KM

After four months in Mexico City, I cannot wait to get on the road again. Ahead of me are the ancient Mayan ruins of the Yucatán Peninsula and eventually Guatemala, and the white-sand beaches of Quintana Roo. With a new bike and new hopes, I am ready for more adventure.

Havana
Varadero
Matanzas
Viñales
Pinar del Río
Santa Clara
Cienfuegos
Trinidad
C U B A
Holguín
Moa
Santiago de Cuba
Guantanamo

HAITI

Jacmel

Mujeres
cún
del Carmen

C A R I B B E A N   S E A

JAMAICA
Kingston

Tocoa
icalpa

N I C A R A G U A

li
Matagalpa

San Andrés

Barranquilla
Santa Marta

Cartagena

Lago Cocibolca

Liberia

C O S T A   R I C A
Volcán Arenal
Limón

San José

Colón
Panama City

Montería

David
P A N A M A
Panama Canal

DARIÉN
NATIONAL
PARK

Medillín

Ibagué

Bogota

Cali

Neiva

Popayán

Altitude (m)
5K
4K
3K
2K
1K
0

Guadalajara
Mexico City
Oaxaca City
Zipolite
Arco del Tiempo
Palenque
Tulum
Cancún
Mérida
Bacalar
Lake Atitlán
Volcán Acatenango
Panama City

Scale

miles   0   50   100   150   200   250
kilometers   0   100   200   300   400

—*The Water that Boils*

In the early evening, a day's ride from Oaxaca City, I come over the top of a hill to encounter these natural pools. Hierve el Agua, "The Water that Boils," is one of those places that is usually shared by many tourists and visitors. I figured it would be a much better experience to camp at the site and be the first to touch the mineral water before opening times, so I pitch my tent nearby. The night is dense and dark and quiet. Before sunrise, I hike down to the pools. Warm colors unfold on a silky smooth horizon, without a breath of wind. The pools are created by freshwater springs that contain calcium carbonate and other minerals, which produce the white residue at their perimeter. I spend some time in the morning sun, enjoying the solitude and silence, and let the worries from Mexico City slide off.

Arco del Tiempo is where the river La Venta
disappears under the rocks. It's located on an
unmarked trail hidden deep in the rainforest
of Chiapas. I hire a local guide from the nearby
village to take me on the steep six-kilometer
walk up and down through thick jungle,
ending with a 30-meter rappel down the cliff.
The gorge is so narrow that in some places, the
clifftops touch each other and close the gap.
Under the arch live thousands of swallows,
whose beating wings create an amazing sound.

A large diversity of people are on the streets of colonial town San Cristóbal de las Casas. Every day indigenous artisans come to the town to sell knitwear, souvenirs, and artifacts to tourists from around Mexico and the world.

PALENQUE, CHIAPAS, MEXICO | *One of the many Mayan temples still intact in Mexico and Guatemala.*

Yucatán
—Cenotes & the Mayans

Everything is far from everything on the Yucatán Peninsula. It's an endless jungle as far as the eye can see. However abundantly green, most of the land visible from the road is hostile and unlovely, and there are many reasons to *not* come here. There are only few people here; these great swathes of wilderness belong to snakes, spiders, and unfamiliar insects. Only a few roads connect the towns, which are mostly on the coast. Cycling here is a claustrophobic experience: the impermeable rainforest looms on both sides and the extreme tropical heat and humidity grip me and cover me in a heavy blanket. Sometimes I can't keep my eyes open because of the sweat pouring down my face. To say I am up for a refreshment is an understatement.

I am heading to a small town called Yaxuna, which is known for its *cenote* (natural pool) and some Mayan ruins. When I arrive at the sleepy village, I stop where the cenote is supposed to be, just a few

blocks from the main road. It is surrounded and completely over-grown by trees—someone passing in a car wouldn't even notice it. The gate to the cenote is locked, but after asking around, I learn it will open at noon, so I look for a restaurant that serves lunch. Of course there isn't one in this forgotten place, but I am pointed to a hut where hamburgers and *panuchos* (refried tortillas stuffed with black beans and topped with chopped cabbage, pulled chicken, onion, and tomato) are being prepared. While I wait, I am invited to sit inside. It's a small, single-room bamboo structure, built simply. Clearly, it's not for tall Europeans, because the top of the doorway reaches as high as my chest. It's like I'm entering a chicken coop. It turns out I'm not that far off; there are actually chickens pecking around a space that seems to be a kitchen. When I sit down on a stool, I am still taller than the women cooking. Mayan wood carvings are scattered around. A stereo and the food packaging are the only signs that I haven't entered

a time machine. As I enjoy the food, the women and I laugh at our size difference, despite the fact that we cannot speak a word of each other's languages.

In Yucatán, the majority of the citizens are Mayan. While that term is often associated with ancient peoples and temples from the distant past, there are actually many direct descendants still living in south-ern Mexico and Guatemala. I'm generally surprised by the variety and concentration of indigenous people in Latin America. They seem more dominant and integrated into the larger culture here than in the US, where the indigenous people often live on secluded reservations, more or less off the grid.

After my lunch, I go for a refreshing swim in the cenote before con-tinuing on the hot road.

LOL-HA CENOTE, YAXUNA, YUCATAN

—Cenotes

Cenotes are natural, crater-like pools sourced from underground water channels. You'll find them in all shapes and forms across the Yucatán Peninsula. Often they are much larger underground than at the surface. Most of the well-known Mayan ruins are found near cenotes because they provided fresh water for the people that lived there. The prettiest one I've seen is the one I found in the middle of Yaxuna. A dive from the edge is about nine meters, and below the surface there are another 16 meters of water at its deepest point. Enormous ceiba trees grow along the edge, their extensive roots reaching all the way down into the water. Because most cenotes are deep, the water is refreshingly cold and clear, great for a quick dive during a hot day of cycling. There are probably many more undiscovered cenotes, deep in the jungle.

Mezcal, served with orange slices and chili.

Tulum
—Unspoiled nature

"In Tulum, everything is beautiful," people would tell me in Mexico City. They were right. The endless white-sand beaches, the turquoise water, the sacred cenotes, and the shores dotted with trendy resorts and boutique restaurants all make Tulum the perfect escape for bohemian eco-tourists. Farther north are the more mainstream beach destinations of Playa del Carmen and upscale Cancún—they do not interest me. Tulum is where the young and attractive come to indulge in unspoiled nature. At least, that is how it's marketed—one could debate how well luxury goes together with unspoiled nature.

I'm staying here for a week to catch up on work and explore some remote beaches. I've even called up Alejandra to join me. I ended up taking the bus here from Mérida. I went too far north into the Yucatán Peninsula and didn't have the energy or will to cycle all the way down. The long roads through the jungle were torturous for my body and mind.

Originally named after a Mayan settlement, Tulum is a small town in the state of Quintana Roo along the main road a few hundred meters from the coast. The town itself is not very interesting; people come here for the coastal road that cuts through the thick rainforest—that is where the countless beach bars and hotels are situated. Most are stylishly constructed from bamboo, palm leaves, and mangrove wood, with Azulik Resort leading the way. For a staggering 800 dollars, visitors can book a night in this clothing-optional, Instagram-hyped jungle paradise. Alejandra and I just go for a drink, and sit in one of the elevated sitting areas above the restaurant. The entire resort looks like one big bird's nest-turned-villa right in the canopy of the green wilderness. The rustle of the palm trees and swell of the sea are ever present, as are the heat and the mosquitoes—unspoiled nature comes with rough edges. Photos of these places are seductive, but once lured here, travelers learn that actually, it's too hot to do anything other than meditate, swim, and serve as part of the thin veneer of civilization contending with nature's inexorable growth. The abundance of greenery is so forceful, I believe that if the people left, the jungle would take over in an instant. Somehow, to me that's a very comforting thought.

GUATEMALA

DAY 400 – SEMUC CHAMPEY, GUATEMALA – 7534 KM

With its historical city of Antigua, trembling volcanoes, and pristine Lake Atitlán, Guatemala is the jewel of Central America. Its steep, meandering jungle roads make it a tough place to cycle, but the rich diversity of its people and nature make it one of the most special countries of this journey.

—Antigua

The historic capital and heart of Guatemala, Antigua has been tested by
the forces of volcanic eruptions and earthquakes for centuries. It is known
for its ubiquitous Spanish Baroque architecture; it seems like around every
corner, one can find a church from a bygone era. Some are restored and
given a new purpose, while many are in ruins and overgrown with purple
flowers. Restaurants employ chefs from all over the world, which means
travelers can find just about anything here, including chocolate makers,
French bistros, and coffee shops. Arguably some of the best coffee in the
world comes from Antigua and the surrounding regions. It's the perfect
place to unwind and plan some nearby excursions.

Sitting in an old plaza, I hunch over a map, figuring out which places
to visit. There's a dry fountain in the middle of the square. Pigeons fly
overhead and Mayan women in traditional dress sell their handicrafts. A
young couple sits against a house making out. It looks like it's his first kiss,
but not hers—she's clearly in charge. An old lady rattles down the cobblestone street in the rustiest Toyota pickup I have ever seen, bouquets of
flowers bouncing in the bed. A chicken bus—an old school bus, often
from the US, which is shipped south, tricked out with loudspeakers and a
paint job, and widely used for cheap transportation—rumbles by with the
usual riot of color, noise, and fumes. Above it all towers Volcán de Agua,
dwarfing the low-slung orange rooftops. There is charm in every detail
my eye lands on. It's the delicate charm of age, which cannot be manufac-
tured, but has to organically grow and survive over time.

Playing with fire

—Central America is one of the most volcanically active regions in the world, and a few of the biggest and most active hot spots are in Guatemala. These days, Volcán El Fuego is the most notorious—just weeks before my arrival, it made headlines around the world with its most violent eruption in recent memory.

When Volcán El Fuego (Volcano of Fire) erupted on June 3rd, nobody was surprised at first. The active stratovolcano spits ash and debris on a daily basis, and usually it's nothing to worry about. The local communities and farmers are used to its rumblings and official warnings to evacuate are often ignored. "I have no time for this. I have work to do on my land," locals tend to respond to such advisories. But this time was different. El Fuego erupted like never before and it turned out to be the deadliest in more than four decades. Pyroclastic flows rushed down the valley. Clouds of ash rose 15 kilometers into the air, resulting in it "raining" burning coals. People panicked and got in their cars, but for many it was too late: the eruption took the oxygen out of the air, killing their engines. The terrifying images of the movie *Dante's Peak* come back to me as the hostel owner in Antigua tells me this horrific story that happened only a month ago. Some say that the locals should have been taking El Fuego more seriously, but that is just one side of the story; others say that officials knew the eruption was coming, but neglected to send out a warning and evacuate the area in time.

Just north of El Fuego is Acatenango, an equally tall but less active volcano. The nearly 4000-meter summit appears to be the ultimate place to witness the eruptions of its sister up close, which has lately been strangely silent. The excessive eruptions seem to have calmed her down, and now there is only a strange red glow and some dust clouds visible. In the hostel in Antigua, I team up with two Israeli girls and we hire a guide, Manuel, to take us to the summit of Acatenango to see what we can see.

This is considered one of the hardest hikes in Guatemala. It is a two-day, eight-hour trip: we will hike 4.5 kilometers and gain 1400 meters on the first day to get to the base camp, where we'll spend the night. On the second day, we will hike another 2 kilometers and gain another 300 meters to the summit and its dormant crater. I am slightly worried on the day of our departure: I remember being sore for days after the trek to Arco del Tiempo in Mexico. Apparently, full days of cycling don't prepare one's legs for a serious hike.

At Manuel's house we rent warm jackets, gloves, and hats to insulate ourselves against the high altitude temperatures. Early in the afternoon, the four of us set off on the steep trail. At first, the volcanic soil is soft and easy to walk. One of the girls is a bit slower than the rest, but I don't mind—it makes it easier for me. As we slowly gain altitude, thick clouds drape around the slopes of the mountain and it gets colder. The slower girl is not doing well; she is shivering uncontrollably. She has made the mistake of wearing a cotton t-shirt, which is damp with sweat and not drying fast enough to combat the plummeting temperature. We stop to eat some food and talk courage into her, and she decides that she wants to continue upward. For hours, we walk slowly through a forest dripping in thick mist. We can't see more than 30 meters ahead of us: basically, there is no view.

After five hours, we reach base camp. A platform is carved into the hillside, equipped with a tarp shelter and some small tents. Still covered in clouds, we warm up around the fire and eat a meal Manuel prepares for us on the stove: spaghetti, black beans, and coffee. The tarp above him is full of holes from the burning stones that came down on June 3rd. He was up here, he tells us, and burned his arm seeking shelter. Hikers were coming down from the mountain with burned limbs and shoulders. It must have been terrifying. We have yet to catch a glimpse of El Fuego or hear any volcanic activity. It seems this long hike has been for nothing. A permanent gray wall of clouds cloaks the mountain. For hours, we wait under the burned tarp for them to clear, our hopes dwindling. But then, out of nowhere, like a curtain revealing a stage, the view of the valley opens up. The clouds clear and the skies turn blue. "Amigos, on your right...Volcán El Fuego!" announces Manuel trium-

> The place feels haunted: at this elevation, there is no sign of life, just the deafening, ice-cold wind and the soft volcanic sand underfoot.

phantly. The volcano rises up in front of us in purple and dark green tones. Our spirits lift as we watch the sunset through the retreating clouds as they create a whirl of light and color that moves like a timelapse film. The fact that we haven't seen anything all day makes it all the better.

It's dark by 7:00, so the two girls retire to their tent. But I stay up with Manuel, keeping the fire burning. It's cold. I wish I'd brought some whiskey to warm us up, and maybe my Kindle. There is nothing to do besides stare into the flames. Because of the language barrier, we don't talk much. At 10:00, when it's close to freezing, I go into my tent. It's too cold to stay up and stare at El Fuego, but Manuel promises to wake us if he sees any activity.

We wake up at 3:00 in the morning for the final push, keeping a close eye on El Fuego while we have breakfast. The girl who was fatigued yesterday decides not to join us on the way to the summit, saying she is afraid of heights. As we pass the tree line, the volcanic soil becomes softer, drier, and sandier, and our feet sink deep into it. It's hard not to slide back down with every step. I use my tripod as a walking stick. Our headlights guide us along the trail, but soon the horizon starts to shimmer with the deep blue of dawn. Lights flicker in the valley, and below, we can see Antigua and, farther away, the modern capital of Guatemala City. The slopes of Volcán Pacaya, the most active volcano at the moment, are tinged with red. I keep turning my head to El Fuego as we climb, hoping it will wake up just a little bit. Near the top of Acatenango, the wind gets stronger. We pull up our collars and raise our voices to talk to each other. There are other groups of hikers converging on the final stretch, too. Clouds sweep violently over the summit, which is getting nearer and nearer. The place feels haunted: at this elevation, there is no sign of life, just the deafening, ice-cold wind and the soft volcanic sand underfoot. Once we reach the rim of the crater, we are met by a gust so strong we can barely keep ourselves upright. We immediately descend into the shallow crater. Throughout this entire hike, El Fuego has remained quiet. Despite the beautiful hike, I'm slightly disappointed, but I have to accept the fact that nature doesn't always give us what we want.

To experience sublime natural beauty is to confront the total inadequacy of language to describe what you see. Words cannot convey the scale of a view that is so stunning it is felt.

—ELEANOR CATTON

VOLCÁN ACATENANGO, GUATEMALA

Lake Atitlán
—Coffee expedition

Through winding and relentlessly steep roads, I reach San Pedro La Laguna, a small coffee town underneath a dormant volcano on the pristine Lake Atitlán. At 1500 meters above sea level, I get a break from the tropical heat in the lowlands I faced after leaving Antigua: it's not too hot and not too cold. In the morning, men bathe and shave in the lake while the women and children do laundry on concrete washboards. In some ways, the culture seems years behind what I'm used to—but it's a relaxing thing to see, and I feel less annoyed that the Wi-Fi is out yet again, preventing me from working. Shrugging it off, I go for a swim and hang out with the shaving men.

Guatemala has been the biggest coffee exporter in Central America for a long time. Café Cristalinas is one of the better roasters. They are supplied beans by the local farms, then roast, package, and sell their coffee all in one small shop. There's no better way to enjoy an espresso than with the smell of freshly roasted beans wafting through the air. Eager to learn more, I park the bike for a few days and connect with Pedro, a local guide who lends me a horse, to show me around. It's very relaxing to wander through the plantations on horseback. It just feels like the right way of traveling through the countryside.

He tells me about the harvesting. The hillsides around the lake provide the perfect climate and elevation for growing coffee, but it's difficult for cars to reach the plantations because the roads are so steep. Most pickers have to walk up the hillsides, and then all the way down to the nearby villages to deliver the coffee beans, sometimes carrying bags weighing up to 50 kilograms. Currently, it's quiet on the plantations. It's not harvesting season, and most of the cherries are still green. When they turn red later in the season, they will be ready for picking, processing, and roasting to get to their recognizable, fragrant form with which we are familiar. Some people are sorting small batches of unroasted beans, but I don't get to see much more. Back at the café, Luis is roasting a batch of coffee, filling the whole street with the gorgeous aroma. After the beans cool off, they are bagged and ready to be sold from the counter.

↑ *Women doing laundry in the lake in San Pedro La Laguna.*
→ *A mysterious traveler: I believe she is from Brazil. Her English is bad and my Portuguese even worse, which I will regret forever.*

—Luxury is the enemy of observation...

Guatemala has been the biggest surprise of this trip so far. I am amazed to witness its long-standing traditional culture and the many adventures available in its spectacular volcanic landscape. Coming from Europe, countries like Guatemala are often pictured as poor, undeveloped, and unsafe, and in some ways, this is accurate. I remember the charity projects organized by my childhood church for local communities here. Back then, roughly 25 years ago, my parents financially sponsored a child, sending money each month to help with her basic needs and get her through school. Seeing the children in Guatemala now reminds me of the picture of her we kept on our fridge for years, every year replaced by a new one that her family sent. As a child, I would look at her picture and see her bare feet and secondhand skirt, both dirty from playing in the unpaved streets, and the tin-roofed houses in the background. It all looked so different from the world I knew, and I pitied her. We were glad we could help by making small donations and sending letters to her family. After some research, I learned that she is now a teacher in elementary school and lives in Patzún, a village I crossed some days ago, though I found out too late to meet her.

The picture from the fridge sticks with me as I cycle through Guatemala and interact with people. Here, I can zoom out and see the beautiful, unspoiled landscape these people live in. That girl's feet and skirt were dirty from playing in the greenest hills, the bluest lakes, and the prettiest sunsets. She was surrounded by chickens, cats, and dogs that roamed freely and were part of her family's domestic life. Maybe she grew up in a small home, but that meant growing up in a place where people spent the majority of their time outside in shared spaces. She must have grown up with a deep connection to nature and to her community.

The other day I saw a woman doing laundry in a stream, far out in a remote village. I stood on a small bridge for a snack break, and to take in the pristine landscape. Tucked in between high palm trees, the stream flowed over the rocks underneath my feet. The woman was on her knees a bit farther downstream, her pink dress standing out in the rich greenery. It was the most idyllic picture. I thought about how we do laundry in our developed homes—the noisy machines in the dark rooms, the dryer spreading damp air, the smell of detergent through the house. And then I looked again at the woman and the simple life she lived in this paradise. It made me realize how quick we always are to judge someone else's happiness. Wealth has led to private space, private land, and private property. That same wealth has created the fear of losing it all, so we get fences, locks, and alarms to protect our stuff, and then we end up shut away in our fancy homes, dealing with anxiety, depression, and loneliness.

When I meet other travelers on my journey, I often ask about "the good life." What does it mean to them? How much is luxury or physical comfort a part of living well? Most bike travelers I know didn't choose the bike because they lacked money for a car—although people in the developing world think that sometimes, which is funny. (In Iran, kind people sometimes stopped me to try to give me money.) I'm not on this journey just to see the world. I'm also retreating to a basic way of living. It's a conscious choice of simplifying life, challenging my abilities, and being open to the beauty that's around me when I stop prioritizing my comfort zone. It's not always easy. Many times, I wish I had a car, or a nice Airbnb instead of my tiny tent. But in the long run, the more vulnerable I make myself, the more I feel I've tapped into something more fundamental and rewarding. I sometimes feel I can get a taste of what it's like for the coffee farmer who labors all day under the sun and returns to his small home with a tin roof, where his family is waiting for him.

Of course, no one's life is perfect, and money is a necessity that too many in the world lack. But clearly, it isn't the only need we have. I'm grateful to have the opportunity to choose to explore simplicity, and I'm aware that that is a privilege. More than ever, I'm coming to learn what wealth really means.

Luxury is the enemy of observation, a costly indulgence that induces such a good feeling that you notice nothing. Luxury spoils and infantilizes you and prevents you from knowing the world. That is its purpose, the reason why luxury cruises and great hotels are full of fatheads who, when they express an opinion, seem as though they are from another planet. It was also my experience that one of the worst aspects of traveling with wealthy people, apart from the fact that the rich never listen, is that they constantly groused about the high cost of living—indeed, the rich usually complained of being poor.

—PAUL THEROUX, THE OLD PATAGONIAN EXPRESS

COSTA RICA & PANAMA

Across Costa Rica, I map a route straight through the coffee plantations, avoiding political unrest on the bigger roads in El Salvador and Nicaragua. If I had known how steep the roads would be, I would have probably taken another route.

—*Crushed by the grades*

After struggling through El Salvador and Nicaragua, I consider taking a break in San José, the capital of Costa Rica, but I find I don't like it there. So, after servicing the bike and buying some new shorts (I cycled a hole in my last pair), I move onward. There are parts of this journey that I desperately want to skip so I can get to the next chapter. This is one of them. Some weeks ago, Nicaragua's capital Managua was in the news because of riots, and across the entire country there was unrest. All the tourists left, and the hotels emptied. I took a bus to Managua to avoid some of the more dangerous areas, and found many streets blocked by police squads. It made me want to be out of the city, and out of Central America entirely. As much as I settled into life in Mexico, I have now had enough of this part of the world. The constant political unrest is unnerving, and the heat of the jungle weighs on me and makes me restless and fatigued. I dream of the highlands of Ecuador and Peru, and the alpacas and cold mountain air of the Andes.

With fresh bike lube and a new chain, I climb out of San José. On top of the hill, I stop for a watermelon break at a roadside fruit stand before plunging in. A green sea of hills spreads out ahead of me, with steep roads winding through coffee plantations and banana nurseries. As was the case in Guatemala, El Salvador, and Nicaragua, it will take forever to cover any serious distance here in Costa Rica. The roads are neither straight nor flat; they meander up and down the hills. Even the descents are slow, because I need to be careful to keep the heavy bike in control. My disc brakes scream: the new pads have not fully broken in since I replaced them. The grades are so extreme, it's impossible to film with my phone because if I brake with only one hand, the bike and I will tumble into the ravine—it's that steep.

The people, however, are extremely friendly. I've come to realize that the more remote I get, the farther away from the touristy areas, the more welcoming the people are. Local farmers greet me cheerfully from their old Toyota Land Cruiser J40s, which seems to be the only car used here. In a small, secluded hamlet at the bottom of a deep valley, I fall into conversation with a villager. When I explain my route, he strongly recommends an alternative way which is much longer, but less hilly. I object, because I don't feel like extending the route, but he keeps looking down at the bike and shakes his head, murmuring, "*Muy difícil...*"

Grades could be as steep as 20% in Costa Rica.

Too late, I learn he is right. No stretch of pavement is level; literally everything is at an angle. I come to a small bridge in a village that feels like a relief, somewhere I can take a rest and stand straight on my feet. On both sides of the bridge, the road ramps upward. I buy some pasta and veggies and fill up my water before continuing uphill. Right out of the village the road resumes climbing at merciless grades between 12 and 25 percent. The pavement is smooth so I'm able to cycle, but eventually my legs are so depleted that I have to walk. It's not much easier, but at least it makes use of a different muscle group. I can barely keep the heavy bike from rolling back. Every 20 meters I hold still and gasp for air. Gravity has never made me fight so hard. I am desperately seeking a place to camp, but there's simply no flat space to pitch a tent. On my right it goes straight up, and on my left, straight down into the jungle. After a while I find a fenced-off track with a sign saying "PRIVATE PROPERTY." Behind the fence the road is overgrown, so I assume I won't meet any people here. It turns out to be a perfect camp spot.

The next day, the same dreaded hills are on the menu, but now the road is also unpaved, adding another level of difficulty. My shoes slide over the gravel when I try to push the bike up. I'm wearing myself out and not making much progress. When a pickup truck passes with some cheerful coffee farmers, they offer me a ride and I eagerly accept. I throw my bags and bike in the back and the diesel truck works its way along in first gear, engine groaning, to the village at the next summit. At each hairpin turn, the truck seems as if it will tip over.

...the more remote I get... the more welcoming the people are.

Large frogs sit in the puddles,
staring into the dark with big eyes lit
up by the headlight. The rain roars
on in the surreal scenery.

The final stretch through Costa Rica turns out to be a much longer ride than I expected. I have aimed to reach the coast before dark so I can be in Panama tomorrow. On Maps.me, the last 40 kilometers *looks* like one long descent, all the way from 2000 meters high to sea level. But it isn't the case. Maybe a navigation app shows a smooth curve down, but in reality, over such a distance on unpaved roads, there's always a number of smaller climbs in between. As a result, the going has been slow and at nightfall, I still have 25 kilometers to do. To make matters worse, it starts pouring, like it can only do in the jungle: hot, sticky showers that continuously pour down and flood the roads. It's like in *Jurassic Park*, when they hide under the truck from the Tyrannosaurus Rex. (The Costa Rican island Isla Nublar from the first scene is actually not too far from here.)

Making my way through the dark is hard—I only have a rear light at the moment because the batteries of my headlight have run out. Essentially blindfolded, I just keep pedaling. My brain is switched off and I'm only focused on not stopping, and on staying on the road. Because of the heavy rain, I can't check the map on my phone anymore, since the screen won't work if it gets wet. This is taking forever. At some point, I pass someone on a motorbike, probably a worker trying to go home. I pass him and he deliberately drives close behind me, lighting my way with his headlight. I can't see his face; it's hidden by his large yellow raincoat. The road is slippery and full of potholes. Large frogs sit in the puddles, staring into the dark with big eyes lit up by the headlight. The rain roars on in the surreal scenery. I drink the water that falls into my face from my rain cap. I start getting excited. When I first felt wet and cold, I was miserable, and then when it grew dark, I was anxious about not being able to check my map. But now, even though I'm wet to the bone and racing across the palm fields, trying to dodge the deepest

puddles, my muscles are on fire and I am exhilarated. The motorbike and I don't stop; we ride fast. The large palm trees with thick trunks are majestic and grim in the twilight. To the left and right, I can make out the long rows in perfect grids. At some point, the motorbike takes a turn and leaves me alone in the dark. He doesn't say goodbye, and we haven't said hello. I still can't check the map, but soon, I reach the paved highway. It stops raining and dries up, and it doesn't take long until I find a motel at a gas station.

After crossing the border to Panama, I stay on the Pan-American Highway for a few days. August is the height of the rainy season, and the showers come every single day. The skies are electric; sometimes lightning strikes nearby. I continue to feel drained and depleted. The entire day, my clothes are sticky and wet. It makes my skin sore. Things only dry out if I spend a night in a hotel with air conditioning. Any other place is too damp. I expected Costa Rica to be beautiful, but I seem to have come to the wrong places at the wrong time. The reality of living on the road in the rainy season is daunting. I'm quite done with it: done with staying in budget motels with clattering air conditioners, done with the cockroaches in the corners, done with the tasteless pre-cooked meals in roadside restaurants, done with the aches in my body from too many hours in the saddle and too many bad mattresses. I'm trying to minimize further issues by taking the smoother Pan-American Highway, but it makes me feel like I'm wasting my time in this country. Panama *does* have pristine beaches, beautiful rainforests, and tall volcanoes, but they are not on my way. The only highlight is crossing the Panama Canal. I take a break on the bridge and watch gigantic ships sail underneath me. Panama City itself looks gray and desolate. The sun doesn't shine in the three days I'm stopped. It barely even gets light. I need to get out of here.

COLOMBIA

The journey through South America starts in Bogota, which I reach by plane since there is no road connecting it to Central America. I take a break in this megacity to gain strength for the most challenging section of the journey: the Andes Mountains.

With Paula in La Candelaria, the historical center of Bogota.

Bogota
—*Latin America's bicycle capital*

The Darién Gap is bad news. It's a lawless stretch of jungle in between Panama and Colombia without any public roads going through. Although there are people who have successfully crossed borders here, albeit illegally, it's strongly discouraged. Not only is the jungle impenetrable and the wildlife dangerous, but there are also reports of robberies and kidnappings. Therefore, I found myself a cardboard box in Panama and disassembled the bike for a flight to Colombia's capital. Everything arrives in one piece at baggage claim.

Walking out into the crisp mountain air from the airport invites a sigh of relief. Bogota is located 2500 meters above sea level, meaning cooler temperatures. I couldn't wait to arrive here after so much time in the tropical heat of Central America. It feels like coming home. Bogota seems much more modern and developed than I expected. My image of the city was poorly constructed by the usual headlines of drug trafficking and violence, and more recently by *Narcos*, the series about Pablo Escobar. The image I see now as I cycle the long bike lane from the airport to the center is totally different. Many people commute by bicycle, the streets are clean and organized, and the architecture is modern. The old center, Candelaria, looks typically Latin American with its colonial architecture, but the majority of the city has red brick facades and more of a European character.

On Sunday, I see a phenomenon I wasn't expecting in Latin America: La Ciclovía. Every Sunday from 7:00 in the morning to 2:00 in the afternoon, some of the main connecting roads are closed to motorized traffic, allowing people to freely bike, run, skate, walk their dogs, or just sit on the curbs to socialize. There are no isolated freeways or expressways in Bogota, so roads get clogged easily, making this an especially welcome break from the tedious everyday traffic. Every Sunday the streets are

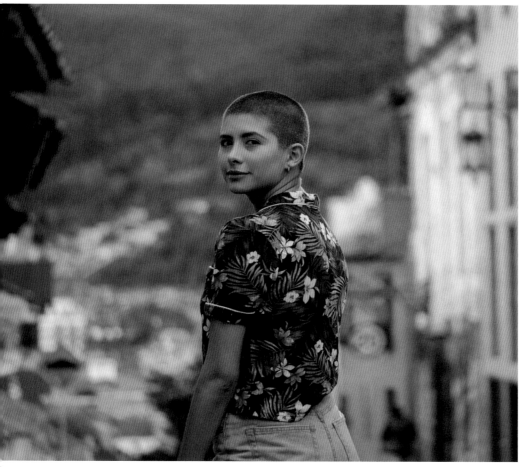

"Aquí la **magia** comienza contigo" #AquelarreLaBruja

quiet and filled with people. The vibe is incredibly uplifting—it's a joy to be outside. And, as it is known for having the most extensive network of bike lanes on the continent, I'm not hesitant to dub Bogota the bike capital of Latin America.

I spend my days in comfortable Airbnbs and catch up on emails, photo editing, and writing for a few days. And it's again time to throw away some clothes and buy new ones. This is an instant upgrade from the gritty lifestyle on the road of the previous leg of my trip. I cherish the clean sheets, the soft bed, the shower that's actually warm, and the bathroom I can stand up straight in. The food is great and the menus are well designed. I even make new friends who speak English. I'm instantly back to the life I used to live, enjoying all the small things I normally take for granted.

As in other big cities, I stay in the capital for a while to connect with people more deeply. Speaking Spanish is still a struggle, so in small towns, communication never goes much beyond small talk. That's different in cities, where people are more educated and speak English. As I

continue to settle in, it appears that I know more people in Bogota than I thought. One guy who has followed me for a couple of years on Instagram invites me to lunch. He has done some cycle touring as well so we have plenty to discuss—this is the wonderful world of social media. It's never been easier to connect with like-minded people instantly, anywhere in the world. But the connections also happen the old-fashioned way. Outside the supermarket, my bike attracts the attention of Dan, a French guy who married a girl in Buenos Aires and has been settled in Bogota with her for the last decade. We chat and he gives me his phone number. A few days later, we have dinner in a downtown restaurant with another cyclist friend. This is how I get to know the city—it's a lot better than hiring a travel guide.

I also get to know Paula, a Colombian model. She's a vibrant personality, with a short blue buzzcut. I ask if she wants to do a photo shoot, and we take some photographs of her in an eclectic apartment with sweeping views over Bogota. We talk about life in Colombia, and about gender equality. She shows me photos of when she had long hair and fit in with everyone else. It's still quite controversial to express yourself in the way

← Bogota's La Ciclovía, where some of the main roads are blocked for motorized traffic from 7:00 a.m. to 2:00 p.m. every Sunday.
→ Plaza de Bolívar.

she does. I admire her courage. I talk about my journey and the adventures in Central America, and she marvels at my courage. For most people, especially women, this style of independent traveling seems far out of reach. Most young people I meet in Latin America haven't traveled beyond their own country. Sometimes it has to do with money, but mostly it has to do with a general fear of everything that could happen on the road. The political unrest and violence of the past decades are still embedded in people's minds. I feel it everywhere: people always warn me when I get out my camera to take pictures outside. When I sit outside at a restaurant, waiters chide me for having my phone on the table. When I go for rides in the hills behind Bogota, people protest that it is too dangerous. The fear is present everywhere.

One day, I participate in a filmed interview for a local clothing brand owned by one of Paula's friends. The story is published on their website, including a photo shoot of us wearing their colorful patterned shirts in Candelaria. Paula also invites me to a techno festival in Medellín, a city farther south. It sounds tempting, but I know if I'm not mindful, I'll be here for months before I know it. I feel I should focus on the bike trip, otherwise I might never finish it. Bogota was another safe haven and a place to call home. I've learned to say goodbye now. After four weeks in the city, I choose the road again.

Trampolín de la Muerte, Colombia.

↗ Restaurante La Cabaña, a family-owned restaurant near Sibundoy, Colombia.
↘ Freshly pressed sugarcane is a popular refreshment.

DAY 496 - SIBUNDOY, COLOMBIA - 9673 KM

—Menú del día

Clif Bars and freeze-dried backpacker meals feel like memories from another lifetime.
As I've traveled south, my diet has shifted to new staples. I often ate in restaurants and
roadside food stands in Central America, and I continue to in Colombia. The food is usually
good, made from real, simple ingredients, cooked with care, and served in family-run
restaurants. The spaces are often less appetizing. A bunch of grimy plastic chairs gathered
in a tiled, oddly colored room, discolored Jesus posters or family portraits on the wall, a
staticky TV in the corner, Wi-Fi that doesn't work... that summarizes most of them.

The food options are limited when I'm on the road, my stomach is growling, and there's
only a small village ahead. Most of the time there's no menu in the little restaurants. I'm
simply told the *menú del día* (menu of the day), and if I don't understand what the meal is,
I simply answer, "Si, por favor." Usually, there's a choice of protein and the rest is default: a
varied combination of rice, cooked potato, yucca, beans, lentils, baked plantain, veggies if
I'm lucky, and *arepas* (Venezuelean corn tortillas). Prior to the main dish, a soup is served,
and the meal comes with unlimited lemonade or other fresh fruit juice depending on the
region. The good thing is that the plates are big and the food is nutritious, not to mention
the price—for no more than three dollars, I can fill up and be ready for the bike again. In
contrast to most places, this little restaurant on the road out of Mocoa was worth a photo.

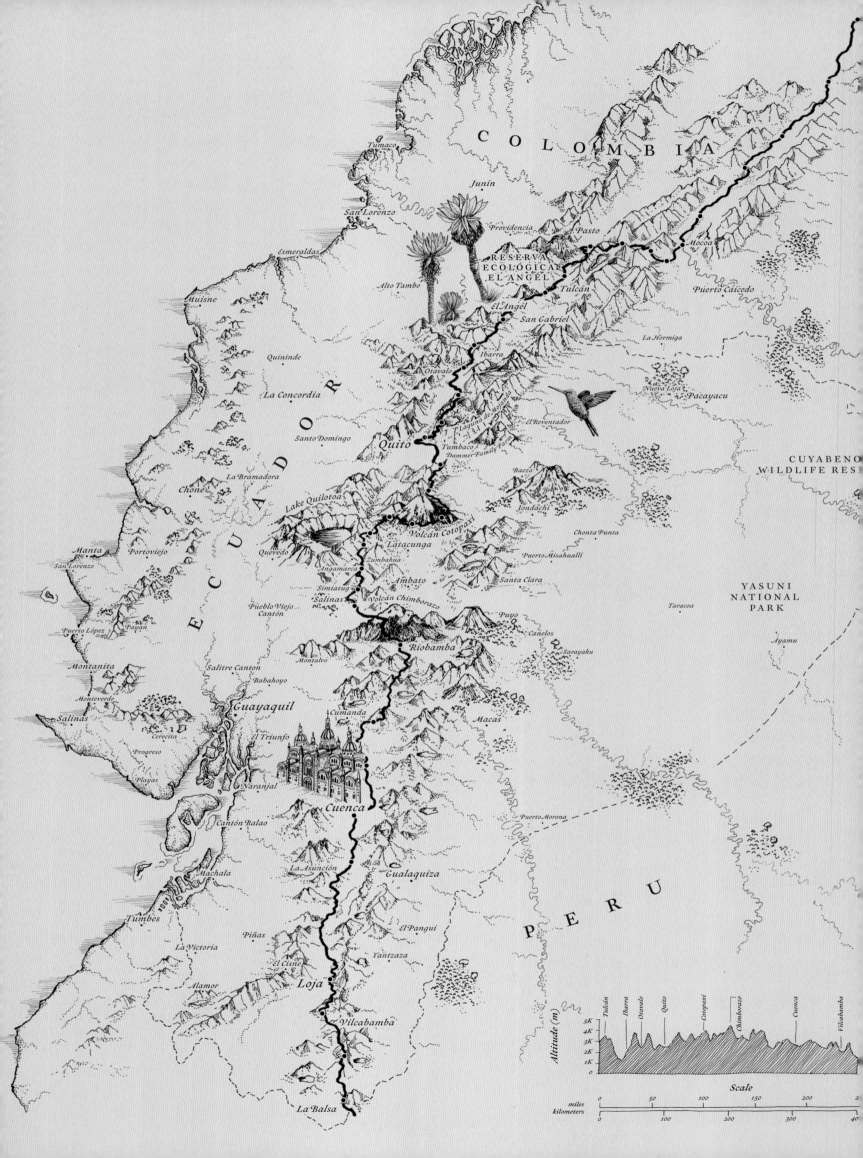

COLOMBIA

Tumaco

Junín

San Lorenzo

Providencia

Pasto

Mocoa

RESERVA
ECOLÓGICA
EL ÁNGEL

Tulcán

Puerto Caicedo

Esmeraldas

Alto Tambo

El Ángel

San Gabriel

La Hormiga

Muisne

Quininde

Ibarra

Otavalo

Nueva Loja

Pacayacu

La Concordia

El Reventador

CUYABENO
WILDLIFE RES

Santo Domingo

Quito

Laguna de Mojanda

Tumbaco
Dammer Family Farm

Baeza

La Bramadora

Chone

Lake Quilotoa

Jondachi

Chonta Punta

Santo Domingo

Volcán Cotopaxi

Latacunga

Puerto Misahualli

YASUNI
NATIONAL
PARK

Manta

Portoviejo

Quevedo

Zumbahua

Santa Clara

San Lorenzo

Ingamarca

Ambato

Simiatug

Salinas

Volcán Chimborazo

Puyo

Pueblo Viejo
Cantón

Taracoa

Canelos

Puerto López

Payan

Sarayaku

Ayamu

Montanita

Salitre Canton

Montalvo

Riobamba

Monteverde

Babahoyo

Salinas

Guayaquil

Cumanda

Cerecita

El Triunfo

Macas

Progreso

Naranjal

Cuenca

Playas

Cantón Balao

Puerto Morona

Machala

La Asunción

Gualaquiza

Tumbes

PERU

La Victoria

Piñas

El Pangui

El Cisne

Yantzaza

Alamor

Loja

Vilcabamba

La Balsa

TEMBR
(TRANS ECUADOR MOUNTAIN BIKE ROUTE)

DAY 500 - TULCAN, ECUADOR - 9673 KM

Popular among adventure cyclists is the Trans Ecuador Mountain Bike Route. It covers almost the entire length of Ecuador, connecting some of the most interesting sights on remote dirt roads through the Andes.

These so-called "frailejones" ("big monks") only grow at high altitude in Venezuela, Colombia, and Ecuador.

On the TEMBR in El Angel National Reserve, dirt road version.

—The beauty of riding dirt

There are two versions of the TEMBR: a dirt road version, and a single track version, where the path is about as wide as the bike. Both are mucky, but the latter involves many more river crossings and hike-a-bikes, and is therefore not recommended for cyclists carrying more than a small pack. Both routes were created by Cass Gilbert (@whileoutriding) and the Dammer brothers (@el_taraumara), experienced adventure bikers who have contributed a lot to the bikepacking community in South America, including improving GPS routes with detailed notes and photography.

I stick to the "easier" dirt road version with a detour here and there. The first day leads me through the ecological reserve El Angél, known for its exceptional plants called *frailejones*. These plants only grow at high altitudes in Ecuador, Colombia, and Venezuela and can stand up to seven meters tall. Their big leaves look and feel like gigantic rabbit ears. They have the unique ability to absorb water from clouds and release it into the soil, which results in lakes at high altitude.

As in Baja California, it's a relief to be away from the everyday traffic.

I was mainly following the paved roads across Columbia. It meant faster progress, but it was stressful at times. I've looked forward to this solitude and quiet. The absence of motorized traffic is a relief, and the lack of infrastructure makes me feel more a part of nature. In one entire day, I see only three motorcycles. It's understandable, because the road is narrow and rocky with deep puddles. A normal car wouldn't be able to make it. The only sign of man is the dirt track in front of me. I can smell the flowers; I can hear the birds and the rustle of the trees. I could take a nap in the middle of the road and nothing would interrupt me.

The tranquility and fresh air come at the cost of a significantly lower average speed. I'm cycling 11 kilometers per hour instead of my usual 17 kilometers per hour on pavement. Dirt roads have more abrupt ups and downs compared to motorways, which have gradual climbs and descents. A downhill ride on pavement compensates for the climb, because gravity makes you fly down the hill. On rougher surfaces, you have to be much more careful, because bigger rocks or mud will make you slide and get into accidents if you go too fast. On these roads, my big tires are a great advantage. I'm finally using the bike to its full potential. Still, it would be much better if I could ship some of my luggage ahead. I resolve to explore the option in the next larger town. Currently, the bike feels overloaded for this type of riding.

OTAVALO, ECUADOR

I go out for a walk to expel the demons I know only exist in my imagination.

Laguna de Mojanda is a small crater lake at 3900 meters. It would be easy to bypass it and cycle through the valley, but I think it would make a worthwhile detour to train for camping at high altitudes. I leave my panniers with the heaviest luggage in a hostel, hoping to make the steep ride on the cobblestones somehow enjoyable.

Early on in the climb, I notice someone pushing a bike up the hill. I assume it's a farmer, but it turns out to be another cyclist. Tomas, from the Czech Republic, started cycling in Alaska on a cheap touring bike, the same one he is now walking. I pinch his hard tires and suggest letting some air out. He shrugs, saying he doesn't mind pushing. Besides, they are so worn, he's afraid they'll pop. Considering myself fortunate to have big tires, I continue the climb in first gear, slowly leaving Tomas behind. We might meet later. Halfway up, I get stuck in a thunderstorm, and, because I forgot my rain gear, I take shelter under the tiny awning over a sign at someone's driveway. The road turns into a small river. I stand there for an hour; the roof barely keeps me dry. I am expecting to see Tomas, because I haven't seen any other option to take shelter from the rain, but he doesn't show up. Eventually, the rain dies down and I continue upward. Some hours later, I reach the little *laguna* just before dusk and set up camp for the night.

The night falls fast. Being only a few kilometers from the equator, it's dark from 6:00 to 6:00 all year round, with hardly any twilight. I want to make some spaghetti, but I've forgotten to bring the spaghetti, so tonight's dinner will be onion soup with bread. For a moment, I slightly panic at the prospect of spending a long night at high altitude, underfed. I calm myself with the fact that it will only be downhill from here. It gets cold quickly, and I tuck myself into the sleeping bag to warm up and watch a show on my iPhone. After that it is still only 8:00, way too early to sleep. So I get out again—and find myself in another realm. The lake is entirely covered in mist. It seems like I have woken up at the bottom of the ocean. Every sound I make is muffled. The peaks surrounding the lake are also invisible and choked up in the clouds. In front of me the shallow waters have turned into a dark mirror. I feel afraid, but I don't know of what. Perhaps to confront the strong forces of nature, to be excluded from everywhere and everything else. I feel alone, but also empowered. I go out for a walk to expel the demons I know only exist in my imagination. The red of my headlight pierces through the night. A bird flies away over the lake and disturbs the deafening silence. I can feel my heartbeat in my throat. I wonder where Tomas ended up. Maybe he found shelter at a farm during the thunder-storm and spent the night there.

In the morning, I get up early, make some coffee, and eat bread with jam and some nuts. The low sun warms me up and I let it dry the tent. The darkness has made way for fresh sunlit views over the laguna and the gray-green páramo grass gently swaying in the wind. The previous night feels like a distant dream. Higher up on the dirt road, I see someone waving. It's Tomas! I walk up to him. He tells me that he hid from the rain by sitting under a tree for an hour. The entire climb—18 kilometers, 1300 meters of elevation gain—he walked, pushing his bike. He is cheerful and doesn't complain about anything.

ers' father, Francisco Dammer, emigrated to Ecuador from Germany about 40 years ago and married an Ecuadorian. He bought the farm, which back then was a regular corn and dairy operation. Michael, Mathias, and Thomas were born and raised here, but have also lived and

Michael shows me around. A narrow cobblestone path leads us to the first house, where Mathias lives with his partner Marcela and their six-year-old daughter Ayra. They have their own piece of land where they have built their house and workshop. Mathias welcomes

That's the thing with handmade items. They still have the person's mark on them, and when you hold them, you feel less alone.

— AIMEE BENDER, THE COLOR MASTER: STORIES

me with a big smile at the front porch of his fantasy house. He wears a long, thin beard and a Bolivian hat. The house is a true work of art. A wooden staircase, the centerpiece of the house, is built on a tree and spirals up to the first floor. Next to it, a swing hangs from the ceiling. Everything is made custom from local wood, stone, and bamboo. No angle is straight; everything has been allowed to whimsically, naturally curve. Mathias tells me they lived in a tent, also self-made, for six years while they built the house and simultaneously worked on the farm. I can't imagine how much effort it took to create.

We walk farther over the hills to Michael's home, where his partner Marcela is taking the youngest out of the bath. They have two children, Koru and Antu, and are slowly growing out of their house. It was the first house built on the farm, in a time when there were no family plans yet. All of the houses are a similar style, with their own unique, personal features. It seems like all of the three brothers are equally talented and gifted.

As we sit down, Michael pours me coffee while we talk about bikes and far-off journeys. On the porch, his little toddler tries to catch a big spider, right on the edge of the platform. I ask Michael if he's not afraid of him falling off the edge. "No, he knows he shouldn't fall," he answers without looking up. On the sofa two children are reading a book together, though I don't know whose they are—I keep mixing it up. They participate in everything together: the work on the farm, the bicycle trips, the projects with the students, and hosting travelers from all over the world who visit them. I wonder what it's like living together so closely knit, and how much privacy there really is. Michael tells me it has a lot of advantages. All of the families have more than enough space for themselves, and the houses are all a 10-minute walk away from each other. At the same time, they can take care of each other's children when one couple wants to travel or visit the city. There seems to be a very healthy social balance and level of collaboration.

As a way of further sharing their expertise, the Dammers have set up an outdoor adventure school. Currently, they have a group of 18 students

at the farm for a semester, where they learn the permaculture lifestyle and outdoor survival skills. Accommodation and all of the required gear is available on the farm, including bicycles, kayaks, climbing gear, backpacks, and cooking equipment. Their upcoming Andes trip will test their knowledge of hiking, biking, rafting, and camping. During the past few weeks, they have been learning about growing and harvesting their own food, and then dehydrating it to reduce it in size and weight, so they can carry meals in their backpacks for plenty of days. They've also made their own knives and spoons. Proudly, they show off each of their hand-crafted tools. They even had to make their own clothes for the journey. The school has had a long-term relationship with Tatoo, one of the largest outdoor brands in Ecuador. This lets the students work on their own clothing line in the factory, where they learn to sew the garments. All in all, it's a highly versatile and varied education program with a healthy dose of fun and adventure.

The group of young people is incredibly disciplined and eager, which shows in an incident that occurred a few days before my arrival. Four of the group went a bit too far with alcohol one night. As a "punishment," they had to spend three days and nights alone in the forest with only a sleeping bag and water, no food. Initially, this sounds quite cruel to me, but Michael explains that they actually *liked* the idea, and all agreed in

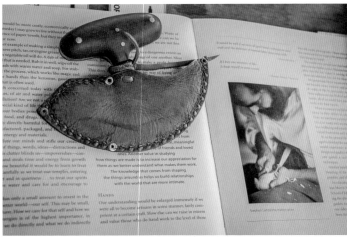

Our main objective is to offer our children and students a space to experience and learn through permaculture, adventure sports, and wilderness living, and it is our hope that they may take us by the hand and help us, and themselves, expand our potential as human beings.

FROM NAHUAL.COM.EC

committing to it. Michael has done it himself and explains that being alone in nature without food allows you to be more aware of what's happening in your body, and the phases it goes through in such an ordeal. I am there when the four students return from their "purgatory," as they call it. They are welcomed and hugged by the entire group. To me, they look exceptionally rested and relieved.

In the evening, we have a gathering and I screen my film *One Year on a Bike* to the students. Afterward, Michael invites me to do a Q&A with them about my travels. They talk my ears off and grill me with questions about long-term travel, cycling, and camping. At 10:00, it is time for all of us to go to bed: daily chores and breakfast preparation start at 6:00 in the morning. I sleep in a guest room above the space where the cows are milked. At dawn, I join everyone at the communal building. The students are gathered in a circle in the outdoor kitchen, singing a ritual song in a language I don't understand—a way of saying grace over the food. Breakfast is served: fresh fruit, yogurt, and pancakes with jam and peanut butter. Even the peanut butter is locally made and scooped from a big white bucket.

After Michael and the group leave for their expedition, I have a chat and some tea with Nicole, Thomas's partner, in their house, which I haven't seen yet. She shows me her medicinal product line, sold in shops all over Ecuador. I just can't stop being surprised and inspired by the creativity of this place and its people, by the versatility of their skills, and by their success in having such a unique commune together. They seem to have mastered a minimalist lifestyle while at the same time embracing an unstoppable drive to create beautiful things. I have seen many times how often family obligations and full-time jobs suck up people's time, preventing them from exploring their wilder, deeper passions. This family seems to have found the perfect solution by combining it all, and by living in harmony with all the things they make, consume, and create, every animal and individual contributing to the reimagined system.

INTO THE WILD

DAY 514 - VOLCÁN COTOPAXI, ECUADOR - 9920 KM

On this next ride, I'm going to take it to another level. While the TEMBR route bypasses Volcán Cotopaxi along the west side, I plan to circle the volcano, following a lesser-known route on the east side. The highest pass will be 4192 meters, higher than I've ever been before—and most of the landscape will be single track.

Ecuadorian "cowboys" returning from a rabbit hunt.

Before I hit the road out of Quito, I ship part of my luggage ahead via a courier, so I will be without it for about a week. After that, depending on the difficulty of the route, I might ship it ahead again. My panniers with my laptop, hard drives, clothes, and some spare bike parts that I can go without for a few days, I send to a hotel near the Pan-American Highway. Not far from the Dammer farm, I pick up the TEMBR again, which leads through small villages on unpaved roads, gradually climbing up toward Volcán Cotopaxi. This route will be far from straightforward, but as I often do, I remind myself that I'm not on these trails to cover lots of distance in a short time. I'm here to experience the paths themselves: in this case, the detour is all about encountering the rugged nature of the Andes and being away from civilization for a while.

From Tumbaco, at 2350 meters, the cobblestone road goes up along green meadows and through small towns and villages, slowly leaving behind the urban sprawl of Quito. The lighter bike is a relief, but still I'm slower than I would be on pavement. Sometimes a bus passes, and when it arrives at a village, it honks the horn and waits for one or two people to hop on. This is also how mail is delivered. Some people suggested just giving my bags to a bus driver, an affordable service most people use for shipping parcels, but I thought it was worth paying 25 dollars for a more official courier company.

At the end of the second day, I reach the refuge at the foot of Cotopaxi at 3900 meters. It's a lodge and restaurant in the middle of nowhere. The landscape is desolate and colorless. Big black boulders are scattered across the wide-stretched páramo. I cycle up to the refuge to charge my electronics and have a meal. Inside is a group of elderly German and French tourists, who will probably hike the volcano the next morning. After dinner, I cycle into the cold night to pitch my tent in the field a few hundred meters from the lodge. I leave my drone batteries inside to charge; the next morning I will pick them up. Apart from the lodge, there's nothing manmade around. Just the gray windswept plains expanding in all directions. Straight to the south, Cotopaxi towers majestically against a black canvas of stars. It's a beautiful and cold night.

In the morning I pack up, have coffee in the warm restaurant, and embark on the trail that leads clockwise around Cotopaxi. I'm as nervous as I am excited. This is my first serious single track, far from any road. It's a different game, because trails are full of unexpected elements. Trails are made by walkers or livestock. Sometimes they disappear because a herd of sheep has scattered at a river or a ditch. Sometimes they disappear because there are multiple alternative routes. Other times, rainfall and mudslides change the landscape, completely erasing the path. I constantly have to look at the map on my phone to make sure that I'm still heading in the right direction. Sometimes the trail is gone for a while and it's better to follow the ridgelines and the

I discover a new level of solitude that is both invigorating and terrifying.

> Trail riding is a completely different way of bike travel compared to using conventional roads, which at some point always provide food, shelter, security, and connectivity.

positions of the sun and clouds. Often, there are hike-a-bikes—places where you need to carry your bike instead of ride it—to get over old fences from long-gone *fincas* or to cross streams. Trail riding is a completely different way of bike travel compared to using conventional roads, which at some point always provide food, shelter, security, and connectivity.

It also comes with a new set of fears. I discover a new level of solitude that is both invigorating and terrifying. Alone here means *really* alone. There are no people, no power lines, no cell phone connection, no gas stations, no power to charge devices, no food, and no way to call for help. What happens if this takes much longer than planned, or if the rain turns the landscape into a swamp? The rainy season has just started, and even in the dry season the weather is very unpredictable. Having plenty of food gives me peace of mind in any situation. It's the essential that will get me through anything. If I have food, I can stay warm, I can cycle, I can walk, I can eventually get out of anywhere. And so naturally, I worry if I have enough. I'm also worried about my phone battery lasting. More than ever, I need it to follow the trail. If the battery dies and the trail vanishes, I won't know how to go on. I'll have to follow my instincts about the right direction. I figure that as long as I keep the peak of Cotopaxi on my right, I will be going the correct way. But even that isn't a constant: sometimes the clouds drift in and I lose all visibility.

The higher I get, the more the landscape changes. New, strangely colored plants and flowers appear that look like coral. The volcano, my anchor point, disappears again in the fog. I lose track of time. Emotions roll through me like waves: restlessness is followed by wonder, and then stillness in the beauty and grandeur of this place. I surrender to it and try to trust my instincts as I navigate in the mist. Then, I arrive at a small settlement. There's one old hut with a grass roof. Around it is a trench and a rotten fence. A well has been dug for water and a cow skull is raised on a stick, marking the entrance. I call out to see if there are any people. After hearing nothing, I walk to the hut and peek over the door, which is locked. It is a small shelter with a bed and some pots and pans, but no signs of life. At the end of the third day, I set up camp to the southeast of the volcano—at least, I think that's where I am. I haven't seen the snowy peak since earlier in the day.

Moments before dragging the bike over the 4192-meter pass.

It's as if your body just doesn't want to perform, like there's a belt around your chest and you can only take in a little air at a time.

The next day, I have one more pass to tackle, and it's at 4192 meters, the highest of my trip so far. The trail has now completely vanished and turned into a swampy grassland with puddles and ditches, so narrow and deep that it is unrideable. The high altitude steals the oxygen from my lungs and quickly wears me out. I take many breaks and eat all the biscuits I can find in my bags. I feel empty; I'm probably not sufficiently nourished. Or maybe I have just reached the limits of capabilities. It's hard to explain altitude sickness. It's as if your body just doesn't want to perform, like there's a belt around your chest and you can only take in a little air at a time. With the last of my energy, I literally drag the bike over the pass. It's more a bare ridge than a pass. Once over it, I continue to struggle as I bike down sandy ditches and trenches. Even going downhill, I feel too weak to control the bike, until at last, the trail has mercy on me and turns into a road. Slowly the landscape becomes more friendly as I lose all the altitude I've gained in the last days in only a few hours. The warmer temperatures and breathable air return. I roll down through young pine forests and before I know it, I've safely returned to the Pan-American Highway.

I have a reservation in a unique hotel where I can recover for two nights, thanks to Martina, a friend in Quito. Her family owns a *hacienda* near Latacunga. She has told me it's a special place, but I'm still bowled over by what I see when I approach the gate. The hotel is at the end of a long, imposing driveway, lined with trees that might even be taller than the Redwoods in California. Hacienda la Ciénega was built as a country house in 1580. At the reception desk, I find a book about it and read up on some of its history, which is mostly a litany of long, impressive names like "Don Mateo de la Escalera y Velasco." Martina's family has owned it for two hundred years, and they were the ones to turn it into a hotel. The long history of the building is one thing, but what has impressed me even more is the 300-meter driveway, lined with giant, 250-year-old eucalyptus trees, rustling in the high, howling winds.

Hacienda la Ciénega.

A hike along the ridge of Quilotoa, a crater lake, at 3900 meters. The round trip is 12 kilometers, but I keep it to a short morning walk, since the ride here through steep canyons was more than enough for my daily exercise.

Drying out clothes after a rainy start to the day while taking one last glance at Volcán Cotopaxi, this time from the southeast.

—The highest volcano in the world

Dark skies over Chimborazo, Ecuador's highest peak (6263 meters). I have spoken with other travelers about their experiences on this volcano. Some have cycled its trails, and others have hiked to the snowy summit, which is technically higher than Everest if measured from the center of the planet instead of sea level (because Earth is wider at its equator). Everyone's story of Chimborazo is unique, depending on their mode of travel, the time of day, and the season.

Here, I'm cycling up to the pass in the early afternoon, just before ending up in a hailstorm at the highest point of the road at 4400 meters. When I set up the drone for the shot, it's already raining a bit. I get it down just before all hell breaks loose. Later, the clouds part for the briefest moment, giving me a clear view of the summit, but I'm wet and cold and want to get to lower altitudes as soon as possible. I'm somewhat disappointed, but there's no sense in being angry with nature. I like this picture because it's on the edge of everything. Nature often doesn't deliver what we want, but it certainly rewards us in the most unexpected ways.

—Cuenca's flower market

I'm stuck for a few days waiting for a shipment to arrive, which is no punishment in the beautiful colonial town of Cuenca. I'm staying in a quaint little hotel overlooking the historic center, where I catch up on my editing and writing. I take walks in the early mornings to explore the streets and squares and see the town come to life.

In the flower market, Quechua women in colorful traditional dress inspect the new harvest of roses being delivered into town. Ecuador is one of the world's largest exporters of roses. Martina, my friend from Quito, is also here, which makes it easier to talk with people. She carries a vintage Polaroid camera, which proves to be an additional blessing because we can give people their photos on the spot. I've taken dozens of people's portraits, but there's usually no way to give people their pictures. Sometimes we swap emails, but most people who live in remote locales don't have the modern devices I use every day to exchange photos and memories. Besides, a printed picture is much more lasting and personal.

The parcel I'm waiting for contains new tires, which I ordered from the US two months ago. The original tires have done about 4000 kilometers and are pretty much worn out. They are an odd, large size, and I haven't been able to find them anywhere, not even in Bogota, which has plenty of professional bike stores. Shipping packages to South America can be problematic, just like in Mexico. There are often delays, added taxes, and an inability to track shipments. Colombia seems to be the exception. Two packages were shipped fairly quickly without unforseen costs. Or maybe it was just luck.

The Ecuadorian mail, however, appears to be the opposite: days pass and there is still no sign of my tires. Luckily, Felix, my hotel host to whom the parcel is addressed, is extremely helpful. He explains how to pay the tax via a website. It's more than 100 dollars, and it's probably going to take some extra weeks. I don't want to wait that long, so I pay him for shipping costs and he promises to forward them to Peru. I hope the old tires, which are growing dangerously thin, can keep up for another 1000 kilometers.

—Vilcabamba

A drastic change of scenery occurs as I cycle through a bamboo forest near
Vilcabamba, one of the last towns in Ecuador. Dropping 1000 meters in altitude
reveals a completely different spectrum of vegetation and climate. Around the
border of Ecuador and Peru, the Andes spread out a bit and the mountains are
not as high, giving me the opportunity to warm up a bit and enjoy the greenery
and the flowers.

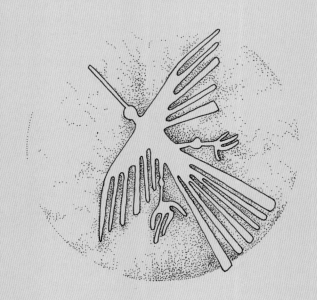

PERU'S GREAT DIVIDE

DAY 541 - LA BALSA, PERU - 10,743 KM

The Andes Mountains separate the Amazon Basin from Peru's arid coastal region. Instead of taking the faster Pan-American Highway along the coast, I opt for the less traveled roads through the Andes. With the rainy season drawing in, I know I am in for a real challenge.

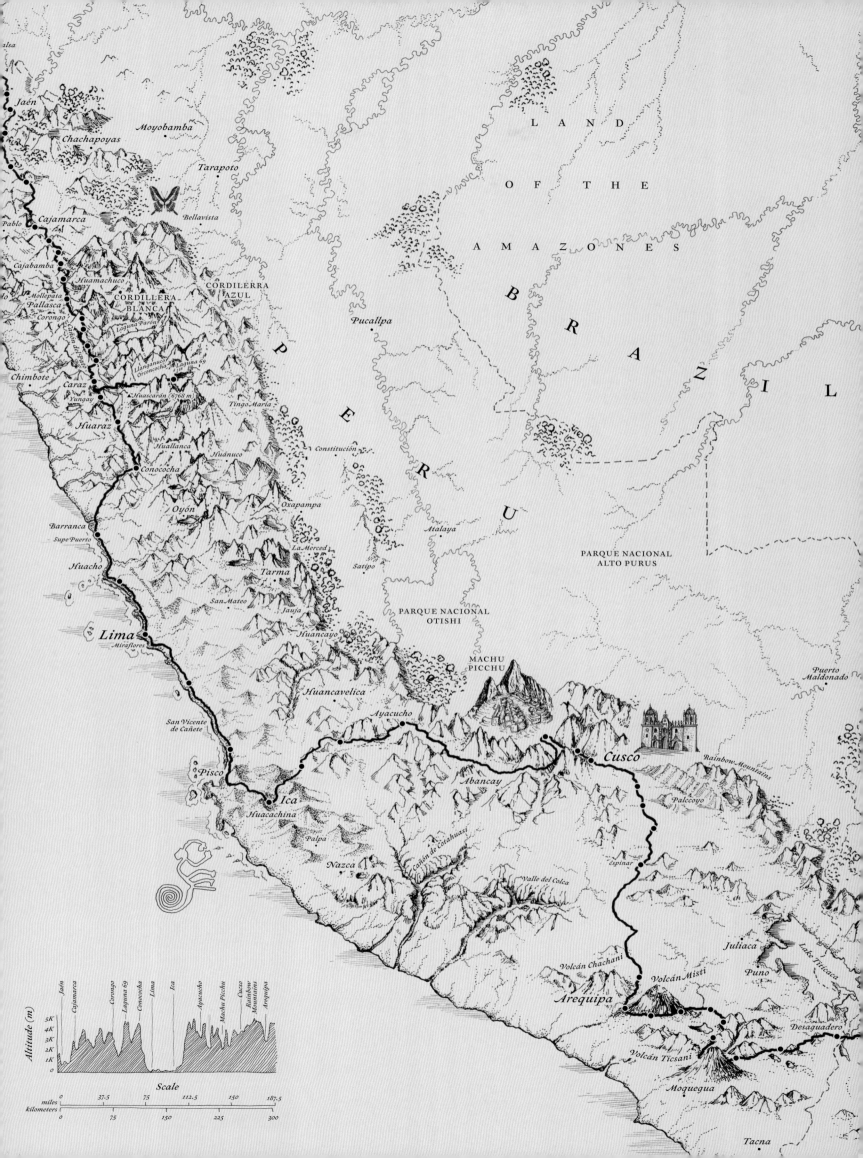

Jaén

Moyobamba

Chachapoyas

Tarapoto

Pablo

Cajamarca

Bellavista

Cajabamba

Huamachuco

Mollepata

Pallasca

CORDILERRA
AZUL

Corongo

CORDILLERA
BLANCA

Chimbote

Laguna Parón

Llanganuco,
Orconcocha Laguna 69

Caraz

Yungay

Huascarán (6.768 m)

Tingo María

Huaraz

Huallanca

Huánuco

Conococha

Oyón

La Merced

Barranca

Supe Puerto

Huacho

Tarma

San Mateo

Jauja

Lima

Miraflores

Huancayo

San Vicente
de Cañete

Huancavelica

Pisco

Ica

Huacachina

Ayacucho

Palpa

Nazca

Cañón de Cotahuasi

Abancay

Valle del Colca

L A N D

O F   T H E

A M A Z O N E S

P
E
R
U

B
R
A
Z
I
L

Pucallpa

Constitución

Oxapampa

Satipo

Atalaya

PARQUE NACIONAL
ALTO PURUS

PARQUE NACIONAL
OTISHI

MACHU
PICCHU

Cusco

Rainbow Mountains

Palccoyo

Espinar

Puerto
Maldonado

Juliaca

Puno

Lake Titicaca

Volcán Chachani

Volcán Misti

Arequipa

Desaguadero

Volcán Ticsani

Moquegua

Tacna

Altitude (m)

Jaén
Cajamarca
Corongo
Laguna 69
Conococha
Lima
Ica
Ayacucho
Machu Picchu
Cusco
Rainbow Mountains
Arequipa

5K
4K
3K
2K
1K
0

Scale

miles   0   37.5   75   112.5   150   187.5

kilometers 0   75   150   225   300

CACHACHI, PERU

Peru
—*A new level of difficult*

As my route develops south into the Andes, the mountains rise higher and the canyons carve deeper. The altitude remains between 3000 and 4500 meters, but I hardly get used to the thin air. Again, I feel the belt tighten around my chest. The road quality decreases, the days become rainier, the nights get colder, and the distances between supplies increase. Gradually, everything becomes more exhausting. What I get in return, however, are unforgettable vistas and a sense of adventure that makes my heart beat fast every time I reach a summit. The question is, when is something *too* adventurous? More and more, this journey is depriving me of long, urban sojourns. Instead it's testing my mental and physical endurance, forcing me to constantly toughen up. I know I am tougher now: I wasn't capable of any of this the day I struggled across the Lions Gate Bridge in Vancouver. I believe that when things become harder, the rewards become bigger too. During this long journey, I've looked forward to Peru, but also dreaded it, because I've always known it to be next level. Peru is the literal summit of the entire journey, and I feel that if I don't really push myself hard, I won't be satisfied. With that in mind, I'm raising the bar again for myself.

"Gringo!" the villagers call out as I pass. Sometimes they use it as a greeting, other times as a warning to their peers. Most people in the remote villages are adorably shy. When I approach one hamlet of mud brick houses, children first run down the grassy hill cheering from excitement. I stop to have a chat. Hesitantly, they come closer, but when I pull out my camera they run away like I'm drawing a gun. When I'm far away enough, they find courage again and scream, *"Plata, plata, Hollanda!"* ("Money, money, Holland!") In another village, there is a young girl who is braver and dares to talk to me. Her little brothers stand firmly at her side, proud to pose for a picture. Other times, strolling children turn away and cover their faces, like I'm a ghost. They probably never see foreigners on these roads.

In Peru, one's traditional dress, and especially the type of hat, identifies from which region one comes from.
This woman wears one of the exceptionally large straw hats from the Cajamarca region.

—61 switchbacks

It's never happened before that I can see an entire day's route at one glance. Tomorrow, it will be 900 meters down and then 1350 meters up, covering 30 kilometers. This capture takes 20 minutes to make, the same time it takes for one car to drive from Pallasca, the small town on the far right of the photo, all the way down to the river. There are only three cars in this picture: one on my side of the canyon going down, and two on the other side. My camera has a maximum shutter speed of 60 seconds. To create the continuous light ray of the moving cars, I take 20 shots from a tripod, one after another, and stack them together in Photoshop.

The man that built this road is a local hero, and also the owner of the inn I'm about to stay in. His full title is Captain Orlando Vladimir Alvarez Castro, a Peruvian soldier who was assigned to build this road to make the town of Pallasca accessible by car. It contains 61 switchbacks in all. Each member of the community—shopkeepers, teachers, and children alike—supported him by preparing food and helping to build the road. On June 24, 1972, Orlando was the first person to drive a car into Pallasca. Before then, it was only accessible by

CORDILLERA BLANCA

DAY 575 - LLANGANUCO ORCONCOCHA, PERU - 11,604 KM

The "White Mountains" are at the center of the Andes in Peru and are some of the highest peaks in the Americas, reaching as high as 6,768 meters. It's a place for long climbs, stunning vistas, breaking altitude records... and getting seriously sick.

—Collapsed

Today is my birthday. I am writing this in Caraz, having been unable to record much of anything in the last 12 days, which have been an ordeal. Bad weather and hard riding aside, I also got sick. Contaminated water was probably to blame: I tend to trust streams above 3000 meters, but you can never be sure, especially in Peru, where high-altitude mining can pollute the groundwater. I don't carry a water filter at the moment; I usually buy bottled water. This time, I underestimated the risk—and paid dearly for it.

Two weeks back I needed to get over a high plateau from Cajamarca toward a small town called Corongo, then all the way down into the valley, then up through Cañón del Pato, and finally to Caraz, a place that would be good for a break. It had already been a difficult few days since Cajamarca. Almost the entire route was over dirt roads above 3500 meters. The roads had loose rocks and deep cracks, built only for occasional mining traffic, and they rattled the bolts off my bike, so to speak. One night after I cooked dinner at camp, my stomach started to roar. That night, I left the tent four times until I was completely empty. It was kind of funny—I had never thrown up with such a great view. The sky was clear and I was 3800 meters above sea level. In between my trips to "look at the scenery," I lay in my tent considering my options, feeling miserable. The idea of continuing up over the high plateau didn't seem a wise decision, let alone a feasible one. The road was going to remain around 4000 meters for at least another day without any resources. The

Notifications poured in on my phone after six days without service, including some worried messages from my father. I texted my family that I was all right, but really I wasn't.

weather forecast was bad news, as usual. Aside from some painkillers, I didn't have Immodium or anything to stabilize my stomach. I considered cycling back down to the main road and trying to catch a bus, but the public buses I had seen around here were minivans, too small to carry a bike. Larger buses didn't come here, because the roads were too narrow and rugged, including the main one. Eventually I worried myself to sleep.

In the morning I woke up feeling weak, but not too sick. I decided to continue upward, just drinking water and eating plain bread. Painstakingly slowly, I made my way up to the pass at 4400 meters. I was doing okay with the altitude, but the lack of oxygen made me tired and sluggish. Luckily, my stomach was handling it well and I kept my food down. Up on the plateau, it started raining again. My hands and feet grew very cold; there was simply no energy in my body to keep myself warm. I was looking forward to the downhill, but the road was so full of cracks and potholes, it was closed to cars. And for a road in Peru to be closed for cars, it needs to be in really, really poor condition. This did not bode well for a bicycle. My entire body hurt when I arrived in Corongo in the dark. The illness and the weather had kept me offline for longer than I intended, and I knew my family would be worried. Notifications poured in on my phone after six days without service, including some worried messages from my father. I texted my family that I was all right, but really I wasn't.

Sometimes I regret that I stayed so long in Mexico City. As a result, I have had to ride through rainy season after rainy season. I crossed Central America during June and July, its wettest months, and now I'm getting rained on in the Andes. South of the equator in Ecuador, Peru, and Bolivia, the rainy season lasts from November to April. Now, it's early December, which means wet clothes almost every day. It's very demotivating to start the morning with rain. Most of the time I'm at high altitudes, where a cloudy day means a foggy day. I cycle with no view at all for hours, just the black mud and gravel underneath me and the páramo grass on the flanks. The beautiful scenery has turned into a damp reality check.

After a night in Corongo, I felt stronger. I said goodbye to the generous, friendly family of my guesthouse, and continued down hill. A single-lane paved road curled around the mountains. I took a break for a moment to take in the sweeping sight of the canyon. To my surprise, the sun came through and the clouds cleared, unveiling the colors of the deepening view. I could see the road going down through yellow and orange rock layers, green patches of farmland, and, in the distance, the bare mountains colored purple in the haze. There wasn't any traffic. I put my headphones on with music and rolled down the mountain roads. I felt like I was flying and like I'd never stop. Deeper and deeper into the canyon I soared; the oxygen came back and the air warmed up.

↑ *Taking a break after a sunburst on the downhill road toward Caraz.*
→ *One of 35 tunnels on the narrow Cañón del Pato.*

Everything changes when you drop fast in altitude; it's like taking a plane to another country with its own vegetation, humidity, and temperatures. I descended from 3200 meters all the way to 1000 meters, to the Santa River in the deep canyon, where it was about 30 degrees Celsius. I still felt a little weak, but the joy of cycling returned again after so much time in the high cordillera.

By now, it had been 11 days and 550 kilometers since leaving Cajamarca. I felt ragged and had lost weight. I couldn't wait to arrive in Caraz, take a shower, and put on a fresh set of clothes from the bag I shipped ahead. But before arriving in Caraz, I had to go up *again*, this time on the mild inclines of Cañón del Pato (Duck Canyon), a narrow, single-lane road of about 30 kilometers passing through no fewer than 35 tunnels. Most of them were relatively short, but some went around bends in the pitch dark, and my light wasn't charged. Sometimes the tunnels were so narrow, I needed to squeeze against the wall to let a truck pass. Halfway up the road, I met Leon, a British traveler who was cycling up and down from Caraz on a rented mountain bike. I was incredibly happy for this sign of civilization, and to meet someone who spoke my language. He joined me on the final stretch.

That was yesterday, and today is my birthday, which I've shared with Leon and some other travelers. I gorged myself on—finally—some enjoyable dinner. I'm done with the big piles of plain rice and cold meat, the staple meals in the mountains. I couldn't stop eating, my body had a lot of calories to catch up on. In the east, the mountains rise up high with their white peaks. I look forward to breaking another altitude record there, but first, I need a few days off.

Cañón del Pato

Everything changes when you drop fast in altitude; it's like taking a plane to another country with its own vegetation, humidity, and temperatures.

BESIDES THE COLD AND WET DAYS, THE RAINY SEASON BRINGS MORE SERIOUS PROBLEMS. I'M GETTING WORRIED ABOUT MY EQUIPMENT. THE CANVAS SADDLE BAG, WHICH STORES MOST OF MY ELECTRONICS, IS GETTING WET INSIDE. THERE'S ALSO AN INCREASED RISK OF LANDSLIDES, FLASH FLOODS, RIVERBANK EROSION, AND BRIDGE WASHOUTS. THE SMALL STREAMS COMING FROM THE MOUNTAINS ARE NOW ROARING RIVERS OF BROWN WATER. ROADS ARE SOMETIMES IMPASSABLE FOR LARGER VEHICLES BECAUSE OF FALLEN ROCKS AND MUDSLIDES. NEWS REPORTS WARN OF THE DANGERS AND POSSIBLE DELAYS OF TRAVELING THROUGH THE ANDES. I'VE CLEARLY UNDERESTIMATED THE IMPACT OF THE SEASONS IN MY PLANNING.

The strenuous downhill through the rain and dark toward Corongo.

Christmas day
—*Another personal record*

Not long after my illness near Corongo, I come down
with yet *another* stomach bug. I spend a few days recovering in Huaraz, the main tourist hub in the area. It rains
every day, which makes me seriously doubt my latest
scheme: a high-altitude loop crossing the Cordillera
Blanca twice, which would allow me to once again break
my personal altitude record. I decide to protect my
health and go for a shorter version: cycling up and down
Road 106, the pass next to Huascarán, Peru's highest
peak. Halfway up, I can squeeze in a hike to Laguna 69
at 4600 meters. I will spend Christmas Eve alone in a
small tent, but when a person is so far from the normal
world, those things don't matter much.

I split the jaunt over two days and camp at 4000 meters
at the trailhead to Laguna 69, so I can acclimatize. Early
the next morning, I hide my bike in the bushes and start
the hike. It's a very popular walk, yet I am the first one
to arrive at the pristine alpine lake with eye-shattering
cyan water. The weather is stable, but the chance of rain
will increase in the afternoon. I still want to cycle to the
top of the pass at 4700 meters, so I don't linger long by
the lake. I hike back, dig out my bike, and start climbing
the countless switchbacks.

I find a good rhythm and make slow progress without
exhausting myself too quickly. Thankfully, the grade
isn't too steep. I'm not sure if it is the knowledge of
being at this high altitude or the actual lack of oxygen,
but I still have to gather my courage to cycle up through
this rough landscape. The two lagoons below are majestically blue against the black landscape and the white
road. Just before I reach the pass, a thunderstorm rolls
in across the high peaks, taking away the opportunity
to photograph the road, which one can only see in its
entirety in clear weather from the top of the pass. It is
4:00 in the afternoon; soon it will get dark. Luckily, I
have my drone, which I send up to take a photo. I have
to be quick, because it's about to pour down. Just in
time, the small machine is back in its pocket and I'm
ready to return. With freezing fingers, I roll down to
the valley, a drop in altitude of 2200 meters. A guy on a
motorbike passes me, his girlfriend on the back holding
a jacket over both of them. It's the only traffic I've seen
on this road. Then I remember: it's Christmas Day.

Laguna 69 at 4600 meters in Huascarán National Park.

With freezing fingers, I roll down to the valley, a drop in altitude of 2200 meters.

HUASCARÁN, CORDILLERA BLANCA, PERU

THE PAN-AMERICAN HIGHWAY

DAY 575 - SUPE PUERTO, PERU - 11,930 KM

It speaks to the incredible diversity of Peru's landscape that one can cycle from the snow-capped mountains of the Cordillera Blanca to the warm sunsets of the central seaside in the same day. I've broken many personal records during the past weeks, and today's is my longest downhill ride, from 4000 meters to sea level. The world that greets me near the coast, however, is not charming: I am now facing dusty, desolate days on the dismal Pan-American Highway.

From Conococha at 4020 meters, I start a descent which could best be compared to a motorbike ride. I fully participate in the car traffic, because my average speed is 50 kilometers per hour with a top speed of 67.5 kilometers per hour. If I wanted to go faster, I'd have to install a bigger sprocket on the front. Pedaling has no effect at this speed. Sand and dust blow in my face as I get closer to the coast. The empty water bottle under my downtube shrinks to half the size and looks like a raisin from the difference in air pressure. After a mind-blowing 150-kilometer downhill ride, the grade slowly evens out and the perfect day is disturbed by a beastly headwind.

The huge drop in altitude changes everything. It's warm and vaguely sunny, though far from picturesque. It's a strange climate I haven't seen anywhere in the world. Usually deserts are dry, with azure skies. Here it's dry and stark, but far from pristine. The sky is smudged with a thin haze called the *garúa*, which coats everything in an oppressive, opaque grayness. The air is so thick, it reminds me of the post-apocalyptic film *The Road*. Along the coastline is one continuous line of black pavement breaking the dim monotony: the Pan-American Highway.

With the notorious Darién Gap in Panama being its only interruption, the highway serves as a continuous motor vehicle route from Prudhoe Bay in Alaska all the way to Ushuaia in Argentina, the construction of which began in the early twentieth century. Of course, nowadays there are many alternatives to this route, but it's still a romantic idea to stick to a single main route connecting the North with the South. Because of the heavy traffic, the Pan-American Highway can be less attractive to cyclists, but sometimes it just feels good to speed up and see some prog-

ress on the map after being tangled in the mountains for so long. Plus, it allows an escape from the rainy season, which is most troublesome in the mountains and Amazon Basin. Here, it looks like I won't need my rain gear for a while.

At the end of the day I arrive in Supe Puerto, a gritty desert town on the coast with nothing of note for a tourist to visit. Sometimes, those are the places that attract me. I am gawked at as I venture through the streets looking for a grocery store. People are surprised to see a gringo cycling through the poor town, though pleasantly, it seems. It's just a few kilometers off El Pana, as they call the international highway. The man behind the counter of a grocery store welcomes me, and when I ask his advice about spending a night at the coast, he assures me: "Of course you can camp on the beach; it's very safe here." I wonder what that means. I've heard the word "safe" in so many situations, from all kinds of people. It's become a hollow word, not signifying much more than one's personal *perception* of safety. To the average white tourist with a decent travel budget, this town looks anything but safe. The streets are full of litter, stray dogs feast on leftovers, and little trash fires burn on the shoulders of the roads. Dingy establishments are built of bare cinder blocks and none of the houses seem to be finished. From the flat rooftops, rebar sticks out randomly, ready to extend into additional floors. I've seen this all over Peru, and later I learn there is a reason for it: if a house is under construction, the owners avoid paying property taxes. Therefore, everyone lives in unfinished houses with unpainted walls, missing doors, and entire floors without ceilings. In the mountains and the rainforest, the pristine nature somewhat disguises the urban ugliness, but here with the colorless desert as a backdrop, it's front and

center. Altogether, Supe Puerto is a place I would rather avoid. It would never be on any traveler's bucket list. On a bike tour, however, a cyclist goes through dozens of such places. The slow pace of travel makes one spend more time in the unwanted, in-between destinations. At the moment, there's hardly any place I feel unsafe anymore. I don't come across as a wealthy white tourist anymore; I've come to blend in. The colors of my bags have faded from many days under the sun. My bike is dusty and scratched, and the tires worn out. My skin is burned and dry, my face grim and unwashed. When I look in the mirror, I see someone who could pass for a beggar on the side of the street staring back.

By sunset I reach the beach. The sand, the dunes, and the hazy horizon are all drenched in one orange-brown color. Celebrating my arrival at the sea with a beer and a cigarette, I sit on the beach, feeling the sand between my toes. I gaze at the sunset and listen to the calming sound of the waves. As always, the waves are high and rough. They remind me of the first time in Washington, even though everything else is so different. By now, I've lost count of the times I've spent a night at the Pacific coast. Despite the dirt, I couldn't be happier to be here.

The next day I continue on the dusty, noisy road. Desert highways can be cathartic, as I experienced in parts of Nevada. The sound of rubber singing on pavement for hours on end, not having to worry about navigating and simply being able to pedal, resting on the handlebar and letting my thoughts wander... it puts me in a serene, contemplative mindset. But if that thin layer of tranquility is disturbed by heavy traffic and a strong headwind, all bets are off. That's what I'm up against today, and so there's nothing positive to say about hours on a bike out on these particular dusty plains.

The next few days, the wind has free reign and tries its best to stop me from reaching Lima, Peru's capital, where I hope to stay for New Year's Eve. I'm hardly making any progress, and I once again catch myself longing to skip ahead to the next stage of the journey. As I battle against the gusts one afternoon, I slowly come to the discovery that I'm not going to make it to the next water supply. I've totally underestimated the circumstances. Only 30 kilometers after having left Huacho, I'm already running out of water, because it took me almost the entire day to get even this far. Being on the busy Pan-American Highway, I assumed there would be plenty of gas stations where I could fill up. Packing too much water with such a headwind was the last thing I wanted to do. With the wind straight in my face, the three liters I have go quickly. After scrolling through Google Maps, it appears there are no gas stations for another 40 kilometers, so I have no choice but to go back and try again the next day. Frustrated, I curse the dust, the highway, the wind, and the obnoxious logistics of the whole thing.

The wind sets me back enough that I end up taking a bus to reach Lima in time for the end of the year, which I celebrate in solitude.

→ *Wild camp spot at the Pacific coast.*
↘ *Unknown settlement along the Pan-American Highway—are these houses, or remnants of some industrial venture? The desert is home to some mysterious, almost apocalyptic settings.*

SUPE PUERTO, PERU

The Nazca Lines are a collection of giant geoglyphs (landscape drawings) depicting various animals, plants, and shapes, dating from around 100 AD. Because of their size they are only vaguely visible from the sky. These are much smaller drawings inspired by the Nazca Lines.

At the moment, there's hardly any place I feel unsafe anymore. I don't come across as a wealthy white tourist anymore; I've come to blend in. The colors of my bags have faded from many days under the sun. My bike is dusty and scratched, and the tires worn out. My skin is burned and dry, my face grim and unwashed.

I PARK MY BIKE AT THE OASIS OF HUACACHINA AND BURST OUT RUNNING INTO THE DESERT UNTIL I SEE NOTHING AND HEAR NOTHING. MY LAST DESTINATION OF THE 600-KILOMETER DESERT RIDE ALONG THE COAST: AT LAST, I AM AWAY FROM THE UGLY CHAOS OF THE PAN-AMERICAN HIGHWAY, AWAY FROM THE CROWDS OF TOURISTS OF THE TOUR BUGGIES. I SIT ON THE HIGHEST DUNE UNTIL THE SUN SETS AND BREATHE. IT IS THE MOST BEAUTIFUL DESERT I HAVE EVER SEEN.

A DECISION HAS TO BE MADE: THE EASY ROAD ALONG THE COAST, OR THE CHALLENGING CLIMB THROUGH THE ANDES. I ALREADY KNOW IT ISN'T A CHOICE.

The oasis of Huacachina.

—Saved from a hailstorm

Only two days into the mountains, I'm unsure if I made the right decision. The rainy season in late February is officially over its peak—thankfully, work kept me in Bogota and New York for the last couple weeks—but the threat of bad weather is still constant. I start almost every day by slipping into wet socks and shoes. Everything is dirty from the mud. The wide views which attracted me to the mountains are often obstructed by clouds. Today started sunny, which gave me hope. I even cycled shirtless for a while through green fields where herds of alpacas grazed peacefully. But by noon, the clouds gathered and I was back in this dark reality.

As I slowly climb to a 4700-meter pass, it rains continuously. I'm sort of doing okay: the cycling effort keeps me warm. Above 4300 meters, the rain turns into hail, which hits my hands and knees relentlessly. At the moment, I do not own long rain pants. I consider putting on my normal long trousers, just to protect my legs from the hailstones, but I don't want to stop. I'd rather keep the momentum of the climb and stay warm. Soon, the landscape turns white as I gain altitude, and the cold at last starts to grip me. I climb faster, looking for shelter, but on these remote roads, there is nowhere to hide. No trees, no buildings, no gas stations, nothing. If there were only a small roof, I could put on dry clothes, eat something, and do squats or push-ups to raise my body temperature. Minutes pass by as the storm worsens. I finally stop to put my trousers on, when a police truck approaches with lights on. It stops, and a window opens.

"Señor. ¿Estás bien?"
Hail still pours down as I fiddle helplessly with my trousers. My knees are dark purple and itchy from the hailstones. I look at the pickup truck's empty bed. They could potentially give me a ride, but I'm too proud to ask them.
"Where going?" the driver asks.
"Busco un hospedaje." I reply and point to the pass asking if they know of a guest-house or hotel. The driver looks at his colleague and they share a few words in Spanish. Without saying a thing, he closes the window and turns off the car. Both step out and one of them opens the trunk.
"Come."

Moments later, I'm in the back of the police car and my legs are turning a normal color again. The policemen give me lift over the pass and drop me off at the hospedaje, where I have lunch and warm up. They show me one of the rooms. A squeaky steel door leads to a dark concrete room where I can't even stand up straight. The mattress is moist and thin. After learning there is also no electricity during the day, I decide to move on. It's still early in the afternoon and I can do another 30 kilometers to another hospedaje. But when I get there, that one appears to be closed and I end up in my wet tent again. It hasn't stopped raining for the entire remainder of the day. I mark today in my diary as the most miserable of the trip.

CUSCO

DAY 619 - CUSCO, PERU - 12,517 KM

As the historic capital of the Incan Empire and the central hub of the Sacred Valley, Cusco is the place to explore some of the best-preserved remains of the Inca Empire, including Machu Picchu. After many days of cycling through the wettest months of the rainy season and the hot, dusty coasts, I couldn't wish for a better place to unwind and soak up the history in comfort.

In Peru, there are only a handful of locations like Cusco that have tourist infrastructure, with public spaces developed according to the globalized standards of leisure. The coffee shops serve coffee from Italian espresso machines, with New York cheesecake and French crêpes on the side. The music is tasteful and perfectly leveled to accommodate the chit-chat of the clientele and the crush of the coffee grinder. Ideally, the cheesecake has a little chocolate alpaca on it, a local touch. There are yoga retreats, Irish pubs, and Mexican restaurants—and everywhere, it's relatively easy to get by in English. Visitors are usually foreign tourists, in practical outdoor gear or shorts and flip-flops, even if it's too cold for that. Organized tours are widely advertised for hassle-free visits to nearby sights, where people can marvel at the historic landmarks and briefly experience the rough edges of an enticing culture before being ferried back safely to their comfortable hotels. It might not be the most authentic way to see the country, but it's *nice*.

I'm also enjoying the balance of comfort and foreign culture. It's where I charge up. Most of the time, as a bicycle traveler, I spend my time in between those places. Order a coffee outside of the tourist zone, and you'll be served a hot can of water with a plastic mug, spoon, and a big Nescafé jar, with the instant coffee powder stuck to the lid. You'll sit on a plastic chair in a concrete-walled room, with a loud TV on the wall and reggaeton blaring through the speakers. Instead of cheesecake with a chocolate alpaca, you'll get a pack of fake Oreos or a plate of bland rice with a limp street dog at your feet, begging for a share. So of course, I take advantage of this luxury while I can.

I have downloaded the Lonely Planet guide to Peru, where I read: "One existential question haunts all Peruvians: What

↗ *Carnaval in Ayacucho.* ↘ *Coffee and pancakes with Cecilia*

You can still see the iconic Incan stonework at the base of some of the Spanish-built walls—the old and new married together.

to eat? Ceviche with slivers of fiery chili and corn, slow-simmered stews, velvety Amazonian chocolate—in the capital of Latin cooking, the choices are dazzling." I delete it from my phone. The opposite couldn't be more true. The choices *aren't* dazzling—yes, maybe Cusco and some neighborhoods in Lima boast that sort of variety, but across the Peru that I've seen, people eat the plain staples of rice and beans with soup. Traveling the secondary roads alone has shown me the real, raw parts of the country, which aren't as flattering and sense-tickling as the commercial travel guides promise. So once I reach a town like Cusco, I revel in it, knowing it is the exception to the rule. I can step out the door of my hotel and choose between delicious Indian food or exquisite Thai food. Some cafés not only have craft IPA, but *more than one* craft IPA. And the Wi-Fi works just like at home, so I can get some tasks done and catch up on movies and Netflix shows. I was slowly getting rid of my addiction to the online feed, since the Wi-Fi in rural areas is often too weak to stream, but here, the addiction returns in full force.

The Cusco region is packed with historic landmarks. Although much has sadly vanished from the Pre-Columbian cultures since the Europeans arrived, there is still a lot to discover. Some of the colonial houses are built on the remains of derelict Incan structures. You can still see the iconic Incan stonework at the base of some of the Spanish-built walls—the old and new married together. Plaza de Armas, the main square boasting two colonial churches, is the business and social center of the city. Peruvian women try to persuade passersby for a massage. "*Masaje*, amigo?" is the question heard on every corner. Many indigenous people also come to Cusco to sell their colorful crafts and garments. On the first day in town, I buy a sweater made of alpaca wool. The next day, I notice that all the other tourists in town are walking around in the same sweater—and that's not because I'm so influential.

I'm not alone in this city. I team up with Cecilia, a Dutch actress who is on a two-month trip through Peru. She crossed Europe on her bike last summer, so we have a lot of stories to share. We become fast friends and explore a lot of places together. We visit

It contrasts so strongly with my life on the road, where I'm alone, eat simply, sleep in the wild, and pedal most of the day.

the San Pedro Market, packed with fruit stands and eateries where mostly Peruvians eat. Salesmen and vendors sell their wares in a labyrinthine mishmash of stalls. It's a typical South American market, a bit rough on the edges, too strong for the stomachs of most tourists, who stick to a quick stroll and leave with an alpaca sweater, scarf, or poncho. After Cecilia and I pass the butchers' alley, where chopped-off cow tongues dangle and pigs' heads stare down at us, decomposing in the warm sunlight among piles of red meat, we move on. The hygiene laws in these *mercados*, if there are any, are not taken too seriously.

Cusco is a city of contrasts, where the tourist area is just a small bubble in the historical center. The apartment we're staying in is a steep walk up cobblestone stairs in San Blas, one of the oldest neighborhoods on the north hill. We're out of breath in no time at this altitude, even when we merely walk home, but drinking lots of coca tea seems to combat altitude sickness. We enjoy sitting on our French balcony and looking over the city, which is situated in a bowl. In the evening we watch the lights dancing in one particularly lively zone, but as beautiful the view is, I know I don't want to be on the other side, where the stray dogs roam the steep, garbage-strewn alleys. I cycled there the other day and thought I was in another town.

We spend a few days here, trying out all the coffee places and restaurants. I desperately needed this: a level of safety, warmth, and predictability, not to mention someone to talk to and be with. It contrasts so strongly with my life on the road, where I'm alone, eat simply, sleep in the wild, and pedal most of the day. Here, I also am able to catch up on some freelance work that I thoroughly enjoy: a graphic design project, a book-editing job, some administrative tasks. I embrace doing all the normal things that would bore me during my life at home. If the road is plain bread, these places are Nutella.

MACHU PICCHU

DAY 616 - MACHU PICCHU, PERU - 12,721 KM

The ruins of Machu Picchu are some of the most intact and complete of the Inca Empire. Situated before a stunning backdrop of smoky mountains rising steeply from the Amazon Rainforest, it's not surprising that Machu Picchu is one of the New Seven Wonders of the World. Getting there is an undertaking in itself, and it requires some planning and research to avoid paying a small fortune in the tourist circuit, but there is true magic in these landscapes that inspires curiosity.

The first moment of the day, at 6am, when the clouds vanished revealing the famous view.

> For a few minutes, there is a concert of camera clicks, until the clouds gather again and hide the structures, like they were never even there.

Machu Picchu revealed to a wider public with this image by Hiram Bingham III in 1911.

The mountains are so steep and hostile that it makes one even more amazed that the Incas were able to build an entire city on the near-vertical slopes, using the ingenious technique of meticulously carving huge boulders to fit to each other like a jigsaw puzzle. Highly developed agriculture is evidenced by the hundreds of terraces curling around the hillsides, and they even constructed a complete irrigation system. The Incas didn't have a written language. We have only the structures from which to make inferences. They communicated via networks of runners—horses were not used for transport—who could run the entire length of the country to relay messages orally or with a communication system called *quipu*, a combination of strings and knots tied to a necklace, which is similar to the binary code used in computers. It's obvious that the Incas were an inventive people, but many questions remain unanswered since we have no written records. One can only marvel at the wonder of this place, the magic of the fecund jungle, the iconic peaks, and the ancient ruins.

There's no easy way into Machu Picchu. With close to 5000 visitors each day in the high season, Machu Picchu is one of the most-visited landmarks in South America. It's also one of the most expensive to visit. To get there on a budget requires eight hours in a small local bus from Cusco, three hours trekking through the jungle, spending the night in the village at the bottom of the citadel, and then a three-hour hike up on the mountain. The return trip is the same. Including the entry ticket, it sets one back about 80 dollars total. People easily spend tenfold for slightly faster and more comfortable accommodations, with train tickets ranging from 50 to 500 dollars. It's an insane money-making circus. I have gone for the affordable option.

So here I am, up on the citadel at dawn, in the rain. I'm in the midst of a crowd of tourists in ponchos waiting for a glimpse of the remarkable ruins. My ticket is for 6:00, the earliest entry slot, so I had to walk 300 meters up the endless slippery stairs through the rainforest in the dark. The Inca city is right in front of us, but it's entirely covered in clouds. Nobody has seen anything yet. Hundreds of phones and cameras are waiting to capture one of the most photographed views of this continent. Some people pose for pictures, but there's nothing to see in the background. I look around a bit, studying the disappointed horde of tourists. Maybe it's just karma, expecting such beauty to be at our beck and call, because it clearly is not. It clearly is not. Nature gives as it pleases, as I've experienced many times before, from San Francisco to the Ecuadorian wilderness. We keep staring into the abyss, and then, all of a sudden, the clouds drift and the labyrinth of stone walls rises from the mist. "Oohs" and "ahs" sound from the crowd. For a few minutes, there is a concert of camera clicks, until the clouds gather again and hide the structures, like they were never even there.

Teaming up with Mark & Hana, two cyclists from New Zealand, on a trail around Cusco, the Sacred Valley, and Salineras de Maras.

THE RAINBOW MOUNTAINS

DAY 625 - RAINBOW MOUNTAIN, CUSIPATA, PERU - 12,663 KM

The higher I go, the more otherworldly it becomes. The south of Peru is known for its mineral-colored mountainscapes which take on the oddest hues. To see them, we have to climb up to breath-snatching altitudes of 5000 meters. The Rainbow Mountain is the most famous peak and receives hundreds of visitors every day, but there are also alternatives that are worth going deeper into the mountains to find.

... if the mountain won't show its colors, the local people will.

The Rainbow Mountain, locally known as Vinicunca, would be a day's bike ride away from Cusco, but most people visit it with an organized tour, as I also do this time. The demanding walk to 5000 meters takes all the breath out of my lungs, and I'm not very lucky with the weather. It's still the middle of the rainy season, so the entire morning is wet and foggy, which makes it impossible to see anything more than 50 meters away.

But if the mountain won't show its colors, the local people will. It's inspiring to see that the poorest groups are by far the most vibrantly dressed, sporting bright outfits with cheerfully clashing patterns—especially considering their circumstances in muddy highlands, where they live in small huts herding alpacas and selling coca tea and snacks to tourists with altitude sickness. It's a far cry from Northern European cities, where people dress in pragmatic, monochromatic fashion. I wait a few hours for the colorful view, but the clouds stay in place. I will have to return one day in the dry season.

—Palccoyo

These lesser known rainbow mountains near Palccoyo, a
much better place with fewer tourists. I travel here with
Cecilia on another day. This time the weather is with us.
We need a guide because the road is not on most maps. A
long dirt trail climbs up slowly via the terraced mountains
past many small alpaca farms. The higher you get the more
red the soil becomes, which contrasts beautifully with the
green grass.

It's inspiring to see that the poorest groups
are by far the most vibrantly dressed...

The Rainbow Mountains showing their vivid colors.
Despite being reasonably close to the Amazon Basin,
it can be quite chilly 4800 meters up.

Arequipa
—*The end of the rainy season*

Watch a sunset over Plaza de Armas in Peru's second largest city, Arequipa, and you will see why it's been nicknamed The White City. Arequipa is largely constructed of local white stone from the nearby mountains, and it enjoys many hours of sunlight every day. Situated at the edge of the Andes at 2300 meters, Arequipa is in the lower, dryer part of Peru, and thus only sees about two weeks of rain in a year. That makes it the perfect place to wait out the rest of the rainy season.

Like Cusco, Arequipa is a pleasant place to stay. Despite being a large city, the colonial center feels like a compact, peaceful town with many informal eateries, coffee shops, and a handful of craft breweries. Tourists don't venture outside of the center, where the real Peru is. A few other friends are taking a break here too. I see Sophie and Jeremy,

two French cyclists who are on a similar journey to mine. I met them briefly in Ecuador by chance, and we've been in touch on social media since then. And there's Pascal from Canada. We all share dinners, discuss routes, and take part in Massa Critica, a friendly protest bike ride through the city. It's organized monthly by a couple who own a bike shop to raise awareness for cyclists in the city. About 200 people join the ride, young and old, on all kinds of bikes. Everyone is dressed up with colorful lights and loud music playing through bluetooth speakers—it's loud and vibrant, as to be expected in Latin America.

Arequipa grows on me quickly. I spend my days working, writing, and making time for Cecilia. She will move on pretty soon as well, which I'm not looking forward to. Maybe I secretly wish to join her and be home-

ward bound. To reference Paul Theroux again, the temporariness of travel often intensifies friendship and turns it into intimacy. On this journey, I often have to disconnect from people at the very moment we are happiest together. We keep the souvenirs and the memories, but we move on before we grow bored. These memories are my most valuable belongings.

I want to keep up my momentum after this and stay focused on the route, so this is probably my last longer break in a city. I look forward to cycling again, but I dread it too. The mountains will be at skull-crushing altitudes, and the most beautiful deserts in the world are all around. When I leave Arequipa, I will say goodbye to lower altitudes for a long time. The sun grows stronger every day and the clouds vanish. I finish my work, my friends move on, and soon, so do I.

THE ALTIPLANO

Toward the south of Peru, the Andes Mountains widen and become the second-highest plateau in the world: the Altiplano, where 3000 meters is the new sea level and natural phenomena like geysers, salt lakes, volcanoes, and outstretched plains are part of the everyday scenery. It covers the majority of Bolivia and reaches all the way into Argentina and Chile. As someone who grew up in the greenery of Northern Europe, I find myself in a landscape that is completely alien to me.

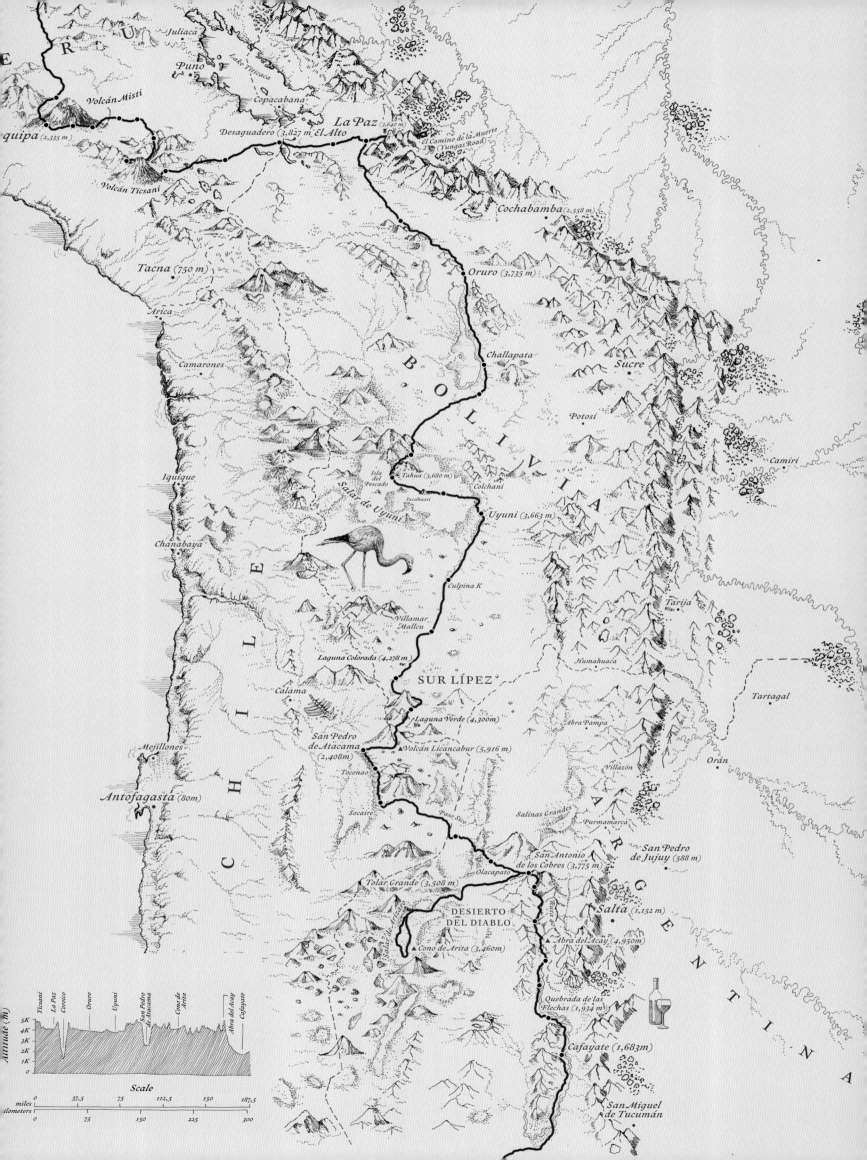

P E R U

Juliaca

Puno

Lake Titicaca

Copacabana

Volcán Misti

quipa (2,335 m)

Desaguadero

La Paz (3,640 m)

3,827 m El Alto

El Camino de la Muerte
(Yungas Road)

Volcán Ticsani

Cochabamba (2,558 m)

B O L I V I A

Tacna (750 m)

Oruro (3,735 m)

Arica

Challapata

Sucre

Camarones

Potosí

Iquique

Tahua (3,680 m)

Isla del Pescado

Salar de Uyuni

Colchani

Camiri

Incahuasi

Uyuni (3,663 m)

Chanabaya

Culpina K

Tarija

Villamar Mallcu

Laguna Colorada (4,278 m)

Humahuaca

Calama

SUR LÍPEZ

Tartagal

Laguna Verde (4,300m)

Abra Pampa

Mejillones

San Pedro de Atacama (2,408m)

▲Volcán Licancabur (5,916 m)

Orán

Toconao

Villazón

Antofagasta (80m)

Socaire

Salinas Grandes

Paso Sico

Purmamarca

San Antonio de los Cobres (3,775 m)

San Pedro de Jujuy (588 m)

A R G E N T I N A

Olacapato

Tolar Grande (3,508 m)

Salta (1,152 m)

Salar de Arizaro

DESIERTO DEL DIABLO

▲Abra del Acay (4,950m)

▲Cono de Arita (3,460m)

Quebrada de las Flechas (1,934 m)

Cafayate (1,683m)

C H I L E

San Miguel de Tucumán

A

Altitude (m)

Ticsani
La Paz
Coroico
Oruro
Uyuni
San Pedro de Atacama
Cono de Arita
Abra del Acay
Cafayate

5K
4K
3K
2K
1K
0

Scale

miles 0   37,5   75   112,5   150   187,5
kilometers 0   75   150   225   300

*Volcán Misti, seen from the north at 4900 meters,
just before the downhill toward Arequipa.*

CHASING VOLCANOES

DAY 662 - VOLCÁN TICSANI, PERU - 13,332 KM

I have one last goal in Peru: breaking my altitude record again by sleeping at the foot of Volcán Ticsani and climbing alone to the summit at 5400 meters. It will be a serious introduction to the Altiplano.

It's not easy to fall asleep at 4850 meters. The air is extremely dry, which dries out my nose and throat and causes a bit of a headache. Some moments, I'm breathing actively just lying still in my sleeping bag.

While in Arequipa I wanted to climb Volcán Misti, but because of the wet season, there was still too much melting snow on the top, which would have been dangerous to navigate on a trek to the summit. Volcán Ticsani, a few hundred kilometers farther south, is slightly lower and, according to weather reports, snow-free.

I leave Arequipa after four weeks of almost no cycling, spending time on my laptop, and exploring places with Cecilia and other travelers. The first days on the road hit incredibly hard. Not just physically, as I work my way back up to altitudes which are unnatural to my body, but mostly mentally. The great paradox of this journey is that when I'm witnessing the most beautiful places on the planet, I am also the most alone. I'm surrounded by the most incredible landscapes, but my mind is somewhere else. Being out on these amazing roads sometimes has an opposite effect. It's like a prison, like being locked up in infinity. All I have is the crackling of the gravel underneath me and the slowly evolving landscapes around me.

Two days after Arequipa, I lose phone connection. Now it's just me and the road. I miss Cecilia; she became a really good friend. I miss the good food, and going to the market, and watching people. I miss hanging out with my other new friends, going out for drinks, and cooking elaborate meals together in the hostel. I miss the internet, social media, and YouTube videos—the stupid things to enjoyably waste time. I miss all the distractions.

I never get used to these hangovers, even when I know they're coming. They're an inevitable part of the traveling lifestyle, which is itself an infinite loop of searching, finding, connecting, collecting, and

Hana's House, a shelter known only by cyclists.

letting go. Christopher McCandless, the protagonist of Into the Wild, concluded in the last chapter of his life that happiness is only real when it's shared. Right now, I feel this keenly. But it doesn't mean that unshared happiness doesn't exist. On the contrary, there are many moments of joy, self-discovery, and growth that must be found alone. I've had many such moments. And of course, there is always writing. That's a way to share as well. Maybe it's less direct, but it's a comfort during the lonely times, and a powerful way to preserve memories for the future. After a few days, my mindset becomes more positive and I get used to the solitude again. The cycling remains tough at these altitudes, but now and then I go through a landscape so stunning, the difficulty is transcended by the strange colors and otherworldly vegetation. In these moments, I'm in pure awe.

After many painstaking climbs, I reach the foot of Volcán Ticsani, which is set in a sandy valley. I stand next to the road gasping for air. It is late afternoon, and it is snowing a little. The plan is to camp here and climb the volcano early in the morning, but I am out of water. The entire day, there were no shops to buy water or streams to fill up my bottles. I tried the nearby lagunas, but the water was green from algae. Finding water is always a gamble in these landscapes. I don't want to carry too much with me, but then there's the risk of running dry. Eventually I make my way to a small town in the valley some 1400 meters below. The next day, I'll return and repeat the plan.

The next morning I hitch a ride back to the foot of
Ticsani and find the rock shelter that was built by
Mark (@highluxphoto) and Hana, the cycling couple I
met in Cusco, when they passed by here a few months
ago. I have plenty of time before sunset, so I make
myself at home and add my own touches to the refuge.
I reinforce the wall and make the floor space large
enough to fit a tent. The shelter is marked as "Hana's
House" on the track downloadable from their Ride-
WithGPS account. It will remain a place known only to
cyclists because it's invisible from the road. The entire
day it stays bright and sunny, with vast views over the
desert and no living soul in sight. It's surreal and enjoyable to hang out here and make camp. The strange
landscape makes me feel like building a house on Mars.

Despite the great camp spot, I sleep poorly, perhaps
from the excitement and the high altitude. It's not easy
to fall asleep at 4850 meters. The air is extremely dry,
which dries out my nose and throat and causes a bit
of a headache. Some moments, I'm breathing actively
just lying still in my sleeping bag. Usually I sleep on
my belly, but here that's almost impossible because it
robs me of oxygen. I think my camp is not totally level
either, so my head is a few centimeters lower than my
feet. This high up, it makes me feel the world is turning
me upside down.

At 2:00 in the morning my alarm goes off, and at 3:00
I'm on my way to the summit, leaving my tent and bags
at the shelter. The majority of the trail is rideable with
an unloaded bike. A bright half moon lights my way
and the stars are plenty. Above 5000 meters, there's
snow on the side of the steep trail, the part where I
have to start walking. My feet sink into the thin, powdery dust. Around the last bend, there's a heavy sulfur
smell. Smoke curls up from the inside of the volcano,
but I can't see the crater. The horizon in the distance
turns light blue. At the summit is a wooden cross and
some empty liquor bottles. It's well below freezing,
and the wind cuts like a knife. I'm trying to take some
drone shots, but the batteries give out immediately in
the cold and the touchscreen of my phone fails under
my cold fingertips. Aches and malfunctions aside, my
soul is grateful. 5408 meters: another crazy personal
record.

At high altitudes, the blue skies are much darker than at sea level because of the lower air density. You can see that in this photo, taken at midday at 4850 meters. It's even more noticeable from the window of a plane, which cruises about 10,000 meters high. At 35,000 meters, the sky is completely black.

The great paradox of this journey is that when I'm witnessing the most beautiful places on the planet, I am also the most alone.

—La Paz

Nighttime in La Paz, one of Bolivia's two capital cities. Situated at the very edge of the Altiplano, La Paz lies in an urban valley rimmed by steeply sloping cliffs. At 4000 meters above sea level, it's the world's highest metropolitan area. I have arrived here via El Alto, its neighboring city, through an endless knot of dense traffic that took hours. Most residents commute on public minibuses, which clog the streets in uncontrolled numbers. There seem to be no bus stops and people board and disembark wherever they want, which meant that all day, I had to be ready to get cut off at any moment. I don't know of anything more overwhelming than cycling into a major capital for the first time. I recall the breathing monsters of Istanbul, Tehran, Kolkata, Bangkok, Mexico City, Lima, Bogota: each causes a uniquely comprehensive sensory overload, and each requires adjusting differently.

Once I'm settled in a new city, I ground myself for a few days behind my laptop. So far, getting work done on the road has proved largely to be a success, but it comes with challenges. When I think I've scored the perfect café or hotel to do some work, I often need to relocate because of bad Wi-Fi. I always ask about the internet connection up front, but even then, you never know. Outside the cities, especially in developing countries, Wi-Fi and cell phone connections are often unreliable. It teaches you to disconnect from your phone more often, but when it breaks up your workflow, it can be quite frustrating. Also, finding a comfortable chair and table sounds easier than it is. A full day of work often starts with two hours on the bed in my hotel room, an hour or two in a café, then another stint in the hotel room before another hour during lunch or dinner in a restaurant. None of these places are suitable to spend a full day of work. And on a trip like this, these problems have to be navigated on a daily basis. I'm starting to catch myself dreaming of being back in Amsterdam, where I don't have to worry about any of this.

Valle de las Animas (Valley of the Souls), which is on the eastern side of La Paz, stands out with its sharp cathedral-like rock formations, which you see everywhere at the edges of the city and in between neighborhoods. One day, I leave the bike in my hostel and go for a hike. There are a few trails to take from the river valley, but I choose my own route. It leads to a serious climb on sandy edges that gradually become steeper and, near the summit, almost vertical. I scramble to the top and find myself on the sharpest summit I've ever seen, with an amazing view over the peaks and city in the distance.

Death Road
—Bolivia's most lethal mountain road

The unpaved Yungas Road connects La Paz on the Altiplano and the Yungas region in the steaming jungle of the Amazon. It was named the world's most dangerous road in 1995, when an estimated 200 to 300 people were being killed every year. Nowadays, there is a two-lane paved highway through another valley, so Death Road is only used by local traffic. It also has been gaining popularity among mountain bikers. You could argue that the title is now exaggerated, since most of the danger came from the fact that the road was too narrow and poorly built to handle a large volume of buses and trucks. During the rainy season the risks of falling rocks and mudslides are higher, but most of the traffic danger is gone.

For cyclists, it's a beautiful ride through the jungle, and a welcome change of scenery for me. The mountains are lush, green, and incredibly steep—sometimes literally vertical. Overhanging ferns and waterfalls sprinkle on me as I ride underneath. As I descend, I feel the air become more fragrant and damp, and the scent of orchids growing stronger. Memories from earlier in the journey return as the greenery unfolds around me. Mexico, Guatemala, Costa Rica, all the humid, noisy jungles, all of the fruit stands along the road selling mangoes and coconuts. I forgot how sweet it is—the plants, the butterflies, the waterfalls in such an abundance of sound, color, and growth. Perhaps Yungas Road needs a new name: The Road of Life.

↗ *A roadside stand selling snacks and beverages in La Paz.*
↘ *A tailor and cobbler's shop in El Alto, La Paz's neighboring city on the Altiplano.*

Making my way south out of El Alto on the busy Highway 1.

↖ Ruta 603 toward Salar de Uyuni, with Cerro Tunupa (5321 meters) in the distance on the left.
↗ Welcome statue of desert town Huari.
↙ Red quinoa fields on the side of the road are a common sight on the Altiplano in Bolivia.
↘ Flamingos on their way to the mineral lakes.

An impact crater left by a meteor, near the community of Jayocota.

SALAR DE UYUNI

Some places make you wonder if you're still on Earth, and this is one of them. Cycling and camping on the world's biggest salt lake is a novel experience in many aspects. Long before I started this bicycle journey, I was struck by the images of this magical area, and it was the prospect of cycling here that sparked my dream of traversing the high plains of South America.

Salar de Uyuni is dry most of the year, but for a few months during the rainy season, it's covered by a shallow layer of water. The depth can range from a meter at the peak of the rainy season (January and February) to only a few centimeters when it dries up. I am here in April, and it is almost completely dry.

This isn't my first time cycling through a desert. I have some long days of solitude behind me on the nearly empty freeways of Bolivia, and I've cycled the deserts of Nevada, Turkey, and Iran. But when I stand at the edge of Salar de Uyuni for the first time, I cringe. I am unnerved to enter the blank canvas. This will be my very first time navigating by compass, without any path to follow. But I am excited to spend a few days in this infinite dreamland. Perhaps it's the closest thing Earth has to heaven, if heaven is an endless, vacant, blinding-white expanse.

Before embarking, I spend a night at the north edge of the lake, in a hamlet called Tahua. There is an exquisite, high-end resort there made entirely of salt, comically out of proportion with the unassuming village. Rooms are expensive at 130 dollars a night, but since this is the only place with Wi-Fi, I go there for dinner. Once on the lake, I don't expect to have any connection for at least three days. The fireplace warms the restaurant and the windows frame a panoramic view of the lake drenched in moonlight—beautiful and haunting at the same time. The hotel is an odd paradise at the edge of civilization. The rest of the village is a collection of mudbrick houses, half of them unhabited. There's no vegetation, and everything is dressed in volcanic dust, making it look apocalyptic under the night sky.

In the morning, I enter the lake. The edge is wet and the tires sink down, but as I gain distance it dries up. The going is much slower than I expected. Despite being the flattest place on earth, the crackling salt has a lot of drag on the bike. The surface at this section is quite rough,

comparable to cycling on a rocky dirt road. After about 10 kilometers, I take a break to get my bearings. It's eerily quiet when I hold still, and the harsh sunlight bounces off the salt, blinding me and making me feel dizzy. Surprisingly, there's no wind at all, and soon it gets hot. To keep from becoming faint, I unpack and do things slowly. I boil all the eggs I just bought in the village before they break from the shaking of the bike. From the ground, I take some salt and crush it between my fingers over the eggs. The salt leaves little cuts on my fingertips.

This is one of those rare places where the sky draws all the attention. The landscape is an unnerving nothingness. Without GPS, it's impossible to determine where I am on the lake. My only anchor points are the mountains in the distance and the moving clouds in the sky. I'm heading to Isla del Pescado for the night, which is 30 kilometers from the shore. It's easy to navigate: the island pops up clearly from the horizon. For hours, nothing changes around me as I pedal forward. It's like riding in a dream. The distance I gain is unnoticeable. The island remains a small bump on the horizon. The only moving things on land are the salt crystals beneath me.

The first night, I camp at the edge of a small island. It turns out not to be Isla del Pescado: that one is a bit farther and larger than I thought. I spy it now: it looks like a giant ship on the white sea and I'm completely fooled by its size. I calculate that a round trip around it is seven kilometers. It's composed of bare cliffs, rocks, and cacti. Families of *viscachas* (rabbits with squirrel-like tails) scurry around. How do they survive

> Without GPS, it's impossible to determine where I am on the lake. My only anchor points are the mountains in the distance and the moving clouds in the sky.

> For hours, nothing changes around me as I pedal forward. It's like riding in a dream.

out here? I cook myself some local quinoa, pumpkin, and tomatoes. The night is chilly but not too cold. I can't sleep for a while because my body aches from a sunburn. Thanks to the salt reflecting light, I've burnt parts of my body that never see sun, like the backs of my arms and legs, the underside of my nose, and even my eye sockets.

Early in the morning, I am strangely knocked back to reality when I receive a phone call from some new tenants who are in front of my apartment in Amsterdam and can't find the keys. It takes a moment before I understand what's going on and how to direct them. I didn't expect to have reception here, but apparently being on this island slightly above the lake lets me pick up a signal from a nearby village. When I prepare to cycle onward, I discover I have a flat tire, so I take the bags off again to deal with it. A few days ago I got a big puncture, which the sealant could just barely fix. When I take out the tube, it's entirely dry. Luckily I still have a spare tube, which I put in. Despite the salt, the drivetrain is doing reasonably well. I put some extra lube on the chain to keep it from rusting, remembering how badly my bike rusted after cycling the salt lakes in Turkey a few years ago.

The next destination is the island of Incahuasi, 25 kilometers ahead. Again, I focus on the small stain on the horizon for hours. Now and then, a car passes as I approach the island. All the tourists visit this particular island, which is the only place on the lake with a restaurant, water tap, and small store. When I arrive, I see a lot of Land Cruisers and SUVs from organized tours. People marvel at the bike and find it hard to grasp that I'm here by human-powered

A full moon during the second night on the salt flat.

travel—the usual reactions. Another cyclist from Spain greets me. He just camped on Incahuasi, but will take a bus back to the town of Uyuni: "It's too much salt for me. I can't stand it any longer." After our chat, I continue on. It's another 90 kilometers and a night on the lake before I'll reach the shore and the next town. The salt still stretches out like a giant snakeskin, but because there's more traffic here, white tracks have formed in the salt, which I use to navigate. Unlike the past two days, there is no anchor point on the horizon. Progress has improved because the car tracks have smoothed out the surface.

The second night is spent directly on the salt. The light is incredible as the full moon rises on one side and the sun sinks behind the mountains on the other—a color spectrum that morphs from deep orange to icy

blue. After dinner, I read for a few hours inside the tent. At 11:00, it's barely dark because the moon is high and tiny clouds cast dancing shadows over the lake. In the far distance, a car roars over the salt crust and sounds like a jet engine. The white and red light beams move fast across the horizon, then dip behind an island for a while and appear again later, like something out of *Star Wars*.

I go for a midnight run to warm up. The tent and the bike quickly turn into tiny specks on the horizon, even from a few hundred meters away. A shiver rolls down my spine: if I ran for some time with my eyes closed, I might never find my tent again. Later, I return and fall into a deep sleep. When the alarm goes off in the morning, the sun and the moon have switched places.

Last day on Salar de Uyuni. Salt lakes are the worst for bicycles. If you don't clean off the salt immediately, many of the parts will rust.

—13 hours on washboard tracks in Bolivia's emptiest province

Sur Lípez is the southernmost province of Bolivia at the edge of the Atacama, the driest desert on earth. It is the gateway to a barren landscape rich with salt flats, volcanoes, geysers, and mineral lakes, all painted in surreal hues. But some of the most colorful places in the world are also the most unlivable. Not many Bolivians call this place home apart from those who run the handful of *refugios* serving adventure tour groups. They are far from cozy places and merely the only available options for food, water, and accommodation.

I have taken some days in the town of Uyuni to rest and clean all the salt off the bike—I was relieved that it came out well without much rust. My next goal is San Pedro de Atacama, just over the border in Chile, but before that, I have to cross the Atacama, which will take about six days. I've planned it in such a way that I can stay at all the refugios, so I won't have to camp. The majority of the road will be far above 4000 meters, and my sleeping bag is wearing thin. I know what it's like to spend the night that high, so any excitement about that particular novelty has been replaced by a dismissive "Been there, done that!"

The only traffic on these roads is from the tour agencies' Land Cruisers. They plow the sandy surface to a washboard that's almost unrideable on a bike. When cars hit bumps on unpaved roads, their suspension systems absorb the shock and then come down hard at the ground, displacing the dirt and starting the washboard pattern. With time and traffic, the bumps only get higher and the depressions only get deeper. In some places, the original road has become such a sandpit, cars get stuck in the deep tire grooves. To avoid this, each vehicle chooses its own way, creating additional tracks that result in a chaotic network of tracks, which is hard to follow. By bike it's an uncomfortable ride for most of the route. My tires are at minimum pressure to soften the shake over the washboard. I'm constantly looking for the smoothest piece of road.

Today I have covered 80 kilometers and 1000 meters of elevation gain, which is too much for a day in these conditions. At the end of the afternoon, I'm struggling through the sand and still have 20 kilometers before the refugio. Near Laguna Colorada, I find a stream where I could possibly camp, but far over the laguna I can see the lights of the refugio twinkling, so I decide to continue in the dark. But I've been fooled by the mirage: it's a lot farther than I think. The road is hard to see in the dark, and many times I have to check if I'm still on the route. For two hours, I cycle under the dim light of the stars and my headlight. When I reach the refugio at 8:30, my cycling app tells me I've been moving for 13 hours.

Some of the most colorful places in the world are also the most unlivable.

The red color of Laguna Colorada is caused by algae and plankton, the staple foods of the resident flamingos and the source of their pink plumage.

↑ *Laguna Tuyajto in Chile, near the border with Argentina.*
↗ *Blinded by boiling geysers in Sur Lípez.*
↘ *Bubbling, gurgling, smelly mudpots at the geysers of Sol de Mañana.*

Chile
—A welcome break

I descend into Chile from the Atacama and have the feeling that I can see the entire country in a glance. It's not only a beautiful downhill ride from 4800 to 2300 meters during sunset, but it's also *smooth*: in stark contrast to Bolivia's bone-breaking washboard roads, Chile's highways are paved. It's like stepping into a warm bath.

San Pedro de Atacama is finally within reach. It's an odd little town in the middle of the desert, a popular hub from which tours are organized to visit the surrounding valleys, volcanoes, hot springs, and geysers. If you zoom in on the map, it looks like there are more hotels than local dwellings. I arrive in the evening eager for a proper meal.

The tourists' demands mean there are many good restaurants here. I haven't checked into a hotel yet, so my bicycle, fully loaded and caked in dirt, waits out front while I devour two hamburgers and keep an eye on it. As I'm eating, a cheerful, middle-aged man walks in and greets me, and I know it's because of the bike. Of all the people in the restaurant, I am obviously the cyclist: exhausted, sunburned, unwashed, and unshaved. From his accent, I can tell that he's Dutch. His name is Arnold, and he's on a northward transcontinental bike tour. He suggests that I sleep at a hostel called La Casa Del Sol Naciente, where he and some other cyclists are staying. I agree to come over, but not before ordering another large portion of fries. My hunger is insatiable.

> Most of us camp in the garden. Maintenance needs to be done on the bikes, bags, and gear.

When I enter the hostel's patio, I get a friendly welcome from Nathan (of Australia) and Toby (of the UK), two other cyclists taking a break from the remote Altiplano. It turns out that they both follow me on Instagram, though I've never spoken with them before. They began their journeys individually, cycling northbound from Patagonia, but since meeting, they have been traveling together the last four months.

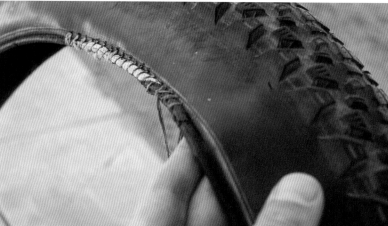

Most of us camp in the garden. Maintenance needs to be done on the bikes, bags, and gear, like stitching tires, bleeding brakes, and sewing tent zippers. I have been having more bad luck with my rear tire. After it exploded on the freeway in Bolivia a few weeks ago, I was forced to travel back to La Paz to get the large tear patched and glued with a piece of plastic. It worked out well, but now new problems have arisen. The wire bead has come off, making the inner tube bulge out from the side, which makes it impossible to pump to high pressure. In the meantime, Maxxis Tires has acknowledged that this should have never happened, and they are shipping a new tire to Santiago. I will have to find a temporary solution in the meantime.

On the streets of San Pedro de Atacama, I ask a random lady if she knows of a shoemaker to stitch the tire as a temporary solution, and she answers, "*I* can do it!" I ask where she lives, and she points a few blocks away. She is on her bicycle, and she takes me all the way to the outskirts of town at the edge of the desert. The street isn't even on my map. She lives with her four children in a one-room wooden chalet. In the corner is a sewing machine. She stitches the tire successfully, and while she's at it, the sleeve of my jacket.

It's enjoyable hanging around the hostel for a few days with other cyclists, eating good food and sharing route information. I haven't planned any of the way forward yet, so I glean inspiration and tips from Nathan, Toby, and Arnold. We cook mythically large meals and eat ourselves round for the coming time on the road. For all of us, it's going to be a lot of remote riding on the dry *puna*. Arnold is persistent and the first one to leave. We wish him tailwinds. The rest of us stick around a little longer, writing and updating travel diaries.

SALAR DE ARIZARO, ARGENTINA

↘ *This dead mule at the side of the road, held together by iron wire, raises a lot of questions.*
↓ *Aerial view of the Martian terrain of Devil's Desert.*

DAY 706 - CONO DE ARITA, ARGENTINA - 14,982 KM

Devil's Desert
—An ill-planned road trip

In San Antonio de los Cobres, a group of young travelers in my hostel invites me for a trip in a borrowed car through a remote part of the Altiplano in Northern Argentina. Many secrets are hidden across its wide plains, connected only by a few dusty roads and abandoned train tracks. It wouldn't be possible to see everything on a bike, so when Véro, Justine, and Maurien suggest I hop on for two days, I can't say no.

The rental car is a ramshackle Chevy Aveo. For the kind of roads we'll be on, it would be advisable to have four-wheel drive, but that was above their budget. Véro, age 21, is behind the wheel and drives too fast, but he seems to have the car under control. He tells me he came to South America on a sailboat from France. With a crew of five, it took them five months to cross the Atlantic Ocean to Ushuaia, my final destination at the tip of Argentina. From there he hitchhiked north to where we are now. On the way he met Maurien and Justine, two other like-minded, (barely) twentysomethings who were backpacking, and they decided to team up for a few days to explore Northern Argentina. I'm amazed how young people are undertaking solo international trips nowadays.

Our goal for the day is Cono de Arita, a strange, almost perfectly conical hill at the far edge of Salar de Arizaro, Argentina's largest salt flat, which covers 1600 square kilometers. We've planned for a five-hour drive, but soon discover that on these washboard roads, it's going to be much longer. We're not even sure if we'll make it to the hill before sunset. This part of the country is virtually uninhabited, except for some nearly abandoned mining villages where a handful of people live simple lives. In between the settlements are desolate, windswept plains known collectively as the puna. Here, raging storms can appear out of nowhere. They call this part of the Argentinean Altiplano the Desierto del Diablo (Devil's Desert), a Martian landscape with strangely shaped buttes and jagged gullies of deep red soil. It would be the perfect location to film a science fiction story.

As Véro steps on the gas on the desert road, the soft sand spirals through the vents and windows of the Aveo. Sometimes he hits the brakes abruptly to avoid a pothole and the rest of us lurch forward. Our noses fill with dust and we squint to protect our eyes. The washboards roads make the car rattle, the kind of rattling that unscrews bolts. My tripod in the trunk loses a leg from the shaking. The lakes we pass glint magically in the sunlight, reflecting the azure sky and revealing the salt caves beneath their surfaces in a myriad of aquas and teals. The shallow parts of the lakes are white, but where their deeper parts dark blue, where caves continue deep below the surface.

The lakes glint magically in the sunlight, reflecting the azure sky and revealing the salt caves beneath their surfaces in a myriad of aquas and teals.

After six hours, we pass through the sleepy town of Tolar Grande. We plan to backtrack and spend the night here later, but we still have to cross the entire Salar de Arizaro to reach Cono de Arita today. This salt lake is not as pristine as the Salar de Uyuni in Bolivia. It looks more like a plowed field whose rows are covered by a thin crust of snow. A seemingly endless dirt road bisects the enormous lake. We drive as fast as the car allows us. Slowly, as the sun begins to sink, we squint and see a tiny triangle shape popping out from the salt flat in the distance. We have no idea how big the thing actually is.

After countless minutes racing through a barely changing landscape we reach the part of the road closest to the cone. We leave the car behind and start hiking. It's an hour before sunset and the plan is to summit it. It only looks a few hundred meters away. As Véro and I lock the car, the other two are already on their way. I check the distance on my phone and say, "It's going to be a 2.5-kilometer hike to the foot of the cone, and a 200-meter climb to the top." Véro smirks and says, "This is going to be a long night." We have no idea what we are up against as we walk out onto the salt flat. It's a tough walk on an uneven surface. We constantly have to keep an eye on where we put our feet, because we could easily get stuck in between the frozen waves of the salt crust and hurt our ankles. Instead of walking straight, I split off and move in a wider circle so I can photograph the others climbing the hill from the side. On the horizon, I see my companions as three dots slowly moving across the flat. Because the surface of the hill is so straight and smooth from a distance, I can keep track of where they are. After an hour, Maurien is the first to reach the foot of the cone. Justine gives up and starts hiking back to the car. Maurien and Véro are two little specks on the side of the giant hill: it's so much bigger than we imagined. I hurry to catch up and reach the summit out of breath, just too late to see the sunset. Still, the view over the salt lake is unbeatable. Maurien reaches out for a high five. As it gets dark, the wind picks up and the temperature plummets. We shouldn't wait too long because there's at least an hour of hiking ahead of us, and walking the salt waves in the dark will be dangerous.

It doesn't take too long before it's pitch black. The meager lights on our smartphones lead the way downhill. Ahead of me I see two dancing lights descending. The walk takes forever, especially since we have no reference point to tell how far we've gone. Justine didn't have the car keys when she turned around, so she must be waiting outside in the cold. At some point it gets so dark that we lose track of where the car is. The GPS on my phone tells us we're close to the road, but I forgot to mark where we parked. We finally get to the road, but we don't know where to go next. Justine ends up being our salvation: we eventually see her flashing a light by the car, 500 meters away.

It's 10:00 at night when we arrive at the guesthouse in Tolar Grande, exhausted. But to our dismay, no rooms are available. We try another guesthouse and knock on some windows, but have no luck there either. It's hard to believe that all the rooms are booked because this town seems almost deserted and we haven't seen any other tourists. Over a late dinner of plain rice and pork fat with the hair still on it in the only restaurant in town, we discuss our options. We haven't brought tents or camping gear. Four of us sleeping in the small car in the cold doesn't sound appealing. Driving back five hours through the night on the treacherous desert roads to San Antonio de los Cobres doesn't sound like a brilliant idea either, but that's what we decide to do. At least we will be warm. I agree to start driving, and Véro will take over in two hours. Before heading out into the night, we knock back some coffee and bring a few bottles of cola to keep us awake.

A thin sliver of moon reveals the contours of the mountains as I grip the steering wheel and hit the gas. The last time I drove was nearly two years ago in San Francisco, in Rachel's car. I enjoy the night drive and listen to music on my headphones. It doesn't

We have no idea what we are up against as
we walk out onto the salt flat.

take long before everyone else is asleep and the car smells like a dorm room and Coca Cola. As we plow through the sand, dust billows in front of the headlights, making it hard to follow the road. My knee hurts from keeping the gas pedal in place. I shiver when we pass the dead mule, still eerily gasping out into the night. My eyes grow heavy with sleep and I fantasize about going to bed. But I keep driving slowly, because I feel responsible for the three sleeping people next to me.

Despite the low speed, we make good time because we don't stop for any sightseeing. After two hours, we reach a crossroads and I wake everyone up to propose an idea. We have two options. We can continue driving to the guesthouse in San Antonio de los Cobres where we left from originally. The hostel will probably be closed, so we will have to sleep in the car until morning. The second option is to stop in Olacapato, a small mining town where I spent the night two days ago in a scruffy motel. It's not far from where we are now, and from what I can recall, we should be able to reach the rooms from the patio, which won't be locked. The dogs might start barking, but they were scared of me when I tried to pet them so they shouldn't be a problem. Unanimously, we choose the second option.

Olacapato is an even more run-down place than Tolar Grande. It's a derelict mining settlement with a railway station to connect the quarries and the town, which itself is not much more than a few blocks of mud brick ruins and sandy streets, with a loud generator house in the center to provide the town with power. We roll into town quietly so as not to disturb anyone. It's 3:00 in the morning, and everyone is asleep. I rehearse the scene in my mind: we will drive onto the patio, and the dogs will start barking. The owners will come out, and I will apologize for the late hour and explain the situation, and they will take pity on us and find us beds. But nothing like that happens as we park the car. No dogs, no owners, nothing: it is silent. Five pickups are parked in front of the rooms, probably belonging to the miners who stay the night. I knock on the door of the restaurant and wait for a response, because I'd prefer to ask if we can sleep here rather than squatting. No one replies. After looking around, we enter a barn where the light is on. There are four numbered doors. It smells like sleeping people. Véro carefully opens one of them and peeks inside. "Full!" he hisses. We try another room: also full. There's lots of snoring all around us. Back outside, I try to open the room I slept in the other day. With my headlamp, I look over the bunks. Someone blocks his eyes from the light. I quietly apologize, realizing this is highly inappropriate. All the beds are occupied with sleeping people. Our last hope is one more room. Véro looks in and finds five empty bunk beds: perfect! We tiptoe back to the car, take our bags, and tuck ourselves in. In the morning, the staff is surprised to meet us when we straggle in to the restaurant for breakfast, but they recognize me. We explain last night's escapades, and it all ends with a laugh.

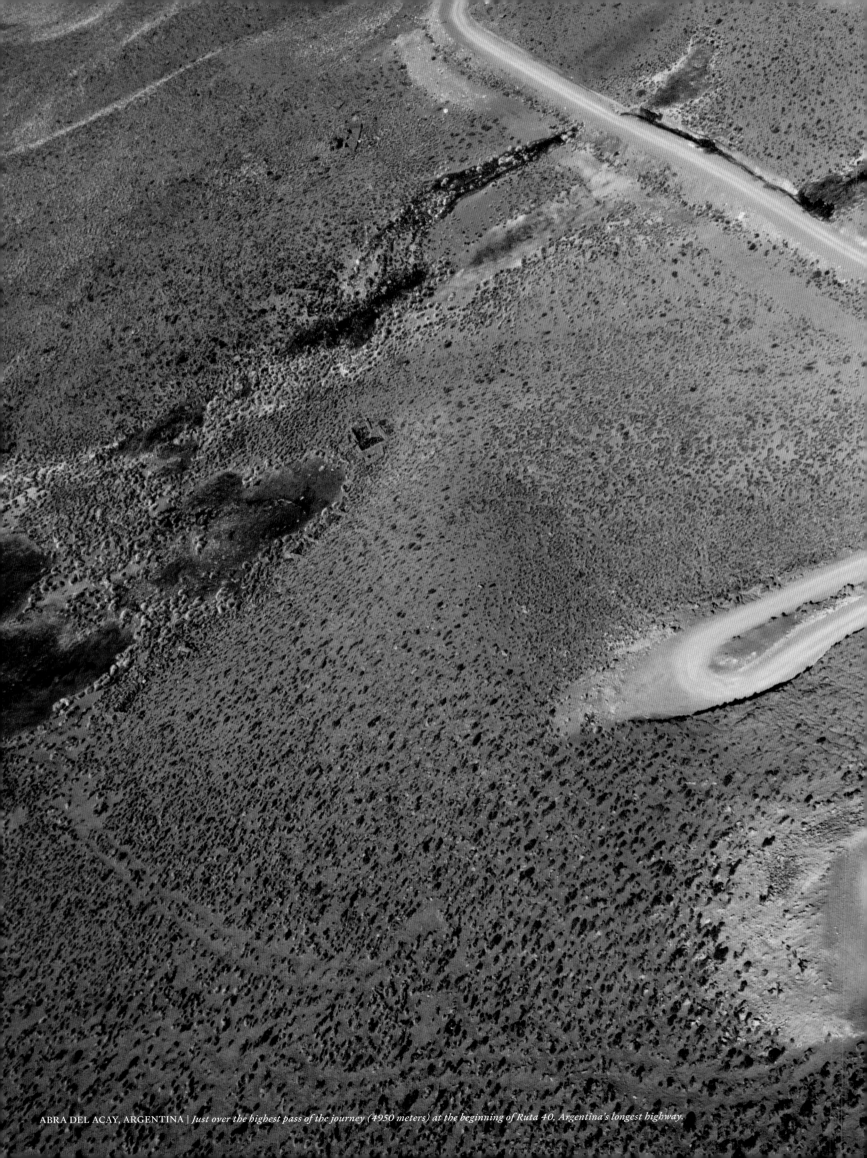

ABRA DEL ACAY, ARGENTINA | *Just over the highest pass of the journey (4950 meters) at the beginning of Ruta 40, Argentina's longest highway.*

Argentina
—*The beginning of the end*

The landscape becomes friendlier and more livable as I say goodbye to the harsh environment of the Altiplano, descending into the warm wine-growing valleys of the Cafayate region. From here, the Andes Mountains start to narrow, forming the long ridge between Argentina and Chile. I have just finished the highest pass I've ever cycled, at 4950 meters, but after so many high routes in Peru, it's nothing new anymore. It is probably my last time at these altitudes, and I'm glad to approach lower ground.

I'm on the famous Ruta 40, Argentina's longest highway, which spans the entire length of the country from north to south. At this point, it is not much more than a dirt track that winds through dusty towns and vineyards and passes fields of red peppers drying in the warm sunlight. Bright green parrots flit around the town squares and provide a delightful contrast to the arid, red landscape. Good wine is available for a bargain anywhere, as well as good meat. The *asador* (barbecue) is the focal point of every kitchen, and Argentineans never rush in preparing a good steak.

As I make faster progress southward, European influence and wealth become more visible. In a way it feels like coming home. Restaurants and supermarkets offer a larger variety and better quality of food, and the infrastructure and architecture are more modern and developed. The climate is also changing quickly. At noon the sun is much lower in the sky, and it shines on my back from the north: clear signs that I am in the Southern Hemisphere and racing farther and farther from the equator. I don't even have to protect my face with sunscreen anymore. I am enjoying this brief dry season, but winter is quickly approaching. It's April, which means late autumn. Soon I'll have to prepare again for cold, wet weather—but not yet. For now, I'm relishing the sunshine in the tranquil countryside, and taking lots of Malbec breaks.

↑ One of the last indigenous people I meet. Farther south, residents are predominantly of European descent.
↗ An encounter with a curious Andean fox on the road near Abra del Acay.

QUEBRADA DE LAS FLECHAS, RUTA 40, ARGENTINA

UNEVENTFUL DAYS ROLL BY. RUTA 40 TURNS INTO A PAVED HIGHWAY THROUGH PALE GREEN, MONOTONOUS DESERT. I NOTICE THAT THIS SOUTHERN LANDSCAPE REFLECTS WHAT I SAW ABOVE THE EQUATOR. RECOGNIZABLE VEGETATION STARTS RETURNING AS I HEAD SOUTH. THE VERDANT JUNGLES, THE PURPLE MOUNTAINS, THE SALT LAKES, AND THE GEYSERS ARE BEHIND ME. I CYCLE MORE THAN 100 KILOMETERS A DAY. I BARELY TAKE ANY PHOTOS, AND I'VE BEEN THROUGH ALL THE AUDIOBOOKS ON MY PHONE. THE DAYS ARE FILLED WITH THINKING, FIGHTING BOREDOM, AND SEEING ARGENTINA LOOK MORE AND MORE LIKE HOME. NOW THAT THINGS ARE BECOMING MORE FAMILIAR, IT'S HARD TO STAY FOCUSED. I FEEL I HAVE SEEN THE BEST PARTS OF THIS JOURNEY, AND THAT THERE ISN'T MUCH TO LOOK FORWARD TO ANYMORE.

Stitching the wire bead of the tires once again. You can see by the different colors of threads how often it has been done.

—*2000 km on low pressure*

My rear tire keeps tearing apart, a problem I've had since San Pedro de Atacama in Chile a few weeks ago. The wire bead broke loose from the tire, and had to be stitched and glued back in. It held for a few days, but then it started to tear even more. I've stitched it several times now, which takes quite a bit of effort because the rubber is so thick and it's hard to get a needle through. By now, it's really not looking good. Soon, the bead is going to tear out completely, and I still have to make it work until I reach Santiago, where my new tire is being shipped. That's roughly 2000 kilometers from San Pedro de Atacama. To slow the deterioration, relieve the tension, and prevent the inner tube from bulging out, I ride on low pressure. This is an undesirable solution, since I have so much distance left to do on pavement.

I wonder why the tire is falling apart so drastically. Obviously, I have been putting them to the test by riding over a variety of terrains with a heavy bike for a long time. But I suspect the problem is the pavement. Despite the Maxxis Chronicle being one of the highest quality tires on the market, it's designed for dirt tracks, and most of my distance has been on roads. I recall constantly pumping them to higher pressures on the Pan-American Highway in Peru, which might have caused the issue.

It's not the only problem I've had. Even earlier, two days out of La Paz, that same tire exploded. A truck driver gave me a lift back to the city where a mechanic stitched the large hole and glued a piece of PET bottle inside to hold it together. Before then, I'd been riding tubeless, but after the explosion I had to put the spare tube back in.

Fast forward, here I am again, sitting in the dirt alongside Ruta 40 north of Mendoza. I have a needle and thread, and once more, I have to stitch this tire and cycle on half pressure all the way to Chile.

Sealant spilling from the rear tire in Bolivia. After it exploded, a truck driver gave me a lift.

Switchback roads can take the oddest shapes to create smooth pathways across the mountains, but the most pleasing to the eye must be the busy Paso Internacional Los Libertadores, which connects Mendoza, Argentina with Santiago, Chile through the Andes Mountains. The pass is designed for heavy traffic, so the curves are wide enough for large trucks to safely pass each other, hence the spaghetti-perfect bends.

Crossing to Chile
—*Teaming up*

Sophie and Jeremy have been in touch with me often over the past year since we first met in Vilcabamba, Ecuador. They are a French couple who have also been on the road for nearly two years, cycling from Alaska to Patagonia. In South America our routes have often overlapped and usually we haven't been more than a few hundred kilometers from each other. In Mendoza, we cross paths again. This time, our plans finally match. So we decide to cycle for a few days together, crossing the Andes once more on our way to Santiago, the capital of Chile, via Ruta 7.

I've crossed paths with dozens of other bikers in my travels, but it's rare that I find people going in the same direction as me. So cycling with Sophie and Jeremy is a treat. It's nice to camp together and give each other wind cover, especially on this road where a strong head-wind comes hard at us from over from the mountains. The road climbs up to 3300 meters, where a tunnel leads through the highest part. Initially, we wanted to take Ruta 7's more rugged, historic pass (Paso Cristo Redentor de los Andes), but it's already covered in a thick layer of snow. Even the tunnel is only open during clear weather windows. We've had to wait out a storm in Mendoza before heading up to the pass, which is a monster this far south and this close to winter. Because it's a single-lane highway, we have to share the road with the many trucks also rushing to the other side during the clear weather. We're constantly pushed off the road by the merciless drivers. Now and then Jeremy loses his temper, and puts his fist in the air. But we're power-less: cyclists are not supposed to even be on this highway. The tunnel is strictly off-limits to us, but the border officials have kindly organized a lift through it for us in a pickup truck.

Once on the other side of the pass, we do not hold back in our grocery shopping. We plan a great feast and stock up on wine, salami, cheese, nuts, local honey, and other delights, taking advantage of the richer food supplies in the Argentinean markets. Why not, since we can make a fire and will have hours to kill under the stars? The last campfire I made was in Colombia, but here, wood is finally available again. The past month, there were no trees at high the altitudes. The fire and the company make camping a lot more attractive than being curled up in a sleeping bag for over 12 hours, fighting the cold and the long, dark nights alone. If I'm honest, I have been very much over that hardship for a while. The solitude has been too much, and on this final leg of the trip, I haven't had any more milestones to be excited for. Sharing the road with Sophie and Jeremy, who are becoming good friends, gives me new energy. The cold doesn't worry us much, because we have good clothing and camping gear. We are just glad to be together around a fire, eating good food and drinking fine wine.

—184 in one day

The average distance I cycle in a day is influenced by a number of factors. There are technical aspects like road quality, elevation profile, wind direction, altitude, availability of food and water, and overall weather. It also depends on what sights there are to see and the time I get up, which varies greatly based on my energy. Overall, my daily average distance is roughly 70 kilometers per day.

It's been a relaxing 11 days in Santiago, Chile's capital. On my way out of town, the circumstances seem perfect for breaking my current distance record. In Peru, I cycled 154 kilometers on a downhill ride from the Andes to the Pacific coast. I could have gone farther, but the ride was spoiled by a headwind at the end of the afternoon. Today there's no wind, the road is paved, and it's almost entirely flat. I finally have a brand new rear tire pumped to high pressure, and it's an early Sunday morning, which means light traffic. So at 8:00 in the morning, I leave my Airbnb from the city center, which is still mostly asleep. I follow Ruta 5, which is Chile's main highway. It runs through most of the country, and since it just goes straight ahead, I don't have to worry about navigation. Bikes are not allowed on some sections, but I ignore the signs. It's an easy ride, and I let my mind wander aimlessly as the kilometers rack up. Today, I'm not worried about finding a scenic camp spot. I'll just pitch my tent at one of the gas stations, which are as modern as the ones in Europe, are open 24 hours, and are found at least every 40 kilometers.

After a dozen podcasts and a few short breaks to eat snacks, I have a big dinner where I plan to stay the night. I've already broken my record, but I feel good, so instead of hunkering down, I continue on in the dark to the next rest stop. At 9:00, long after sunset, I set up camp at a gas station in the midst of the trucks with their loud, running engines. It's far from pretty, and I don't believe I've taken any photos today. I've spent almost 14 hours in the saddle. Some parts of my body didn't like it—I probably won't do it again soon.

Editing photos is often done on the road. All the raw files are stored on a hard disk and edited in Adobe Lightroom.
The exported jpgs are then synced with my phone so they are ready to be shared on my blog and social media.

SOUTH PACIFIC OCEAN

SOUTH ATLANTIC OCEAN

Buenos Aires

Montevideo

Santa Rosa

Santa Teresita

Villa Gesell

Mar del Plata

Necochea

Bahía Blanca

Neuquén

Las Grutas

A R G E N T I N A

Trelew

C H I L E

Concepción

Los Angeles

Ruta 5

Chillán

Temuco

Pucón

Villarica

Junín de los Andes

Valdivia

San Martín de los Andes

Osorno

Villa la Angostura

San Carlos de Bariloche

Puerto Varas

Puerto Montt

Ancud

Esquel

Chaitén

Puerto Cárdenas

Puyuhuapi

Villa Amengual

P A T A G O N I A

Villa Mañiguales

Puerto Aysén

Coyhaique

Villa Cerro Castillo

Chile Chico

Puerto Río Tranquilo

Comodoro Rivadavia

Caleta Olivia

Pico Truncado

Cochrane

Caleta Tortel

Puerto Deseado

Paso Mayer

Villa O'Higgins

Gobernador Gregores

PARQUE NACIONAL BERNARDO O'HIGGINS

El Chaltén

Perito Moreno

El Calafate

FALKLAND ISLANDS

PARQUE NACIONAL TORRES DEL PAINE

Puerto Natales

Puntas Arenas

Porvenir

Río Grande

TIERRA DEL FUEGO

Tolhuin

Ushuaia

CARRETERA AUSTRAL

Altitude (m)

5K
4K
3K
2K
1K

Santiago *Villarica* *San Martín de Los Andes* *Puerto Montt* *Cerro Castillo* *Cochrane* *Villa O'Higgins* *El Chaltén* *Torres del Paine* *Puntas Arenas* *Ushuaia*

Scale

miles   0   50   100   150   200   250
kilometers 0   100   200   300   400

CARRETERA AUSTRAL

DAY 769 - PUERTO VARAS, CHILE - 17,423 KM

There's only one continuous road through Chile that reaches the far south. It winds through dark green forests, fjords, and glaciers, and it is flanked by hundreds of streams and waterfalls. Ruta 7, better known as Carretera Austral (Southern Highway), connects many remote communities in rural Patagonia and is mostly unpaved. While a popular tourist destination in summer, this road is a daunting undertaking in the winter, guaranteed to test my mettle as I grow numb to the charms of the road and long more and more for home.

VILLA LA ANGOSTURA, ARGENTINA

Everyone I meet thinks I'm insane. But quitting is not
an option, so I have to get over it and keep focusing
on the highlights, as faint as they are.

I've reached Patagonia, but this is just the beginning of the end. There's a long way ahead of me still. Patagonia is the sparsely populated southern tip of South America and is shared by both Chile and Argentina. After a comfortable break for a few days at someone's house in Puerto Varas, at the start of the Carretera Austral, I am reluctant to get back on the road. From Santiago I've been cycling alone, because Sophie and Jeremy wanted to stay in the city far longer than I did. Since parting ways, my reluctance to continue pedaling has come flooding back. I am road-weary and I long for rest. Not just a few days' rest to heal my muscles: a long rest from cycling entirely. Often, I catch myself thinking that I don't even want to finish this journey anymore. I am sick of always being in public places, of camping outside, of being on the move. I have the sinking feeling that this adventure is for all intents and purposes over, that I have already seen everything there is to see on my route. The fact that it is now winter greatly impacts my mood, so I remind myself that I have dreamed of cycling the famous Carretera Austral for years.

But my head is clouded, and so is the weather. The forecast promises ten days of rain. No wonder this region is called Patagonia Verde (Green Patagonia), which receives by far the most precipitation in Chile. At the moment the grim weather makes it look more like Black Patagonia— and I am about to cross it on a bicycle. The climate here could be compared to winter in Northern Europe or the US: the most dismal setting for spending days outside. This is the kind of weather Europeans travel to *escape* from, not to pedal through. Everyone I meet thinks I'm insane. But quitting is not an option, so I have to get over it and keep focusing on the highlights, as faint as they are.

The segment begins with a ferry ride bypassing the urban port of Puerto Montt. It sails during the night, and at 8:00 in the morning I arrive at Chaitén, where I walk off the boat in the rain with a flat tire—a *great* start. Ashore, I patch the tube under the tin roof of the waiting area. The small, gray town looks abandoned in the early morning. I connect with the Wi-Fi in the central square, buy some food, and get on my way. The Carretera is empty of the tourists who flock here in the summer. The silence is only disturbed every few minutes when a lonely car zooms past.

I put on headphones and listen to audiobooks as I make my way through forest after misty forest. I am immersed in the soothing voice of the narrator and the raindrops tapping on my coat: it almost makes me forget I'm cycling. It continuously drizzles, but I am somewhat comfortable, thanks to my newly acquired rain gear. Unlike the rainy season in Peru, I'm better prepared this time with long rain pants and overshoes to keep my legs and feet dry. My winter gloves keep me warm, even when they are soaking wet. This is all thanks to Rapha: the cycling brand has sent some winter gear to keep me warm and dry during these days.

A few days go by like this: rain, audiobook, pedal. Now and then, there's a patch of blue sky and I enjoy the sunlight, but it's never for long. I take shelter under bus stops to eat quickly. Just for a few minutes, otherwise my wet clothes will cool me off too much. Even the best rain gear lets water through at some point, so the trick is not to stay dry, but to stay warm. The insulating effect of neoprene, the fabric used in wetsuits, also works for some clothing, as long as it is quick-drying and breathable.

I spend the nights in cabins designed for travelers passing through. They often have wood-burning stoves inside, which I use to warm up. This is the highlight of each day, enjoying the fire and drinking wine. I need to dry all of my clothes every time I stop, as well as my camera bag and the saddle bag containing my laptop. Everything is always damp. It's a wonder the electronics are still working. With this much rain, no bag is completely waterproof except for the Ortlieb panniers, and even those now have some holes.

On the worst day of rain, I arrive after sunset in the tiny community of Villa Amengual. At the edge of town, I come across a small cabin and see a paper on the door with a phone number and a note in English

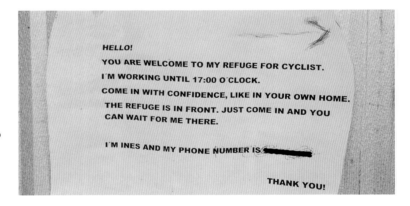

from someone named Ines, inviting cyclists to take shelter in her home. She lives there with her only son, and she has free space for cyclists to spend the night. I let myself in and survey it. It's a very basic room with a woodstove in the middle. The wall is covered with writings from other cyclists, mostly from the summertime. Some of the windows have no glass and are covered with plastic. I'm soaked: it has poured all day and there have been no places to take shelter. My lunch was wet peanut butter sandwiches, which I prepared in the rain and ate in the rain. It was total misery. The pogies on my bike have absorbed maybe a liter of water, and my tent is entirely wet even though I haven't used it. So when Ines shows up and chops wood for me to light the stove, it feels like I'm at a five-star resort. The fire burns all evening and warms the little room. While there is nothing else there except a mattress on the floor, I deeply appreciate the comfort. Warmth and shelter are so valuable after being out there for days in the elements.

It takes a tremendous effort to get a fire going from the soaked kindling ... In the end, I have a pretty enjoyable evening scavenging wood and staying warm while drying out my clothes by the fire.

Winter is sometimes a fight. You have to work much harder to make things work, regardless of the terrain, but I am finding that you also gain greater, more intangible rewards. The past few days, I've hardly seen any daylight. It isn't always easy to find shelter, either. Many hotels and campsites close for the winter in Patagonia and their proprietors migrate to warmer climates until spring. One night, I end up in a scruffy cabaña at an abandoned campsite along a lake. The structure is barely standing, and the wind roars through giant gaps in the wall, but it suits my needs for the night. It takes a tremendous effort to get a fire going from the soaked kindling I find strewn about. I constantly have to waft air into the fire with my sleeping mat, otherwise it starts to suffocate from the moisture and smoke. It's true when they say that one that chops his own wood is twice warmed. After an hour of work, the fire is burning on its own, the flames dancing playfully in the dark. In the end, I have a pretty enjoyable evening scavenging wood and staying warm while drying out my clothes by the fire. I even cook *longanizas*, the most mouthwatering chorizo in Chile, on the fire. I feel I've won the battle between nature and man.

It's a powerful feeling when nature is about to consume you, and you succeed in fighting back. These are the moments that make me deeply grateful to be alive—and they are borne of simple, physical struggles, of blood rushing through my veins, of muscles tingling, of my rubberized skin softening again at the warmth of a fire I built myself.

—White winter days

After some extremely wet days, it gets colder and the rain turns to snow. The snow is worse than the rain, but then the sun comes, and everything changes. This is the winter we all hoped to see. Powdery white fields stretch out under a blue sky. Sophie and Jeremy are nearby again, so we share the road for a few more days. We're happy to leave behind the miserable rain of the past weeks. I'm glad to be reunited: once more, they give me new energy.

The landscape is even whiter as we approach the highest climb of the Carretera Austral at 1200 meters above sea level. Because the snow is fresh, the roads can be slippery. Sophie and Jeremy have each brought a set of ice tires for this section that prove very useful, even

though they're only needed for a few days. They have learned the hard way how to pedal in this weather. They started their trip all the way in Alaska, and because Sophie had a traffic accident from which she needed to recover, they were forced to cycle through the North in winter with a lot of cold days. They have told me endless stories of wet clothes and miserable, freezing limbs. After sharing experiences, we all went on a shopping spree and equipped ourselves to the max: down jackets, winter gloves, pogies, extra merino wool socks, insulated rain pants, overshoes, thicker sleeping bags, large fuel bottles, extra foam pads for heat reflection, and thermoses to have warm tea at all times.

Our bikes are a bit heavier than before, but I don't worry about it too much. The grades promise to be subtler and the (literally) breathtaking altitudes of the Altiplano are behind us. Cycling in colder temperatures isn't much of a problem for me, and I know from experience that I'll usually generate enough body heat to be comfortable. On the coldest days, I make sure my entire face is covered, using a headscarf over my nose paired with glasses and a wool

hat to keep the chill out. I make sure to regulate my clothing, taking something off when I start to sweat and adding an extra layer as soon as I cool down. You can catch a cold before you know it if you don't pay attention to your body's needs, especially on freezing downhill rides. The bike itself also requires extra attention. Once, while cycling through a mild snowstorm in Kyrgyzstan, clumps of ice seized up my brakes and derailleur. I had to change gears by pushing the derailleur with my foot, or even dismounting and manually shoving it. It's cold enough another day to freeze the brake cable and housing to each other. Before a downhill ride I have to check if everything is still working.

But the hardest aspect of bikepacking in winter are the long, cold nights underneath the fabric roof of a tiny tent. At midday in the sun, it is just below freezing, but during the nights it can be 10 below or colder. Since crossing the equator, the days have grown shorter. When I'm alone, I spend up to 14 hours in the dark, disconnected from the outside world, curled up in my sleeping bag, trying to stay warm. It's something I won't soon miss about this journey. It's especially tough

when there's no firewood around, making it a long, claustrophobic wait for dawn. I have downloaded heaps of TV shows and films to my smartphone, as well as e-books and audiobooks. Anything to stave off the boredom and avoid going completely nuts.

Being in a team makes everything easier. One night, we stay at a refugio that is little more than an oversized bus stop with only three walls. At least we are covered from the wind a bit. Sophie and Jeremy have had a particularly tough day because Sophie's seat post broke off. They switched it with Jeremy's because he didn't mind standing on his pedals. Thanks to our thick down sleeping bags and some extra help from our good friend Johnny Walker, they cheer up and we are cozy the entire evening.

On other days, we rent cabañas together, always equipped with the requisite woodstove. Our evenings consist of preparing hearty meals, drying out clothes, maintaining and thawing out the bikes, and playing Yahtzee. I will have warm memories of these days, which demand so much attention and discipline, yet are so sweet and rewarding.

—Frozen knuckles

The highest pass of the Carretera Austral is only 1200 meters up, but being this far south means a lot of snow. Just after the summit, the road curves down beautifully toward the town of Cerro Castillo. The sun has just set and I need to be quick to fly the drone up for a photo. The temperature is quickly dropping below zero, which could make the batteries fail at any time. My hands freeze as I hold the remote control. I put it in sport mode to fly it up as fast as possible and take some shots before my hands go numb. Before continuing my ride, I swing my arms wildly to get some warm blood back into my fingertips, a quick trick that always works. Painstakingly slowly, I descend in the dark. I want to avoid a nasty fall on the black ice. Despite the big tires, the bike doesn't have much grip on the frozen road. An hour later, I arrive in Cerro Castillo, and after some asking around, I find the cabin where Sophie and Jeremy are staying—they are currently about half a day ahead of me. When I arrive, Sophie is making pancakes and Jeremy is firing up the woodstove—impeccable timing on my part.

↗ *One night before arriving in Villa O'Higgins, the last town on the Carretera Austral.*
← *A short stop at Río Cochrane.*

It's a powerful feeling when nature is about to consume you, and you succeed in fighting back.

PASO MAYER

DAY 792 · PASO MAYER, ARGENTINA · 18,845 KM

The border crossing to Argentina via Paso Mayer takes a full day, and is a new kind of thrilling. I won't soon forget the 15-kilometer, roadless no-man's-land, the relentless rain, the multiple river crossings, the thick bushland, or the precarious rope bridge separating me from my journey's end.

The Carretera Austral comes to a dead end in the small town of Villa O'Higgins. This part of the country is so sparsely populated that the road options are nearly nonexistent. From here, there are two possible border crossings into Argentina, accessible only by foot or bike. Any car traffic that wants to go south has to cross borders farther north. The most common option for bike travelers is straight south to El Chaltén, which includes two ferry trips—but of course, the crossing is closed for winter and the ferries don't run. This leaves the second option: eastward via Paso Mayer, where the Chilean and Argentinian border posts are separated by the Mayer River and 15 kilometers of swampy no-man's-land marked only by cattle trails. Although it's an official crossing, nobody really comes here except for some local gauchos as they move their livestock.

Sophie and Jeremy go ahead of me early in the morning from Villa O'Higgins, and I stay to finish up some things on my laptop. I don't leave until the afternoon, and so I end up making camp on the Chilean side of the border, planning to cross in the morning. At the refugio, I see a note from Sophie and Jeremy—they came through here early this afternoon. I expected that they'd continue on: they left so much earlier this morning and probably wanted to move while the weather was on their side.

Heavy rain begins in the evening. I don't know it yet, but it will continue without ceasing for the next 48 hours. In the morning I start slow, reluctant to get going in the drizzle. At 11:00, I arrive at the Chilean border post, already soaking wet. A *carabinero* welcomes me with a handshake and I join him in the customs office, which looks more like someone's living room. There are four officers, one of them preparing lunch for the group. It takes a while before my passport can be stamped because they need to send an email to another office for approval with an unreliable internet connection. The men are very kind and offer me food in the meantime. With an officer's help, I put markers on Maps.me on the trails to choose for my trek between the borders, because there are many. Another officer tosses me a can of tuna to put in my bag. I read pity in his eyes. He probably knows exactly what I'm up against for the coming hours. I don't dare ask how bad it is.

An hour and a few cups of coffee later, my passport is stamped and I am ready to go. Still wet from the morning's ride, I head out into the no-man's-land. First, I pass a small farm. The dogs come after me because the road crosses their property, but then the farmer comes out and explains to me in rapid Chilean Spanish which way to go. I can barely follow what he says. He leads me to the official divide between Chile and Argentina: a shoddy old barbed wire fence. The farmer lifts up the wire and I clumsily shove my bike underneath, the bags getting caught on the wire and items falling out into the mud. Once over the border, I get my bike back in order and look to see what's next. Ahead of me is a tangle of vague trails and low, thorny bushes disappearing into the mist. This is a dreamscape, not a border crossing. I start to pedal in the mud; the going is slow. There is no way to tell which path is correct, so I keep an eye on my phone to see if I am still heading in the right direction. The screen is having trouble in the rain. If it gets too wet, it won't work. Usually I dry it on my undershirt, but if that is also wet, I have a useless device. And today, everything is getting wet. I pray for it to keep working. Despite my phone's help, there are many trails that are not on the map, often with

dead ends, and I get stuck in the bushes more than once. Some of the flooded trails are turning into puddles, and some of the puddles are turning into ponds.

After a few hours of this, the first true river presents itself: a threatening torrent of brown water, many meters wide, fed even more by the long night of rain and the glacial melt from last week's mild temperatures. I look for the widest part, thinking it will be the shallowest. I take my shoes off to keep them dry, but keep my socks on. The water is nearly freezing and grips my ankles like sharp claws as I step into the river. It's much deeper than I expected, and I struggle not to lose hold of the bike in the current. My socks are made of thick wool, but the stones still cut into my sensitive soles. Once I reach a little island in the middle of the water, I drop the bike and gasp for air. Now I need to wade back to pick up my camera, which has been filming my labored crossing, before attacking the rest of the river. When I finally reach the opposite bank, my feet are numb and my skin feels stiff. This was not a good idea; I should have worn my shoes. I rub my toes to warm them as much as I can, put dry socks on, and continue.

I reach the *pasarela*, a simple suspension bridge that will take me over the roughest parts of the river. It's in a state of decay, and not more than 50 centimeters wide. Most of my bags need to be taken off and carried separately. I lift the bike on its rear wheel to maneuver it vertically across. The bridge swings dangerously, and I keep thinking it will tip me over into the river. The going is slow, but all my stuff eventually makes it to the other side. I take a short break to eat. The rain makes the bread easier to chew quickly. It gives me some energy. But I can't stand still

The water is nearly freezing and grips my ankles like sharp claws. It's much deeper than I expected, and I struggle not to lose hold of the bike in the current.

for long. I need to keep moving so I don't get cold. I wade through a few more rivers, this time keeping my shoes on. It is cold for a short while, but then my efforts generate enough body heat to warm up the water in my shoes.

All day, I have to reorient myself, cross streams, pedal through the mud, hoist my bags, and drag my bike through shrubs. With the amount of time I spend lugging my bike around, I would hardly call what I'm doing "cycling." At the end of the afternoon, I reach the Argentinean border post in a state of fatigue I've never experienced before. The officers are expecting me: Sophie and Jeremy were here in the morning and informed the *gendarmerías* that I was on my way. They are probably doing better than I am. They did most of this crossing a day earlier in dry weather. Sophie's note told me it was sunny.

Flooded roads at Paso Mayer, Argentina.

↗ *Looking out the back of the camioneta driving through rivers, with the Argentinean border office in the distance.*
→ *Dinner with the gendarmerías.*

> It's a dangerously rough ride, and I have to hold on to keep myself and the cargo in place.

After the passport stamps, I ask the gendarmerías if I can camp nearby and dry my clothes inside. A junior officer shows me an outdoor place on the property, but the weather is so miserable, they soon enough invite me to sleep inside, where there are a few bunks available. Above the stove, I dry my clothes and let my skin thaw. I discover that my Android has completely died. It's waterlogged: I can literally shake rain out of it. Normally, I would be upset, but not now. I'm just lucky it didn't happen earlier; I wouldn't have made it here without GPS keeping me on track. Luckily, my iPhone is still still working.

The border post on the Argentinean side of Paso Mayer has been here since 1994. It's a simple prefab building with a few rooms. Because it's in the middle of nowhere, it generates its own electricity and has tall antennae to stay in touch with the outside world. The nearest town is 230 kilometers away, and the next nearest one, 400 kilometers away. In between is nothing but the vast Pampas. Because there's no road, there's no traffic coming through, which means these guys are isolated. Only at the end of summer, when the river is at its lowest, can a truck with four-wheel drive and a skilled driver make it through the rivers. The gendarmerías barely have anything to do besides keep the place clean and do mundane errands. Perhaps my presence is as refreshing for them as theirs is for me.

They invite me for dinner: asado (barbecue) as usual, served with bread and potatoes. There are a few kilos of lamb on the table for only five men—Argentineans love their meat. A local farmer joins too, and they ask me all kinds of questions: about my two-year journey, about smoking weed, about the price of a prostitute in Amsterdam. It's a man's world out here, and they make me feel welcome.

The next morning, I wake up to see that the rain has transformed into snow. I cannot imagine how flooded yesterday's fields and valleys must be by now: it hasn't stopped for 36 hours. The stream behind the border post is a lot higher than it was last night; it's almost flowing over its banks. As trying as yesterday was, I am relieved. If I had come here one day later, I wouldn't have been able to cross the rivers with the bike or even find any of the trails in the snow.

My new friends are moving north to another office today, and so they offer me a lift to Ruta 40. I accept, even though it's 95 kilometers to the east and my destination of Ushuaia is to the south. It is the only way. It will at least be dry there because it's on the arid Pampas, far from the wet climate of the southern Andes. At the end

of the afternoon, we leave in a *camioneta*, a small army pickup truck. The bed is covered by a canvas hood that flaps in the wind, which is where I sit: there's no room in the cabin. It's filled with bales of straw, fuel barrels, and other junk, and it smells like mud and gasoline. First, we stop to pick up some large sheets of corrugated steel from a nearby farm, which end up on my lap while I sit on a straw bale. It's a dangerously rough ride, and I have to hold on to keep myself and the cargo in place. Through an opening in the canvas, I can see the white landscape and our tires leaving two brown stripes in the wet snow. We cross numerous rivers and mud lakes. I am deeply grateful I don't have to get through this with the bicycle. I think about Sophie and Jeremy; I wonder how they are doing. It must be a crazy ride, despite their being a day ahead of the snow.

After four hours, we reach Ruta 40. It's a completely different world. Everything is dry and the road is smoothly paved. Even the temperatures are mild. The gendarmerías help me unload my bike, and I thank them for all their help and hospitality. Before finding a spot to camp, I decide to cycle a bit so I can warm up from the ride in the back of the truck. A strong tailwind catapults me onto the wide Pampas—and into the final days of my journey.

Some of the most famous peaks in Patagonia. From left to right: Cerro Torre (3133 meters), Aguja Poincenot (3002 meters) and Fitz Roy (3375 meters). A straight, 90-kilometer road goes off Ruta 40 to the village of El Chaltén at the foot of the mountains. It's a two-day bike detour if the winds are merciful.

↑ Sunset in Torres del Paine.
→ A typical bus stop in Chile.
↓ Eye to eye with a wild puma in Torres del Paine. From the corner of my eye, I see it walking along, and stop abruptly. About 30 meters away, it hides behind a bush and stares at me. Maintaining eye contact, I slowly reach for my camera. I don't know how happy he is about me scaring away his lunch: behind me are the screeching cries of guanacos. Through the excitement, I nervously toggle between video mode and stills mode. A few brief moments of staring later, he casually walks away.

...the hardest aspect of bikepacking in winter is the long, cold night underneath the fabric roof of a tiny tent... I spend up to 14 hours in the dark, disconnected from the outside world, curled up in my sleeping bag, trying to stay warm. It's something I won't soon miss about this journey.

—*Last shower in sub-zero temperatures*

For the last time, I gaze around the interior of my little tent. I'm warming up in the sleeping bag after setting up camp. The layout is so familiar; every bag and item has its place. My canvas duffle with valuables is there in the middle: dirty, aged by the road, and falling apart. And a carton of wine. I've stopped bothering with bottles, since in Argentina, even a carton is of acceptable quality and saves weight on the bike. "Best served between 18 and 20 degrees Celsius," states its label. That's not going to happen tonight. A fridge would be warmer than tonight's bedroom. But I'm used to the cold. When I stay in hotels, my face swells and turns red from the heat.

I'm contemplating whether or not I will take a "shower." I know it will make me feel better, but the thing is that it is literally freezing outside. There's a crust of ice on the tent, and a chilling wind grips my throat and makes it hard to inhale. I build up my strength and fight the instinctive fear of getting colder. On my stove, I heat some water and put it in a bottle. I wrestle myself out of the sleeping bag in the cramped two square meters I've been calling home for two years. I take off my socks, cycling tights, down jacket, wool sweater, and underwear, and step out naked into the cold night, the sharp pebbles scratching the soles of my feet. The water in the bottle is just a bit too hot, but I unscrew the cap and throw it over my face while I regulate the flow by keeping my thumb on the mouth. Usually a bike bottle would be much better for such showers, but I lost it on the way. In the freezing wind, the hot water feels nice and warm. From my head, I work my way down to my feet, until the bottle is empty.

Now comes the hardest part: I shiver uncontrollably, wet and cold. It's that moment we all know, when it's time to open the shower curtain and grab a towel. Even in a comfortable bathroom it can be unpleasant, but here, it's seven degrees below freezing. As fast as I can, I dry myself off. Every muscle and nerve is tense, and my skin feels hard. Ahead of me is a frozen lake under a sea of stars. I stare into the distance, and the fact that I am standing here naked with numb feet in the snow makes me chuckle. Once I'm dry, the worst is over. In the tent, I put on my clothes and wrestle myself back into the sleeping bag. My body returns to a comfortable temperature. I feel renewed as never before.

Tierra del Fuego (Land of Fire), Argentina.

—*Final ride*

As I set out early, the white mountain peaks of Tierra del Fuego are rosy with the coming dawn. The cold morning air coursing through my lungs is refreshing. I've come to enjoy the winter. With hardly any traffic and a smoothly paved road, this should be an easy ride of 100 kilometers. After a few hours of climbing, I'm on a mountain pass at 500 meters with expansive views over Lago Escondido, with Lago Fagnano behind it. I pull out my camera and take a few shots, more out of habit than excitement. The specific landmarks may be different, but there is nothing new to see today. It's another wintry landscape, with old polluted snow piled up on the roadside. Then the downhill starts, and before I know it, it is early afternoon and I see Ushuaia. A sigh of relief escapes me when I see the skyline unfold. I take out my phone to record something, but I have nothing grand to say. The entire journey is a blur. I only recall the last couple weeks.

To be frank, I'm happy it's over. The incessant travel has made me numb and uninspired. My writings and photos have been sparse over the last few weeks. I've rushed over the Argentinean Pampas, fighting the boredom of the empty roads. Everything romantic I had envisioned about the desolate landscapes was gone; the dream was dead. Even the physical challenges dwindled as I grew used to the cold weather. I have finished this journey today not because I've enjoyed it, but because giving up would have been unacceptable. The motivation to cycle here had to come from my toes.

I've struggled with putting any of this into words for my social media audience, because I've feared appearing ungrateful for the opportunity to live a beautiful life on the road. This nomadic life has allowed me to achieve travel milestones, bucket list items, and personal records constantly. It is a lifestyle many only dream of—but, like anything done regularly, it's become routine. Two weeks ago, I did some of the famous hikes in El Chaltén and camped near the majestic peak of Fitz Roy. I visited the Perito Moreno Glacier, and I cycled through the national park of Torres del Paine, which is perhaps the top tourist attraction for hikers in Patagonia. And none of it impressed me. It felt like ticking boxes on a to-do list. I've learned that journeys need careful planning, and that taking breaks from travel are just as important as taking breaks *to* travel during normal working life. But I have been smelling the finish line for a while now, and it's propelled me southward in a mindless, ceaseless trance, at the cost of my enthusiasm.

Ushuaia is not interesting or dramatic—it's simply the quiet end of the line. It is a small winter sports destination and a starting point for

expeditions to Antarctica, however, so it's not unpleasant to spend a few days here and catch my breath. I'm not interested in sightseeing because home is the only thing on my mind, but there are some nice restaurants and bars, though not all of them are open now. After two days by myself, Sophie and Jeremy roll into town, and we celebrate together. We're all tired and eager to go back. My next task is to prepare everything for the flight back to Amsterdam. The main challenge is to find a box that fits the bike and most of its parts, which is easier said than done. Airlines all have different restrictions on special baggage. I'm flying with three different ones, so some research is required to avoid any unpleasant surprises halfway through the return trip. After a few visits to all the bike shops in town, I'm lucky to find a box that's big enough.

Two days later, I'm on the plane. Through the tiny window, I see the gray, snowy landscapes of Tierra del Fuego vanishing into the mist below. It's taken two years to cycle half the globe, and now, it will take me two days to fly it. It is a hectic itinerary with layovers in Buenos Aires and London, but soon enough, I'm in Amsterdam waiting for the bike box at baggage claim, tired and fulfilled. I notice myself tearing up a bit: it must be all the Dutch chatter around me, and the small details of this world I know so well. From the remarks on the weather to the complaints about anything that's not practical enough—I love my country. When I walk out to the arrival hall, my family is waiting for me. My dad is the first one who sees me, and he holds me for a long time. Then my mother, three brothers, and their spouses take turns hugging me. We stare and smile at each other and say silly things that don't matter.

Some hours later I'm back home in my apartment, alone. I've rented it out these past two years, but everything is still the same as when I left: the smell of the century-old building, the sounds from the street, the pale Dutch afternoon light in the windows. I sit down behind my piano and play a song I know well. Flashbacks rush through my head of the ten years I've lived here and the thousands of memories connected to this place. A cold sweat breaks out for a brief moment. It's all a bit weird, being in this old place after becoming a new person. How things have changed since I first lived here a long time ago, dependent on a partner, dependent on a full-time job. I take a deep breath and ground myself.

In the following weeks, I shamelessly indulge in my favorite Dutch things. *Stroopwafels, hagelslag, bitterballen*, pickled herring: everything culinary we have no right to be excessively proud of, but love anyway. Sitting in my own home on my own furniture, I feel waves of peace crashing over me. I've never felt so much in harmony with all the things around me. Travel all you want, but there's nothing like the comfort of your own place, decorated just the way you like it. It takes years for a house to be a home, and this little corner of Amsterdam is the truest home I know. My long absence makes it all the clearer: I don't have to change light bulbs here, or move the chairs around to make the place cozy. I don't have to walk to reception to ask them to restart the Wi-Fi. Things just work, and it all makes me feel safe. I have even been planning to do some work on my house, and soon, I am wrapped up in the process of renovating and painting. This journey has changed me, and my house needs to follow.

Old friends and colleagues ask me what it's like to get back to normal life. I suppose they assume that I'm finding it difficult, that after my adventures on the road, I'm struggling with getting back to the daily grind. But it's nothing like that—even to my own surprise. It's not the same as returning from a short holiday, where you live like a god for two weeks with all the pleasures you can afford in a beautiful resort under the sun. It's also not like I've come back to nothing and have to start from scratch, as so many backpackers do. I imagine that could be hard, starting at square one with no money, no furniture, no plan for the future. But no. I have been looking forward to the end of the trip for a long time, and being home again is full of sweetness.

In more reflective moments, I find myself trying to remember segments of the trip. Two years on a bike is a lot to process. When I flick through photos on my phone and read the writings in my diary and WhatsApp conversations, it stirs up memories; many of which I forgot about. I contemplate the images and words from these two years in the Americas, and I can see a myriad of lessons that have shaped me, but a few stand out.

For one, I notice that I'm becoming less fearful and more able to trust in the goodness of others. If your circle is small, you naturally have a general fear of the unknown: of other countries, cultures, and races. I still remember the look on my mother's face five years ago when I told her I was going to cycle through Iran. Since then, I've been to dozens of countries, and have found that Iran is perhaps the most hospitable of them all. The perception of "the big bad world" has completely changed for me. A handshake and a smile have the same impact everywhere, transcending cultural differences and beliefs. Kindness can always be found in many forms. From Sarkis inviting me into his house, to the unknown driver who lit my way on that rainy road in Costa Rica, to the woman who sewed my tire back together in Chile, I believe more than ever that people are generally good and want to make a positive connection. Even wild pumas can be nice.

I also have developed a greater capacity for appreciating experiences instead of things. There have been so many people—Kent and Joy, the Dammer family, the countless little communities I've gone through—that have tapped into an inspiring way of life driven by simplicity and community, rather than material possessions. Of course, I don't mean to preach that wealth is bad: it's what allowed me to take such a grand trip and return to a nice home. But living from the bike gave me the opportunity to dive into a minimalist lifestyle to a degree inaccessible in everyday life. I had to constantly be mindful of my possessions since it was up to me to carry them. Having less made me feel mentally lighter and less cluttered. Since I had fewer things, I had less to worry about. It allowed me to look outward instead of inward, and to recalibrate my priorities. Physical possessions accumulate so easily, weighing people down before they know it. On a bike, the metaphor becomes literal: a lot of baggage makes for slow, tough going. With this lesson in mind, I make an effort to go through my attic and get rid of the piles of stuff that have accumulated. I get rid of the junk, and my home grows lighter and more spacious. What was once a dumping ground for unneeded things becomes a guest room. After so much time being hosted by others, I can now be the one to welcome guests.

Lastly, I've learned that "the good life" is a mercurial idea rather than a set and secret absolute. Everything you do affects the next thing you do. Over the years, I've painted many different pictures of my ideal life, and all of those pictures have been correct in their own ways. The passion I have for the road and the love for my place of origin are engaged in a dance full of tension and shifting rhythms, a dance that keeps me alert, bold, and light on my feet. It isn't about choosing one or the other, but learning to live in both. Traveling is not the only answer to finding meaning, but it is certainly one of the best ways I have found to grow toward bigger, better life choices, precisely because it can be so daunting and far from "normal" life. Embarking on something scary like a long bike trip for the first time makes it easier to do an even greater one next time. But simply walking out of the house and going somewhere new has the potential to turn your life in another direction. Small, courageous choices get the wheels spinning. Make enough of them, and you'll see that the world is yours to explore, and that your best life is a bigger, better monster than you ever imagined.

Cycling log.

This chart shows all the places where I spent one or more nights. The day number refers to the day I left a place. Only the cycled distances are registered, meaning any sections done by plane, car, bus, or ferry are logged as 0.

DAY NO.	LOCATION	COUNTRY	DAILY DISTANCE	ACCUMULATED DISTANCE
1	Vancouver, BC	Canada	117	117
2	Nanaimo, BC	Canada	71	188
3	Ganges, BC	Canada	109	297
4	Clallam County, WA	USA	76	373
5	Bear Creek, WA	USA	49	422
6	La Push, WA	USA	53	475
8	Rain Forest Hostel, WA	USA	80	555
9	Lake Quinault, WA	USA	106	661
11	Twin Harbor St. P., WA	USA	82	743
12	Bay Center, WA	USA	62	805
14	Astoria, OR	USA	0	805
22	Portland, OR	USA	72	877
23	Eagle Creek, OR	USA	59	936
24	Kent & Joy, WA	USA	68	1004
25	The Dalles, OR	USA	59	1063
26	Maupin, OR	USA	81	1144
27	Jefferson Country, OR	USA	76	1220
30	Mitchell, OR	USA	74	1294
31	Prineville, OR	USA	66	1360
33	Bend, OR	USA	57	1417
34	Elk Lake, OR	USA	99	1516
35	Crescent, OR	USA	105	1621
36	Crater Lake, OR	USA	86	1707
37	Shady Cove, OR	USA	66	1773
38	Grants Pass, OR	USA	137	1910
42	Crescent City, CA	USA	95	2005
43	Patricks Point, CA	USA	46	2051
44	Bayside, CA	USA	89	2140
46	Avenue of the Giants, CA	USA	49	2189
47	Garberville, CA	USA	44	2233
48	Leggett, CA	USA	54	2287
49	Westport, CA	USA	60	2347
50	Albion, CA	USA	61	2408
51	Anchor Bay, CA	USA	44	2452
52	Ocean Cove, CA	USA	45	2497
53	Samuel Taylor St. P., CA	USA	67	2564
91	San Francisco, CA	USA	122	2686
92	Tracy, CA	USA	52	2738
93	Modesto, CA	USA	94	2832
95	Modesto, CA	USA	81	2913
96	Chinese Camp, CA	USA	56	2969
97	Rainbow Pool, CA	USA	53	3022
98	Siesta Lake, Yosemite, CA	USA	39	3061
99	Mono Pass, Yosemite, CA	USA	24	3085
100	Lee Vining, CA	USA	27	3112
101	desert, CA	USA	108	3220
102	desert, NV	USA	75	3295
104	Tonopah, NV	USA	81	3376
105	Warm Springs, NV	USA	95	3471
106	Rachel, NV	USA	80	3551
107	desert, NV	USA	55	3606
109	Caliente, NV	USA	193	3799
113	St George, UT	USA	93	3892
114	Zion National Park, UT	USA	56	3948
115	forest, UT	USA	72	4020
116	Bryce, UT	USA	15	4035
117	Bryce, UT	USA	94	4129
118	desert, UT	USA	82	4211
119	Salina, UT	USA	0	4211
120	Monticello, UT	USA	0	4211
122	Green River, UT	USA	72	4283
124	Canyonlands, UT	USA	41	4324
125	Dead Horse Point, UT	USA	69	4393
126	Moab, UT	USA	71	4464
127	Montichello, UT	USA	37	4501
129	Durango, CO	USA	0	4501
130	Albuquerque, NM	USA	55	4556
131	Bernalillo, NM	USA	45	4601
134	Santa Fe, NM	USA	42	4643
135	Española, NM	USA	0	4643
138	Taos, NM	USA	0	4643
139	Monument Valley, AZ	USA	0	4643
140	Flagstaff, AZ	USA	0	4643
141	Sedona, AZ	USA	0	4643
142	Wenden, AZ	USA	0	4643
143	Los Angeles, CA	USA	0	4643
146	Venice Beach, CA	USA	0	4643
147	Rosarito, MX	Mexico	0	4643
150	Venice Beach, CA	USA	0	4643
160	San Francisco, CA	USA	0	4643
161	Venice Beach, CA	USA	82	4725
162	Huntington Beach, CA	USA	90	4815
163	Carlsbad, CA	USA	40	4855
165	San Diego, CA	USA	79	4934
167	Rosarito	Mexico	79	5013
168	Ensenada	Mexico	37	5050
172	Santo Tomas	Mexico	63	5113
173	Ejido Eréndira	Mexico	42	5155
174	Colonet	Mexico	80	5235
175	Rancho los Pinos	Mexico	57	5292
176	El Rosario	Mexico	52	5344
177	desert	Mexico	77	5421
178	Cataviña	Mexico	26	5447
179	Vizcaíno	Mexico	81	5528
180	desert	Mexico	41	5569
182	Santa Rosalía	Mexico	63	5632
183	Mulegé	Mexico	91	5723
184	desert	Mexico	49	5772
186	Loreto	Mexico	0	5772
190	La Paz	Mexico	0	5772
191	Baja ferries	Mexico	0	5772
195	Mazatlán	Mexico	0	5772
203	Guadalajara	Mexico	0	5772
206	Mexico City	Mexico	0	5772
217	Amsterdam	Mexico	0	5772
222	Mexico City	Mexico	0	5772
225	Xilitla	Mexico	0	5772
233	Mexico City	Mexico	0	5772
241	Puerto Vallarta	Mexico	0	5772
336	Mexico City	Mexico	63	5835
337	forest	Mexico	36	5871
338	Amecameca	Mexico	78	5949
339	Cholula	Mexico	11	5960
340	Puebla	Mexico	0	5960
341	Tehuacán	Mexico	62	6022
342	Chazumba	Mexico	61	6083
343	Huajuapan	Mexico	41	6124
344	Tamazulapam	Mexico	0	6124
346	Oaxaca City	Mexico	68	6192
347	Hierve el Agua	Mexico	0	6292
348	San José del Pacifico	Mexico	100	6307
349	Pochutla	Mexico	15	6307
351	Zipolite	Mexico	15	6322
352	Juchitán	Mexico	90	6412
353	Santo Domingo Zanatepec	Mexico	0	6412
355	Tuxtla	Mexico	0	6412
356	General Cárdenas	Mexico	0	6412
357	Tuxtla	Mexico	0	6412
359	San Cristóbal d/l Casas	Mexico	0	6412
360	Palenque	Mexico	55	6467
361	Escárcega	Mexico	0	6467
370	Tulum	Mexico	0	6467
374	Playa del Carmen	Mexico	0	6467
375	Cancún	Mexico	0	6467
376	Pisté	Mexico	49	6516
379	Mérida	Mexico	99	6615
380	Temax	Mexico	90	6705
381	Tizimín	Mexico	88	6793
382	Las Coloradas	Mexico	72	6865
383	Tizimín	Mexico	0	6865
388	Playa del Carmen	Mexico	0	6865
389	Tulum	Mexico	96	6961
390	Felipe Carrillo Puerto	Mexico	81	7042
392	Pedro Antonia Santos	Mexico	46	7088
394	Bacalar	Mexico	110	7198
395	Orange Walk	Belize	90	7288
396	Los Lagos	Belize	95	7383
397	Unitedville	Belize	66	7449
398	backcountry	Guatemala	85	7534
399	Machaquila	Guatemala	0	7534
400	Semuc Champey	Guatemala	0	7534
402	Cobán	Guatemala	0	7534
403	Antigua	Guatemala	0	7534
404	Acatenango	Guatemala	0	7534
407	Antigua	Guatemala	48	7582
408	Patzún	Guatemala	49	7631
415	San Pedro La Laguna	Guatemala	0	7631
429	Antigua	Guatemala	0	7631
430	Pacaya	Guatemala	70	7701
431	Cuilapa	Guatemala	44	7745
432	Jalpatagua	El Salvador	71	7816
435	Santa Ana	El Salvador	66	7882
436	San Salvador	El Salvador	0	7882
437	Managua	Nicaragua	54	7936
438	Granada	Nicaragua	75	8011
439	Rivas	Nicaragua	58	8069
440	Liberia	Costa Rica	59	8128
441	Lake Arenal	Costa Rica	69	8197
442	La Fortuna	Costa Rica	0	8197
446	San Jose	Costa Rica	36	8233
447	Monterrey	Costa Rica	70	8303
448	Paquita	Costa Rica	10	8313
449	Panama border	Costa Rica	55	8368
450	David	Panama	79	8447
451	Las Lajas	Panama	125	8572
452	Santiago	Panama	10	8582
455	Panama City	Panama	0	8582
456	Bogota	Colombia	15	8597
481	Bogota	Colombia	66	8718
482	Soacha	Colombia	109	8827
483	Girardot	Colombia	89	8916
484	Natagaima	Colombia	62	8978
485	Villavieja	Colombia	70	9048
486	Campoalegre	Colombia	86	9134
487	Garzón	Colombia	74	9208
490	Pitalito	Colombia	35	9243
491	Pitalito summit	Colombia	102	9345
493	Mocoa	Colombia	31	9376
494	Trampolín d/l Muerte	Colombia	31	9407
495	Trampolín d/l Muerte	Colombia	37	9444
496	Sibundoy	Colombia	45	9489
497	Laguna d/l Cocha	Colombia	36	9525
498	Pasto	Colombia	69	9594
499	San Juan	Colombia	26	9620
500	Tulcán	Ecuador	53	9673
501	El Ángel	Ecuador	70	9743
502	Ibarra	Ecuador	27	9770
503	Otavalo	Ecuador	21	9791
504	Laguna de Mojanda	Ecuador	23	9814

505	Otavalo	Ecuador	0	9814
508	Quito	Ecuador	0	9814
509	Palugo farm	Ecuador	0	9814
512	Tumbaco	Ecuador	38	9852
513	Pintag	Ecuador	34	9886
514	Cotopaxi north	Ecuador	34	9920
515	Cotopaxi southeast	Ecuador	50	9970
517	Lasso	Ecuador	24	9994
518	Güingopana	Ecuador	58	10052
519	Quilotoa	Ecuador	20	10072
520	Zumbahua	Ecuador	59	10131
521	Angamarca	Ecuador	50	10181
522	Simiatug	Ecuador	22	10203
523	Salinas de Bolivar	Ecuador	71	10274
525	Riobamba	Ecuador	0	10274
526	Alausí	Ecuador	59	10333
535	Cuenca	Ecuador	51	10384
536	Loja	Ecuador	49	10433
538	Vilcabamba	Ecuador	66	10568
539	Valladolid	Ecuador	69	10605
540	Zumba	Ecuador	37	10650
541	Namballe	Peru	45	10743
542	San Ignacio	Peru	93	10768
543	San Augustín	Peru	25	10818
544	Jaén	Peru	50	10888
545	Cuyca	Peru	70	10941
546	Cutervo	Peru	53	10941
547	Chota	Peru	0	10941
552	Cajamarca	Peru	42	10983
553	Jesús	Peru	51	11034
554	Cachachi	Peru	56	11090
555	Cajabamba	Peru	56	11146
556	Huamachuco	Peru	41	11187
557	lake 4000m	Peru	56	11243
558	Mollepata	Peru	37	11280
559	Pallasca	Peru	42	11322
560	3800m (puked here)	Peru	51	11373
561	Corrongo	Peru	67	11440
562	Nueva Esperanza	Peru	64	11504
565	Caraz	Peru	0	11504
569	Huaraz	Peru	63	11567
570	Yungay	Peru	37	11604
571	Laguna 69	Peru	69	11673
572	Yungay	Peru	147	11820
573	Conococha	Peru	110	11930
574	Puerto Supe	Peru	0	11930
575	Huacho	Peru	0	11930
576	Lima	Peru	0	11930
588	Bogota	Colombia	0	11930
595	NYC	USA	0	11930
600	Lima	Peru	76	12006
601	beach	Peru	117	12123
602	Chincha Alta	Peru	106	12229
605	Ica	Peru	0	12229
606	Huaytará	Peru	19	12248
607	Inca Wasi	Peru	63	12311
608	Rumichaca	Peru	95	12406
609	Casacancha	Peru	47	12453
612	Ayacucho	Peru	0	12453
615	Cusco	Peru	0	12453
617	Machu Picchu	Peru	0	12453
619	Cusco	Peru	64	12517
621	Cusco	Peru	35	12552
624	Cusco	Peru	86	12638
625	Rainbow Mountain	Peru	25	12663
626	Pitumarca	Peru	50	12713
627	Sicuani	Peru	92	12805
628	Espinar	Peru	0	12805
635	Arequipa	Peru	59	12864
646	Yura	Peru	84	12948
641	Arequipa	Peru	0	12948
646	Cusco	Peru	0	12948
655	Arequipa	Peru	37	12985
656	Cachamarca	Peru	50	13035
657	Salinas Moche	Peru	82	13117
658	Lloque	Peru	17	13134
659	4500 m	Peru	59	13193
660	Titire	Peru	87	13280
661	Calacoa Bellavista	Peru	5	13285
662	Volcán Ticsani	Peru	47	13332
663	Huaytire	Peru	84	13416
664	Desaguedero	Peru	0	13416
671	La Paz	Bolivia	138	13554
675	La Paz	Bolivia	64	13618
677	Pico Austria	Bolivia	72	13690
678	La Paz	Bolivia	67	13757
680	La Paz	Bolivia	70	13827
681	Oruro	Bolivia	128	13955
682	Challapata	Bolivia	88	14043
683	desert	Bolivia	90	14133
684	Tahua (Salar)	Bolivia	32	14165
685	Isla Pescado (Salar)	Bolivia	58	14223
686	Salar de Uyuni	Bolivia	72	14295
688	Uyuni	Bolivia	0	14295
689	Culpina K	Bolivia	75	14370
690	Vila Mar	Bolivia	81	14451
691	Laguna Colorada	Bolivia	66	14517
692	Laguna Chalviri	Bolivia	106	14623
699	San Pedro de Atacama	Chile	41	14664
700	Toconao	Chile	53	14717
701	Socaire	Chile	68	14785
702	Piedras Rojas	Chile	69	14854
703	customs Argentina	Argentina	65	14919
704	Olacapato	Argentina	63	14982
705	San Ant. d/l Cobres	Argentina	0	14982
706	Olacapato	Argentina	0	14982
707	Purmamarca	Argentina	0	14982
709	Salta	Argentina	0	14982
710	San Antonio d/l C.	Argentina	31	15013
711	Abra del Acay	Argentina	64	15077
712	La Poma	Argentina	60	15137
713	Cachi	Argentina	37	15174
714	Seclantás	Argentina	65	15239
715	Angastaco	Argentina	78	15317
717	Cafayate	Argentina	0	15317
719	Belén	Argentina	76	15393
720	Salicas	Argentina	119	15512
721	Chilecito	Argentina	115	15627
722	Villa Unión	Argentina	125	15752
723	Huaco	Argentina	98	15850
724	desert	Argentina	108	15958
725	San Juan	Argentina	0	15958
728	Mendoza	Argentina	68	16026
729	Potrerillos	Argentina	60	16086
730	Uspallata	Argentina	43	16129
731	Polvaredas	Argentina	49	16178
732	La Cueva	Argentina	86	16264
733	Los Andes	Chile	82	16346
744	Santiago	Chile	184	16530
745	Curicó	Chile	93	16623
746	Maule	Chile	113	16736
747	San Carlos	Chile	28	16764
748	Temuco	Chile	102	16866
749	Villarrica	Chile	63	16929
750	Curarrehue	Chile	97	17026
751	Junín de los Andes	Argentina	45	17071
752	San Martín d/l Andes	Argentina	30	17101
753	Meliquina	Argentina	82	17183
755	Villa La Angostura	Argentina	0	17183
761	Buenos Aires	Argentina	0	17183
763	Villa La Angostura	Argentina	71	17254
764	Licán Ray	Chile	102	17356
765	Las Cabañas	Chile	67	17423
769	Puerto Varas	Chile	0	17423
770	Chaitén	Chile	76	17499
771	Villa Santa Lucía	Chile	70	17569
772	La Junta	Chile	61	17630
773	Puyuhuapi	Chile	75	17705
774	Villa Amengual	Chile	60	17765
775	Villa Maniguales	Chile	41	17806
776	Villa Ortega	Chile	15	17821
778	Coyhaique	Chile	36	17857
779	El Blanco	Chile	73	17930
781	Villa Cerro Castillo	Chile	73	18003
782	abandoned house	Chile	49	18052
783	Puerto Río Tranquilo	Chile	29	18081
784	riverside refugio	Chile	72	18153
785	Río Baker	Chile	15	18168
787	Cochrane	Chile	65	18233
788	forest	Chile	62	18295
789	Tortel	Chile	60	18355
790	Río Bravo	Chile	80	18435
791	Villa O'Higgins	Chile	46	18481
792	Paso Mayer refugio	Chile	26	18507
793	Gendarmerías	Argentina	4	18511
794	Las Horquetas	Argentina	126	18637
796	Gobernador Gregores	Argentina	0	18637
800	El Chaltén	Argentina	100	18737
801	La Leona	Argentina	115	18852
802	El Calafate	Argentina	65	18917
804	El Calafate	Argentina	62	19052
805	Torres del Paine	Chile	68	19120
806	Torres del Paine	Chile	67	19187
807	Puerto Natales	Chile	58	19245
808	pampa	Chile	92	19337
810	Punta Arenas	Chile	0	19337
811	Porvenir	Chile	61	19398
812	refugio	Chile	96	19494
813	San Sebastian border	Argentina	116	19610
814	Río Grande	Argentina	72	19682
815	Tolhuin	Argentina	106	19788
816	Ushuaia	Argentina	0	19788

Total distance cycled: 19,788 km
Total elevation gain: 242,496 m
Max. distance in one day: 184 km
Highest point by bike: 4,972 m
Highest point by foot: 5,408 m
Max. speed: 67,5 km/h
Average speed: 16,8 km/h

Two Years On A Bike
—From Vancouver to Patagonia

This book was conceived, written and edited by	**Martijn Doolaard** *(@_espiritu.libre_)*
Text, images, and layout by	**Martijn Doolaard**
Illustrations by	**Alex Hotchin** (@alex_hotchin)
Editing and proofreading by	**Chelsea Greenwood** (@chelsea_the_writer)
Typefaces:	**Heldane, MVB Sirenne, Operator, Brandon Grotesque**
Printed by	**Gutenberg Beuys Feindruckerei, Langenhagen Made in Germany**
Published by	**gestalten, Berlin 2021 ISBN 978-3-96704-050-0**

2nd printing, 2022

© Die Gestalten Verlag GmbH & Co. KG, Berlin 2021
and Martijn Doolaard

For more information, and to order books, please visit
www.gestalten.com

Bibliographic information published by the Deutsche
Nationalbibliothek.
The Deutsche Nationalbibliothek lists this publication in the
Deutsche Nationalbibliografie;
detailed bibliographic data is available online at www.dnb.de

This book was printed on paper certified according to the
standards of the FSC®.